Everyone's
GUIDE TO COPYRIGHTS, TRADEMARKS, AND PATENTS

The Comprehensive Handbook for Protecting Your Writing, Inventions, and Other Creative Work

With Official, Ready-to-Use Application Forms

Running Press
Philadelphia, Pennsylvania

Canadian representatives: General Publishing Co., Ltd., 30 Lesmill Road, Don Mills, Ontario M3B 2T6.

International representatives: Worldwide Media Services, Inc., 115 East Twenty-third Street, New York, New York 10010.

9 8 7 6 5 4 3 2 1

The digit on the right indicates the number of this printing.

ISBN 0–89471–752–9

Cover design by Toby Schmidt
Interior design by Stephanie Longo
Printed in the United States of America

This book may be ordered by mail from the publisher. Please add $2.50 for postage and handling for each copy. *But try your bookstore first!*
Running Press Book Publishers
125 South Twenty-second Street
Philadelphia, Pennsylvania 19103

CONTENTS

INTRODUCTION

If you're a writer, a graphic designer, a video artist, a musician, or an inventor, you should know how to protect your work.

Just as you can own personal property and real estate, you can own your creations—the property of your intellect. Copyrights, trademarks, and patents are designed to protect the category of property called intellectual property. This book will show you how to protect this kind of property—your writing, your art, your inventions, and much more.

The information compiled in this book is reprinted, excerpted, and adapted from the most recent materials published for public use by the U.S. Copyright Office and by the U.S. Patent and Trademark Office.

You'll find complete information about how to register your copyright or trademark, and how to apply for a patent. Official application forms are included at the end of each section. These forms are exact reproductions of U.S. government forms, so you can tear them out, fill them in, and mail them (or, in some cases, fax them) directly to the Copyright Office or the Patent and Trademark Office.

For more information about copyrights, you can call or write the U.S. Copyright Office. To request information, phone (202) 479-0700, or write:

> Copyright Office
> Information Section, LM-401
> Library of Congress
> Washington, D.C. 20559

To request publications, phone the Forms and Publications Hotline at (202) 707-9100, or write:

> Copyright Office
> Publications Section, LM-455
> Library of Congress
> Washington, D.C. 20559

For further information about trademarks or patents, phone:

> General Trademark or Patent Information, (703) 557-INFO; or
> Patent and Trademark Office Public Information Line,
>   (703) 557-7800; or
> Status Information for Particular Trademark Applications,
>   (703) 557-5249

or write:

> Commissioner of Patents and Trademarks
> Washington, D.C. 20231

Keep in mind that any creation may have individual characteristics that make it exceptional. This book does not contain legal advice. In some cases it may be wise to consult an attorney.

PART

COPYRIGHTS

This section explains the basics of copyright, tells how and when to use the symbol ©, provides detailed instructions for registering all types of work with the U.S. Copyright Office, and describes how to renew and transfer copyright.

You'll find application forms for registering your copyright, and instructions for filing, in Chapter 8, beginning on p. 71.

1 THE BASICS OF COPYRIGHTS

WHAT IS COPYRIGHT?

Copyright is a form of protection provided by the laws of the United States (title 17, U.S. Code) to the authors of "original works of authorship" including literary, dramatic, musical, artistic, and certain other intellectual works. This protection is available to both published and unpublished works.

Section 106 of the Copyright Act generally gives the owner of copyright the exclusive right to do and to authorize others to do the following:

- *To reproduce* the copyrighted work in copies or phonorecords;
- *To prepare derivative works* based upon the copyrighted work;
- *To distribute copies or phonorecords* of the copyrighted work to the public by sale or other transfer of ownership, or by rental, lease, or lending;
- *To perform the copyrighted work publicly,* in the case of literary, musical, dramatic, and choreographic works, pantomimes, and motion pictures and other audiovisual works, and
- *To display the copyrighted work publicly,* in the case of literary, musical, dramatic, and choreographic works, pantomimes, and pictorial, graphic, or sculptural works, including the individual images of a motion picture or other audiovisual work.

WHAT WORKS ARE PROTECTED

Copyright protects "original works of authorship" that are fixed in a tangible form of expression. The fixation need not be directly perceptible, so long as it may be communicated with the aid of a machine or device. Copyrightable works include the following categories:

- literary works;
- musical works, including any accompanying words;
- dramatic works, including any accompanying music;
- pantomimes and choreographic works;

9

- pictorial, graphic, and sculptural works;
- motion pictures and other audiovisual works; and
- sound recordings.

These categories should be viewed quite broadly: for example, computer programs and most "compilations" are registrable as "literary works"; maps and architectural blueprints are registrable as "pictorial, graphic, and sculptural works."

WHAT IS NOT PROTECTED BY COPYRIGHT

Several categories of material are generally not eligible for statutory copyright protection. These include among others:

- Works that have *not* been fixed in a tangible form of expression. For example: choreographic works that have not been notated or recorded, or improvisational speeches or performances that have not been written or recorded.
- Titles, names, short phrases, and slogans; familiar symbols or designs; mere variations of typographic ornamentation, lettering, or coloring; mere listings of ingredients or contents.
- Ideas, procedures, methods, systems, processes, concepts, principles, discoveries, or devices, as distinguished from a description, explanation, or illustration.
- Works consisting *entirely* of information that is common property and containing no original authorship. For example: standard calendars, height and weight charts, tape measures and rulers, and lists or tables taken from public documents or other common sources.
- Blank forms, such as time cards, graph paper, account books, diaries, bank checks, scorecards, address books, report forms, order forms and the like, which are designed for recording information and do not in themselves convey information.
- Works created by the United States Government (see p. 15).

WHO CAN CLAIM COPYRIGHT

The copyright in the work of authorship **immediately** becomes the property of the author who created it. Only the author or those deriving their rights through the author can rightfully claim copyright.

In the case of works made for hire, the employer and not the employee is presumptively considered the author. Section 101 of the copyright statute defines a "work made for hire" as:

(1) a work prepared by an employee within the scope of his or her employment; or

(2) a work specially ordered or commissioned for use as a contribution to a collective work, as a part of a motion picture

10

or other audiovisual work, as a translation, as a supplementary work, as a compilation, as an instructional text, as a test, as answer material for a test, or as an atlas, if the parties expressly agree in a written instrument signed by them that the work shall be considered a work made for hire. . .

The authors of a joint work are co-owners of the copyright in the work, unless there is an agreement to the contrary.

Copyright in each separate contribution to a periodical or other collective work is distinct from copyright in the collective work as a whole and vests initially with the author of the contribution.

Because the Copyright Office cannot give legal advice, it cannot determine whether a work is "made for hire" in specific cases. This decision must be made by the parties involved; it may be necessary to consult an attorney for professional legal advice.

In 1989, the U.S. Supreme Court further defined a "work made for hire."

Any work prepared by a regular, salaried employee within the scope of his or her employment still falls into this category. However, it's no longer enough to cause a work to be created for it to be considered a "work made for hire." The Supreme Court has ruled that freelance artists and writers retain some or all of copyright ownership for their works unless a written agreement expressly assigns copyright ownership to the individual or organization that caused the work to be created.

If you are a freelancer, and would like to retain copyright to your works, you may be able to negotiate an agreement confirming that you hold the copyright to your works. If your organization hires freelancers, do not assume that your organization owns the copyright to their work. Make sure you have a written agreement.

Any written agreement should be prepared or reviewed by an attorney before it is signed.

HOW TO SECURE A COPYRIGHT

The way in which copyright protection is secured under the present law is frequently misunderstood. No publication or registration or other action in the Copyright Office is required to secure copyright (see NOTE below). There are, however, certain definite advantages to registration (see p. 13).

Copyright Secured Automatically Upon Creation

Copyright is secured *automatically* when the work is created, and a work is "created" when it is fixed in a copy or phonorecord for the first time. In general, "copies" are material objects from which a work can be read or visually perceived either directly or with the aid of a machine or device, such as books, manuscripts, sheet music, film, videotape, or microfilm. "Phonorecords" are material objects embodying fixations of sounds (excluding, by statutory definition, motion picture soundtracks), such as audio tapes and phonograph disks. Thus, for example, a song (the "work") can be fixed in sheet music ("copies") or in phonograph disks ("phonorecords"), or both.

If a work is prepared over a period of time, the part of the work that is fixed on a particular date constitutes the created work as of that date.

NOTE: Before 1978, statutory copyright was generally secured by the act of publication with notice of copyright, assuming compliance with all other relevant statutory conditions. Works in the public domain on January 1, 1978 (for example, works published without satisfying all conditions for securing statutory copyright under the Copyright Act of 1909) remain in the public domain under the current Act.

Statutory copyright could also be secured before 1978 by the act of registration in the case of certain unpublished works and works eligible for ad interim copyright. The current Act automatically extends to full term (section 304 sets the term) copyright for all works in which ad interim copyright was subsisting or was capable of being secured on December 31, 1977.

PUBLICATION

The Copyright Act defines publication as "the distribution of copies or phonorecords of a work to the public by sale or other transfer of ownership, or by rental, lease, or lending." An offering to distribute copies or phonorecords to a group of persons for purposes of further distribution, public performance, or public display also constitutes publication.

The following do not constitute publication: printing or other reproduction of copies, public performance or display of a work, or sending copies to the Copyright Office.

Publication is no longer the key to obtaining statutory copyright as it was under the Copyright Act of 1909. However, publication remains an important concept in the copyright law for several reasons:

- When a work is published, all published copies should bear a notice of copyright. *(For an explanation of copyright notice, see Chapter 2, beginning on p. 15. See also Chapter 7, beginning on p. 67, for recent changes in copyright law.)*
- Works that are published with notice of copyright in the United States are subject to mandatory deposit with the Library of Congress. (See Chapter 3, "Mandatory Deposit," beginning on p. 22.)
- Publication of a work can affect the limitations on the exclusive rights of the copyright owner that are set forth in sections 107 through 118 of the law.
- The year of publication may determine the duration of

copyright protection for anonymous and pseudonymous works (when the author's identity is not revealed in the records of the Copyright Office) and for works made for hire (see pp. 58–61).
- Deposit requirements for registration of published works differ from those for registration of unpublished works.

COPYRIGHT REGISTRATION AND ITS ADVANTAGES

In general, copyright registration is a legal formality intended to make a public record of the basic facts of a particular copyright. However, registration is not a condition of copyright protection. Even though registration is not generally a requirement for protection, the copyright law provides several inducements or advantages to encourage copyright owners to make registration. Among these advantages are the following:

- Registration establishes a public record of the copyright claim;
- Registration is ordinarily necessary before any infringement suits may be filed in court;
- If made before or within 5 years of publication, registration will establish prima facie evidence in court of the validity of the copyright and of the facts stated in the certificate; and
- If registration is made within 3 months after publication of the work or prior to an infringement of the work, statutory damages and attorney's fees will be available to the copyright owner in court actions. Otherwise, only an award of actual damages and profits is available to the copyright owner.

For more information about registration and international conventions, see "Registration as Prerequisite to Suit" and "Benefits of Registration," p. 69.
For detailed instructions on how to register copyrights for all types of work, see Chapter 4, beginning on p. 27.

TRANSFER OF COPYRIGHT

Any or all of the exclusive rights, or any subdivision of those rights, of the copyright owner may be transferred, but the transfer of *exclusive* rights is not valid unless that transfer is in writing and signed by the owner of the rights conveyed (or such owner's duly authorized agent). Transfer of a right on a nonexclusive basis does not require a written agreement.

A copyright may also be conveyed by operation of law and may be bequeathed by will or pass as personal property by the applicable laws of intestate succession.

Copyright is a personal property right, and it is subject to the various state laws and regulations that govern the ownership, inheritance, or transfer of personal property as well as terms of contracts or conduct of business. For information about relevant state laws, consult an attorney.

Transfers of copyright are normally made by contract. The Copyright Office does not have or supply any forms for such transfers. However, the law does provide for the recordation in the Copyright Office of transfers of copyright ownership. Although recordation is not required to make a valid transfer between the parties, it does provide certain legal advantages and may be required to validate the transfer as against third parties. *(For information on recordation of transfers and other documents related to copyright, see Chapter 6.)*

INTERNATIONAL COPYRIGHT PROTECTION

There is no such thing as an "international copyright" that will automatically protect an author's writings throughout the entire world. Protection against unauthorized use in a particular country depends, basically, on the national laws of that country. However, most countries do offer protection to foreign works under certain conditions, and these conditions have been greatly simplified by international copyright treaties and conventions. For a list of countries which maintain copyright relations with the United States, write to the Copyright Office and ask for Circular 38a.

The United States is a member of the Universal Copyright Convention (the UCC), which came into force on September 16, 1955. Generally, a work by a national or domiciliary of a country that is a member of the UCC or a work first published in a UCC country may claim protection under the UCC. If the work bears the notice of copyright in the form and position specified by the UCC, this notice will satisfy and substitute for any other formalities a UCC member country would otherwise impose as a condition of copyright. A UCC notice should consist of the symbol © accompanied by the name of the copyright proprietor and the year of first publication of the work.

Since March 1, 1989, the United States also has been a member of the Berne Convention. For a description of this international agreement, and related changes in U.S. copyright law, see "Highlights of U.S. Adherence to the Berne Convention," beginning on p. 67.

An author who wishes protection for his or her work in a particular country should first find out the extent of protection of foreign works in that country. If possible, this should be done before the work is published anywhere, since protection may often depend on the facts existing at the time of first publication.

If the country in which protection is sought is a party to one of the international copyright conventions, the work may generally be protected by complying with the conditions of the convention. Even if the work cannot be brought under an international convention, protection under the specific provisions of the country's national laws may still be possible. Some countries, however, offer little or no copyright protection for foreign works.

2 HOW AND WHEN TO USE THE NOTICE OF COPYRIGHT

When a work is published under the authority of the copyright owner, it is strongly recommended that a notice of copyright be placed on all publicly distributed copies and on all publicly distributed phonorecords of sound recordings. This notice is recommended even on works published outside of the United States.

Before March 1, 1989, all works published in the United States were required to bear a notice of copyright. On that date, however, the law changed so that use of the notice is now recommended, not required (see "Highlights of U.S. Adherence to the Berne Convention," beginning on p. 67).

For works published prior to March 1, 1989, use of the copyright notice is still required (see "Notice Unchanged," p. 68).

The use of the copyright notice is the responsibility of the copyright owner and does not require advance permission from, or registration with, the Copyright Office. As mentioned above, use of the notice makes the published works subject to mandatory deposit requirements. (See Chapter 3, "Mandatory Deposit.")

UNPUBLISHED WORKS

The copyright notice is not required on unpublished works. However, because the dividing line between a preliminary distribution and actual publication is sometimes difficult to determine, the copyright owner may wish to place a copyright notice on copies that leave his or her control to indicate that the author's interests are reserved. An appropriate notice for an unpublished work might be: Unpublished work © 1986 John Doe.

PUBLICATIONS INCORPORATING UNITED STATES GOVERNMENT WORKS

Works by the United States Government are not subject to copyright protection. Whenever a work is published in copies or phonorecords consisting preponderantly of one or more works of the United States Government, the notice of copyright shall also include a statement that identifies one of the following: those portions protected by the copyright law *or* those portions that constitute United States Government material.

For amendments to this law, see the second paragraph under "Voluntary Use of Notice Is Encouraged," p. 68.

FORM OF NOTICE

The form of the copyright notice recommended for "visually perceptible" copies—that is those that can be seen or read, either directly (such as books) or with the aid of a machine (such as films)—is different from the form recommended for phonorecords of sound recordings (such as records or cassettes).

Visually Perceptible Copies

This notice must contain three elements; they should appear together or in close proximity on the copies. Example:

© 1986 John Doe

The elements are:

1. *The symbol* © (the letter C in a circle), or the word "Copyright," or the abbreviation "Copr.";
2. *The year of first publication.*

    If the work is a derivative work or a compilation incorporating previously published material, the year of the first publication of the derivative work or compilation is sufficient. Examples of derivative works are translations or dramatizations; an example of a compilation is an anthology;

    The year may be omitted when a pictorial, graphic, or sculptural work, with any accompanying text, is reproduced on greeting cards, postcards, stationery, jewelry, dolls, toys or useful articles;
3. *The name of the owner of copyright,* or an abbreviation by which the name can be recognized, or a generally known alternative designation of the owner.*

(The "C in a circle" notice is required only on "visually perceptible" copies. Certain kinds of works—for example, musical, dramatic, and literary works—may be fixed not in "copies" but by means of sound in an audio recording. Since audio recordings such as

---

*The United States is a member of the Universal Copyright Convention (the UCC), which came into force on September 16, 1955. For protection in UCC member countries, the notice must consist of the symbol © (the word "Copyright" or the abbreviation are *not* acceptable), the year of first publication, and the name of the copyright proprietor. Example: © 1986 John Doe. For information about international copyright relationships, write to the Register of Copyrights and request Circular R38A.

audio tapes and phonograph disks are "phonorecords" and not "copies," there is no requirement that the phonorecord bear a "C in a circle" notice to protect the underlying musical, dramatic, or literary work that is recorded.)

Phonorecords of Sound Recordings

The copyright notice for phonorecords of a sound recording is different from that for other works. Sound recordings are defined as "works that result from the fixation of a series of musical, spoken or other sounds, but not including the sounds accompanying a motion picture or other audiovisual work." Copyright in a sound recording protects the particular series of sounds fixed in the recording against unauthorized reproduction, revision, and distribution. This copyright is distinct from copyright of the musical, literary, or dramatic work that is recorded on a phonorecord.

Phonorecords may be records (such as LP's and 45's), audio tapes, cassettes, or disks. The notice should contain the following three elements appearing together on the phonorecord. Example:

℗ 1986 X.Y.Z. Records, Inc.

1. *The symbol* ℗ (the letter P in a circle);
2. *The year of first publication* of the sound recording;
3. *The name of the owner of copyright* in the sound recording, or an abbreviation by which the name can be recognized, or a generally known alternative designation of the owner. If the producer of the sound recording is named on the phonorecord label or container, and if no other name appears in conjunction with the notice, the producer's name shall be considered part of the notice.

The notice on phonorecords should appear on the surface of the phonorecord or on the phonorecord label or container in such manner and location as to give reasonable notice of the claim of copyright.

> **NOTE:** Because of problems that might result in some cases from the use of variant forms of the notice, any form of the notice other than these given here should not be used without first seeking legal action.

POSITION OF NOTICE

The copyright notice should be placed on copies or phonorecords so that it gives reasonable notice of the claim of copyright. The notice should be permanently legible to an ordinary user of the work under normal conditions of use and should not be concealed from view upon reasonable examination.

The Copyright Office has issued regulations, summarized below, concerning the position of the notice and methods of affixation (37 C.F.R., Part 201). To read the complete regulations, request Circular R96 201.20 or consult the Code of Federal Regulations in your local library.

The following locations and methods of affixation are acceptable; these examples are not exhaustive.

Works Published in Book Form

- Title page;
- Page immediately following the title page;
- Either side of the front or back cover;
- First or last page of the main body of the work.

Single-Leaf Works

- Front or Back.

Works Published as Periodicals or Other Serials

- Any location acceptable for books;
- As part of or adjacent to the masthead or on the page containing the masthead;
- Adjacent to a prominent heading, appearing at or near the front of the issue, containing the title of the periodical and any combination of the volume and issue number and date of the issue.

Works Published as Separate Contributions to Collective Works

For a separate contribution reproduced on only one page:
- Under the title or elsewhere on the same page;

For a separate contribution reproduced on more than one page:
- Under a title appearing at or near the beginning of the contribution;
- On the first page of the main body of the contribution;
- Immediately following the end of the contribution;
- On any of the pages where the contribution appears if the contribution consists of no more than 20 pages, the notice is reproduced prominently, and the application of the notice to the particular contribution is clear.

Works Reproduced in Machine-Readable Copies

- With or near the title or at the end of the work, on visually perceptible printouts;
- At the user's terminal at sign on;
- On continuous display on the terminal;
- Reproduced durably on a gummed or other label securely affixed to the copies or to a container used as a permanent receptacle for the copies.

Motion Pictures and Other Audiovisual Works

A notice embodied in the copies by a photomechanical or electronic process so that it ordinarily would appear whenever the work is performed in its entirety may be located:
- With or near the title;
- With the cast, credits, and similar information;
- At or immediately following the beginning of the work;
- At or immediately preceding the end of the work.

The notice on works lasting 60 seconds or less, such as untitled motion pictures or other audiovisual works, may be located:
- In all of the locations specified above for longer motion pictures; and,
- If the notice is embodied electronically or photomechanically, on the leader of the film or tape immediately preceding the work.

For audiovisual works or motion pictures distributed to the public for private use, the locations include the above, and in addition,
- On the permanent housing or container.

Pictorial, Graphic, and Sculptural Works

For works embodied in two-dimensional copies, a notice should be affixed directly, durably, and permanently to:
- The front or back of the copies;
- Any backing, mounting, framing or other material to which the copies are durably attached, so as to withstand normal use.

For works reproduced in three-dimensional copies, a notice should be affixed directly, durably, and permanently to:
- Any visible portion of the work;
- Any base, mounting or framing or other material on which the copies are durably attached.

For works on which it is impractical to affix a notice to the copies directly or by means of a durable label, a notice is acceptable if it appears on a tag or durable label attached to the copy so that it will remain with it as it passes through commerce.

For works reproduced in copies consisting of sheet-like or strip material bearing multiple or continuous reproductions of the work, such as fabrics or wall paper, the notice may be applied:
- To the reproduction itself;
- To the margin, selvage, or reverse side of the material at frequent and regular intervals; or
- If the material contains neither a selvage nor reverse side, to tags or labels attached to the copies and to any spools, reels, or containers housing them in such a way that the notice is visible in commerce.

OMISSION AND ERRORS IN NOTICE

The publication of copies or phonorecords with no notice or with an incorrect notice will not automatically invalidate the copyright or affect ownership. However, certain errors in the notice or publication without a notice, if not corrected, may eventually result in the loss of copyright protection or in a change in the length of the term of copyright protection. The extent of the remedies available to a copyright owner may also be affected when someone innocently infringes a copyright by relying on an authorized copy or phonorecord with no notice or with an incorrect notice.

Omission of Notice

"Omission of notice" is publishing without a notice. In addition, some errors are considered the same as omission of notice. These are:

- A notice that does not contain the symbol © (the letter C in a circle), or the word "Copyright" or the abbreviation "Copr." or, if the work is a sound recording, the symbol ℗ (the letter P in a circle);
- A notice dated more than one year later than the date of first publication;
- A notice without a name or date that could reasonably be considered part of the notice;
- A notice that lacks the statement required for works consisting preponderantly of U.S. government material; and
- A notice located so that it does not give reasonable notice of the claim of copyright.

The omission of notice does not affect the copyright protection and no corrective steps are required if:

1. The notice is omitted from no more than a relatively small number of copies or phonorecords distributed to the public; *or*
2. The omission violated an express written requirement that the published copies or phonorecords bear the prescribed notice.

In all other cases of omission, to preserve copyright:

1. The work must have been registered before it was published in any form or before the omission occurred or it must be registered within five years after the date of publication without notice; *and*
2. The copyright owner must make a reasonable effort to add the notice to all copies or phonorecords that are distributed to the public in the United States after the omission is discovered.

If these corrective steps are not taken, the work will go into the public domain in the United States five years after publication. At that time all U.S. copyright protection will be lost and cannot be restored. *(For works published on or after March 1, 1989, see pp. 67–68.)*

Error in Year

Copyright protection under the current law generally lasts for the life of the author plus 50 years. However, in the case of anonymous and pseudonymous works and works made for hire, the copyright term lasts for 75 years from the date of publication or 100 years from the year of creation, whichever expires first. If the copyright duration depends on the date of first publication and the year given in the notice is *earlier* than the actual publication date, the year in the notice could determine the length of protection. (For later date in the notice, see *Omission of Notice.*)

Example: A work made for hire is created in 1980 and is first published in 1986. However, the notice contains the earlier year of 1985. In this case, the term of copyright protection would be measured from the year in the notice and the expiration date would be 2060, 75 years from 1985.

Error in Name

When the person named in the notice is not the owner of copyright, the error may be corrected by:

1. Registering the work in the name of the true owner; *or*
2. Recording a document in the Copyright Office executed by the person named in the notice that shows the correct ownership.

Otherwise, anyone who innocently infringes the copyright and can prove that he or she was misled by the notice and that the above steps were not taken before the infringement, will have a complete defense against the infringement.

> **NOTE:** Before 1978, the copyright law required, as a condition for copyright protection, that all copies published with the authorization of the copyright owner bear a proper notice. If a work was published under the copyright owner's authority before January 1, 1978, without a proper copyright notice, all copyright protection for that work was permanently lost in the United States. The current copyright law does not provide retroactive protection for those works.

3 MANDATORY DEPOSIT

Although a copyright registration is not required, the Copyright Act establishes a mandatory deposit requirement for works published with notice of copyright in the United States. (See "Publication," p. 12.)

The basic requirement of the deposit provisions, found in section 407 of the copyright law, is that within three months after a work has been published with notice of copyright in the United States, the "owner of copyright or of the exclusive right of publication" in that work must deposit the required number of copies of the work in the Copyright Office.

If the required deposit is not made within three months of the demand, the person or organization obligated to make the deposit is liable for a fine of not more than $250 for each work plus the retail price of the copies; if the refusal to comply is willful or repeated, an added fine of $2500 may be incurred.

In general, the deposit must consist of **two** complete copies or phonorecords of the best edition (see below) of the work.

If the work is a sound recording, the deposit must include **two** complete phonorecords of the best edition, **plus** any text or pictorial matter published with the phonorecord. Examples of the textual material include record sleeves, album covers, and separate leaflets or booklets included in the sleeve or album.

If the work is a motion picture, the deposit consists of **one** complete copy of the best edition, **plus** a separate description of its contents such as a continuity, press book, or synopsis.

In general, you can satisfy the deposit requirements when you register. However, to make a deposit without registering, send the copies to the Copyright Office, Library of Congress, Washington, D.C. 20559, specifying that this is a 407 deposit. To receive a receipt, send a check for $2.00 made out to Deposits and Acquisitions.

For details about deposit requirements with registration for various types of work, see Chapter 4, beginning on p. 27.

THE "BEST EDITION"

When two or more editions of the same version of a work have been published, the one of the highest quality is generally considered to be the best edition. In judging quality, the Library of Congress will adhere to the criteria set forth below in all but exceptional circumstances. The criteria to be applied in determining the best edition of each of several types of material are listed in descending order of importance.

Where differences between editions represent variations in

copyrightable content, each edition is a separate version and "best edition" standards based on such differences do not apply. Each such version is a separate work for the purposes of the copyright law.

I. Printed Textual Matter

A. Paper, Binding, and Packaging
   1. Archival-quality rather than less-permanent paper.
   2. Hard cover rather than soft cover.
   3. Library binding rather than commercial binding.
   4. Trade edition rather than book club edition.
   5. Sewn rather than glue-only binding.
   6. Sewn or glued rather than stapled or spiral-bound.
   7. Stapled rather than spiral-bound or plastic-bound.
   8. Bound rather than looseleaf, except when future looseleaf insertions are to be issued. In the case of looseleaf materials, this includes the submission of all binders and indexes when they are part of the unit as published and offered for sale or distribution. Additionally, the regular and timely receipt of all appropriate looseleaf updates, supplements, and releases including supplemental binders issued to handle these expanded versions, is part of the requirement to properly maintain these publications.
   9. Slip-cased rather than nonslip-cased.
   10. With protective folders rather than without (for broadsides).
   11. Rolled rather than folded (for broadsides).
   12. With protective coatings rather than without (except broadsides, which should not be coated).

B. Rarity
   1. Special limited edition having the greatest number of special features.
   2. Other limited edition rather than trade edition.
   3. Special binding rather than trade binding.

C. Illustrations
   1. Illustrated rather than unillustrated.
   2. Illustrations in color rather than black and white.

D. Special Features
   1. With thumb notches or index tabs rather than without.
   2. With aids to use such as overlays and magnifiers rather than without.

E. Size
   1. Larger rather than smaller sizes. (Except that large-type editions for the partially-sighted are not required in place of editions employing type of more conventional size.)

II. Photographs

A. Size and finish, in descending order of preference
   1. The most widely distributed edition.
   2. 8 x 10-inch glossy print.
   3. Other size or finish.

B. Unmounted rather than mounted

C. Archival-quality rather than less-permanent paper stock or printing process

III. Motion Pictures

A. Film rather than another medium. Film editions are listed below in descending order of preference.
    1. Preprint material, by special arrangement.
    2. Film gauge in which most widely distributed.
    3. 35 mm rather than 16 mm.
    4. 16 mm rather than 8 mm.
    5. Special formats (e.g., 65 mm) only in exceptional cases.
    6. Open reel rather than cartridge or cassette.

B. Videotape rather than videodisc. Videotape editions are listed below in descending order of preference.
    1. Tape gauge in which most widely distributed.
    2. Two-inch tape.
    3. One-inch tape.
    4. Three-quarter-inch tape cassette.
    5. One-half-inch tape cassette.

IV. Other Graphic Matter

A. Paper and Printing
    1. Archival quality rather than less-permanent paper.
    2. Color rather than black and white.

B. Size and Content
    1. Larger rather than smaller size.
    2. In the case of cartographic works, editions with the greatest amount of information rather than those with less detail.

C. Rarity
    1. The most widely distributed edition rather than one of limited distribution.
    2. In the case of a work published only in a limited, numbered edition, one copy outside the numbered series but otherwise identical.
    3. A photographic reproduction of the original, by special arrangement only.

D. Text and Other Materials
    1. Works with annotations, accompanying tabular or textual matter, or other interpretative aids rather than those without them.

E. Binding and Packaging
    1. Bound rather than unbound.
    2. If editions have different binding, apply the criteria in I.A.2–I.A.7, above.

3. Rolled rather than folded.
4. With protective coatings rather than without.

V. *Phonorecords*

A. Compact digital disc rather than vinyl disc
B. Vinyl disc rather than tape
C. With special enclosures rather than without
D. Open-reel rather than cartridge
E. Cartridge rather than cassette
F. Quadraphonic rather than stereophonic
G. True stereophonic rather than monaural
H. Monaural rather than electronically rechanneled stereo

VI. *Musical Compositions*

A. Fullness of Score
   1. Vocal music
      a. With orchestral accompaniment—
         i. Full score and parts, if any, rather than conductor's score and parts, if any. (In cases of compositions published only by rental, lease, or lending, this requirement is reduced to full score only.)
         ii. Conductor's score and parts, if any, rather than condensed score and parts, if any. (In cases of compositions published only by rental, lease, or lending, this requirement is reduced to conductor's score only.)
      b. Unaccompanied: Open score (each part on separate staff) rather than closed score (all parts condensed to two staves).
   2. Instrumental music
      a. Full score and parts, if any, rather than conductor's score and parts, if any. (In cases of compositions published only by rental, lease, or lending, this requirement is reduced to full score only.)
      b. Conductor's score and parts, if any, rather than condensed score and parts, if any. (In cases of compositions published only by rental, lease, or lending, this requirement is reduced to conductor's score only.)

B. Printing and Paper
   1. Archival-quality rather than less-permanent paper.

C. Binding and Packaging
   1. Special limited editions rather than trade editions.
   2. Bound rather than unbound.
   3. If editions have different binding, apply the criteria in I.A.2–I.A.12, above.
   4. With protective folders rather than without.

VII. *Microforms*

A. Related Materials

1. With indexes, study guides, or other printed matter rather than without.

B. Permanence and Appearance
   1. Silver halide rather than any other emulsion.
   2. Positive rather than negative.
   3. Color rather than black and white.

C. Format (newspapers and newspaper-formatted serials)
   1. Reel microfilm rather than any other microform.

D. Format (all other materials)
   1. Microfiche rather than reel microfilm.
   2. Reel microfilm rather than microform cassettes.
   3. Microfilm cassettes rather than micro-opaque prints.

E. Size
   1. 35mm rather than 16mm.

VIII. Works Existing in More Than One Medium

Editions are listed below in descending order of preference.

A. Newspapers, Dissertations and Theses, Newspaper-Formatted Serials
   1. Microform.
   2. Printed matter.

B. All other materials
   1. Printed matter.
   2. Microform.
   3. Phonorecord.
   (Effective: January 1, 1978)

SPECIAL RELIEF

The regulations also set up a procedure under which the copyright depositor may request "special relief" from the deposit requirements for published motion pictures. The "special relief" provisions are intended to assist in cases where extenuating circumstances make it difficult or impossible for the copyright owner to provide a deposit copy which meets the "complete copy" or "best edition" standards. Any decision to grant "special relief" and the conditions under which it is granted are made by the Register of Copyrights after consultation with other appropriate officials of the Library of Congress. The decision is based upon the acquisitions policies then in force and the archival and examining requirements of the Copyright Office.

Requests for "special relief" are made in writing to the Chief of the Examining Division of the Copyright Office, and must be signed by or on behalf of the person signing the application for registration. Please include specific reasons why the request for "special relief" should be granted.

4 HOW TO REGISTER YOUR WORK

To register a work, send the following three elements *in the same envelope or package* to the Register of Copyrights, Copyright Office, Library of Congress, Washington, D.C. 20559:

1. A properly completed application form (See Chapter 8, beginning on p. 71);
2. A nonrefundable filing fee of $10 for each application;
3. A nonreturnable deposit of the work being registered.

The deposit requirements vary in particular situations. The *general* requirements follow. Also note the information in "Mandatory Deposit," Chapter 3, beginning on p. 22. For works in the performing arts, the visual arts, and other types of work, see the sections that follow in this chapter.

- If the work is unpublished, one complete copy or phonorecord.
- If the work was first published in the United States on or after January 1, 1978, two complete copies or phonorecords of the best edition. (See "The 'Best Edition'," p. 22.)
- If the work was first published in the United States before January 1, 1978, two complete copies or phonorecords of the work as first published.
- If the work was first published outside the United States, whenever published, one complete copy or phonorecord of the work as first published.

Registration may be made at any time within the life of the copyright. Unlike the law before 1978, when a work has been registered in unpublished form, it is not necessary to make another registration when the work becomes published (although the copyright owner may register the published edition, if desired).

EFFECTIVE DATE OF REGISTRATION

Please note that **a copyright registration is effective on the date of receipt in the Copyright Office of all the required elements in acceptable form,** regardless of the length of time it takes thereafter to process the application and mail the certificate of registration. The length of time required by the Copyright Office to process an application varies from time to time, depending on the amount of material received and the personnel available to handle it. It must also be kept in mind that it may take a number of days for mailed material to reach the Copyright Office and for the certificate of registration to reach the recipient after being mailed by the Copyright Office.

If you are filing an application for copyright registration in the Copyright Office, you *will not* receive an acknowledgement that your application has been received, but you can expect within 120 days:

- A letter or telephone call from a copyright examiner if further information is needed;
- A certificate of registration to indicate the work has been registered, or if the application cannot be accepted, a letter explaining why it has been rejected.

If you want to know when the Copyright Office receives your material, you should send it by registered or certified mail and request a return receipt from the post office. Allow at least three weeks for the return of your receipt.

APPLICATION FORMS

You can find these forms beginning on p. 71.

For Original Registration

Form TX: for published and unpublished non-dramatic literary works

Form PA: for published and unpublished works of the performing arts (musical and dramatic works, pantomimes and choreographic works, motion pictures and other audiovisual works)

Form SR: for published and unpublished sound recordings

Form VA: for published and unpublished works of the visual arts (pictorial, graphic, and sculptural works)

Form SE: for serials, works issued or intended to be issued in successive parts bearing numerical or chronological designations and intended to be continued indefinitely (periodicals, newspapers, magazines, newsletters, annuals, journals, etc.)

For a Group of Contributions to Periodicals

Form GR/CP: an adjunct application to be used for registration of a group of contributions to periodicals in addition to an application Form TX, PA, or VA

For Corrections and Amplifications

Form CA: for supplementary registration to correct or amplify information given in the Copyright Office record of an earlier registration

For Renewal Registration

Form RE: for claims to renewal copyright in works copyrighted under the law in effect through December 31, 1977 (1909 Copyright Act)

The Privacy Act

The U.S. government is required by law to furnish the following advisory statement along with any application for copyright registration.

PRIVACY ACT ADVISORY STATEMENT
Required by the Privacy Act of 1974 (Public Law 93–579)

AUTHORITY FOR REQUESTING THIS INFORMATION:
• Title 17, U.S.C., Secs. 409 and 410

FURNISHING THE REQUESTED INFORMATION IS:
• Voluntary

BUT IF THE INFORMATION IS NOT FURNISHED:
• It may be necessary to delay or refuse registration
• You may not be entitled to certain relief, remedies, and benefits provided in chapters 4 and 5 of title 17, U.S.C.

PRINCIPAL USES OF REQUESTED INFORMATION:
• Establishment and maintenance of a public record
• Examination of the application for compliance with legal requirements.

OTHER ROUTINE USES:
• Public inspection and copying
• Preparation of public indexes
• Preparation of public catalogs of copyright registrations
• Preparation of search reports upon request

NOTE:
• No other advisory statement will be given you in connection with this application
• Please keep this statement and refer to it if we communicate with you regarding this application

MUSICAL COMPOSITIONS AND SOUND RECORDINGS

To register your songs, lyrics, and other musical compositions and sound recordings, use Form PA or Form SR (see pp. 76 and 80).

The information in this section supplements, but does not replace, the basic information on copyright procedures and regulations contained in Chapters 1–3.

The copyright law of the United States (title 17 of the United States Code) provides for copyright in "musical works, including any accompanying words," which are fixed in some tangible medium of expression. Musical works include both original compositions and original arrangements of other new versions of earlier compositions to which new copyrightable authorship has been added.

The copyright law also provides for copyright protection in sound recordings. Sound recordings are defined in the law as "works that result from the fixation of a series of musical, spoken, or other sounds, but not including the sounds accompanying a motion picture or other audiovisual work." Common examples include recordings of music, drama, or lectures.

Copyright in a sound recording protects the particular series of sounds "fixed" (embodied) in the recording against unauthorized reproduction and revision, and against the unauthorized distribution of phonorecords embodying those sounds.

Generally copyright protection extends to two elements in a sound recording: (1) the contribution of the performer(s) whose performance is captured, and (2) the contribution of the person or persons responsible for capturing and processing the sounds to make the final recording.

A sound recording is not the same as a **phonorecord**. A phonorecord is simply the physical object in which works of authorship are embodied. Examples of phonorecords are disks, audio tapes (reels, cassettes, and cartridges), and the like.

A MUSICAL COMPOSITION is normally registered in Class PA as a work of the performing arts. It consists of music and/or words created by composers and/or lyricists. A musical composition may be sent to the Copyright Office in the form of a notated copy (for example, a lead sheet or sheet music) **or** in the form of a phonorecord (for example, tape, cassette tape, 45 rpm or LP disk, compact disk). Sending a musical composition in the form of a phonorecord does **not** mean that any claim to copyright in a SOUND RECORDING is intended or assumed. Example:

> A composer may create a musical work at the piano and either notate or record the work. The manner in which the work is fixed does not affect its classification as a musical composition.

The author of a MUSICAL COMPOSITION is generally the composer, and the lyricist, if any.

A SOUND RECORDING is always registered in Class SR. It is a work that results from the fixation of a series of musical, spoken, or other sounds. There are generally two copyrightable elements in a sound recording:

1. The contribution of the performer(s) whose performance is fixed, and,
2. The contribution of the record producer who processes the sounds and fixes them in the final recording.

The author of a SOUND RECORDING is the performer, the record producer, or both.

Copyright in a sound recording protects ONLY against the unauthorized reproduction and revision of the particular sounds in a phonorecord, and the unauthorized distribution of phonorecords embodying them.

Copyright in a sound recording is not the same as, or a substitute for, copyright in the underlying musical composition—an underlying musical composition is copyrightable itself, apart from the recording of its performance.

CHOOSING THE RIGHT FORM FOR MUSICAL COMPOSITIONS AND SOUND RECORDINGS

How the work was created; what is being registered	Form to use	How to describe the authorship in space 2, "Nature of Authorship"*	What should be deposited:	
			Published in the United States**	Unpublished
Composer/author creates a song, wishes to claim copyright in the song	PA	Music and Words	2 complete copies of the "best edition" if published in a notated copy; 1 phonorecord of the "best edition" if published only on a phonorecord (disk, tape, cassette, etc.)	1 complete copy (lead sheet, etc.) or phonorecord (disk, tape, cassette, etc.)
Composer/author creates musical composition, wishes to claim copyright in the musical composition	PA	Music	2 complete copies of the "best edition" if published in a notated copy; 1 phonorecord of the "best edition" if published only on a phonorecord (disk, tape, cassette, etc.)	1 complete copy (lead sheet, etc.) or phonorecord (usually disk, tape, cassette, etc.)
Performer(s) (for example, vocalist and band) perform and record musical work; wish to claim copyright in the recorded performance only	SR	Performance and Sound Recording	2 complete phonorecords of "best edition"	1 complete phonorecord
Composer/author/performer creates music and performs it, recording the performance; wishes to claim copyright both in the music and the recording	SR	Music and performance *OR* Music, Words, Performance	2 complete phonorecords of "best edition"	1 complete phonorecord

*DO NOT LEAVE SPACE 2 BLANK. DO NOT USE "entire work" to describe "Nature of Authorship"
**For foreign publications, 1 copy or phonorecord of the first published edition.

> **NOTE:** To make a single registration, copyright ownership in the recorded work and in the sound recording must be the same.

31

MOTION PICTURES, INCLUDING VIDEO RECORDINGS

To register your home movies, videotapes, and other motion pictures, use Form PA (see p. 76).

The information in this section supplements, but does not replace, the basic information on copyright procedures and regulations contained in Chapters 1–3.

Definition

The definition of "motion pictures" in the copyright law is very broad, covering theatrical features and short subjects, television films and video recordings, documentaries and news films and programs, educational and instructional motion pictures, and every other form of cinematographic work including amateur movies and home video recordings.

In common speech the terms "motion picture" and "audiovisual work" are often used interchangeably, but they are not synonymous under the present law. As defined in section 101 of the statute, "motion pictures" are a special kind of "audiovisual works"; the broader classification of "audiovisual works" includes not only motion pictures but also certain types of works such as filmstrips that consist of sequences of images but do not give any impression of motion when shown.

The definitions of both "motion pictures" and "audiovisual works" also cover any sounds accompanying the images (such as a motion picture soundtrack, the sound channel of a video recording, or an audio recording cued directly to the images of a filmstrip). The definitions make clear that these "accompanying sounds" are considered part of the "motion picture" or "audiovisual work" and are included in the copyrighted work as a whole. The sounds do not need to be physically integrated with the visual images to be considered "accompanying sounds."

A work must meet the following criteria to be considered a "motion picture" for copyright purposes:

1. It must first of all be an "audiovisual work": It must consist of a series of related images that are "fixed" in some tangible medium of expression (such as film, tape, or disk), and that are, by their nature, intended to be shown by means of projectors or other viewing equipment;
2. These images must be capable of being shown a certain successive order; and
3. The images must impart an impression of motion when they are shown successively.

The Requirement for "Fixation"

Like all other types of copyrightable works, motion pictures must be "fixed" in tangible form as a condition of Federal statutory copyright protection.

Section 102 of the new law provides copyright protection for "original works of authorship" if they are "fixed in any tangible

32

medium of expression, now known or later developed, from which they can be perceived, reproduced, or otherwise communicated, either directly or with the aid of a machine or device."

Section 101 defines the concept of "fixation" as follows:

A work is "fixed" in a tangible medium of expression when its embodiment in a copy or phonorecord, by or under the authority of the author, is sufficiently permanent or stable to permit it to be perceived, reproduced, or otherwise communicated for a period of more than transitory duration. A work consisting of sounds, images, or both, that are being transmitted, is "fixed" for purposes of this title if a fixation of the work is being made simultaneously with its transmission.

A purely live performance or telecast would not be considered a "motion picture" for copyright purposes. Once an authorized fixation of the performance or telecast has been made in the form of a film or video recording, the resulting work is a "motion picture."

The Meaning of ''Publication'' in Relation to Motion Pictures

A copy must exist before publication can occur: In order for a motion picture to be considered "published" under the present copyright law, one or more copies (that is, for example, film prints, videotapes, or videodisks of the finished motion picture) must exist. Advertising and catalog or other distribution offers made before or during production of the motion picture would not constitute publication until the date when one or more copies are actually ready for distribution.

Public distribution: Publication of a motion picture takes place when one or more copies are actually distributed in some way to a member or members of the public at large, regardless of how the copy or copies changed hands—whether by sale, rental, lease, or lending.

Offering to distribute: Publication also takes place when an offer is made to a group of persons (whether members of the public at large or not) to distribute copies of the motion picture to them for purposes of further distribution to the public, or for purposes of public performance or exhibition. This provision means that publication takes place whenever copies are ready for distribution and are actually offered for distribution to a group of wholesalers, retailers, broadcasters, motion picture distributors, or motion picture exhibitors.

Performance is not publication: Merely showing a motion picture (by screening or performing it on television) is not by itself a publication, even if the viewing audience is very large. There must be some actual or offered distribution of a copy of the work before publication is considered to have taken place under the law.

Publication of component parts: For purposes of registration, the Copyright Office has taken the position that publication of a motion picture constitutes publication of the component parts (both visual and aural) embodied in the motion picture. Therefore, the registration of the motion picture will cover all portions of the screenplay, musical score, etc., to the extent they are actually embodied in the published motion picture.

Certain elements not contained in the published motion picture, for example, character descriptions, directions for the camera or actors, or omitted dialogue, may be registered as unpublished.

Deposit Requirements for Registration of Motion Pictures

In all cases, whether the motion picture is published or unpublished, your deposit must include a written description of the contents of the motion picture. This may be a shooting script or continuity, a pressbook, or a detailed synopsis.

SEPARATE DESCRIPTION

The separate description should contain as full, complete, and detailed information about the work as possible. If a shooting script is available, it is the preferred form of the description. The description should include all of the following:

1. The title of the work. If the work is part of a series, both the continuing title and the episode title and/or number, if any, of the particular episode, installment, or segment should be given;
2. A statement of the nature and general theme of the work and a summary of its plot or contents;
3. The date when the motion picture was "fixed" (that is, generally when the filming or video recording was completed). *If the motion picture consists of an authorized video recording of a live television program made simultaneously with the telecast, the description should make this clear and should contain information about the telecast;*
4. If the work has been transmitted on television, the date of the first telecast;
5. The running time; and
6. The credits appearing on the work, if any.

UNPUBLISHED MOTION PICTURES

If you are registering the motion picture in unpublished form, the Form PA and registration fee of $10 should be accompanied by a deposit consisting of the written description and one of the following:

1. One complete copy of the motion picture containing all the visual and aural elements that you want the registration to cover.

OR

2. Identifying material consisting of one of the following:

    Either an audio cassette or other audio recording reproducing the entire soundtrack or other sound portion of the motion picture;

    Or a set of prints consisting of one frame enlargement or similar visual reproduction from each 10-minute segment of the motion picture. Prints taken from the viewing monitor are the preferred deposit form.

> **NOTE:** If you elect to submit an alternative deposit in lieu of an actual copy of the unpublished motion picture, the written description *must* include all six of the items listed above.

PUBLISHED MOTION PICTURES

If you are registering a published motion picture, the Form PA and $10 registration fee must be accompanied by one complete copy of the best edition (see p. 22) as well as the written description.

What is a "Complete Copy"? A copy is "complete" if the reproduction of all of the visual and aural elements comprising the copyrightable subject matter in the work is clear, undamaged, undeteriorated, and free of splices, and if the copy itself and its physical housing are free from any defects that would interfere with the performance of the work or that would cause mechanical, visual, or audible defects or distortions.

MOTION PICTURE AGREEMENT

The regulations permit a motion picture copyright depositor to enter into an agreement with the Library of Congress allowing for the temporary (or, in some cases, the permanent) return of deposit copies to the depositor under certain conditions. The Motion Picture Agreement provides that after copyright registration has been completed, the deposit copy will be returned to the depositor (at the depositor's expense) and is subject to recall for the permanent collections of the Library of Congress within a period of 2 years. The depositor, in signing the Motion Picture Agreement, agrees to provide the Library of Congress with a copy of archival quality if and when such a copy is requested. For detailed information concerning the Motion Picture Agreement and the related shipping and insurance procedures, write:

The Deposits and Acquisitions Section
Acquisitions and Processing Division
Copyright Office, Library of Congress
Washington, D.C. 20559

Visual Arts

To register your drawings, paintings, sculpture, and other works of visual art, use Form VA (see p. 84).

The information in this section supplements, but does not replace, the basic information on copyright procedures and regulations contained in Chapters 1–3.

Types of Works Protected

Copyright protects original "pictorial, graphic, and sculptural works," which include two-dimensional and three-dimensional works of fine, graphic, and applied art. The following is a list of examples of such works:

Advertisements, commercial prints, labels
Artificial flowers and plants, floral arrangements
Artwork applied to clothing or other useful articles
Bumper stickers, decals, stickers
Cartoons, comic strips
Collages
Dolls, toys
Drawings, paintings, murals
Enamel works
Fabric, floor and wallcoverings designs
Games, puzzles
Greeting cards, postcards, stationery
Holograms, computer and laser artwork
Jewelry designs
Logo artwork
Maps: cartographic works, globes, relief models
Masks
Models
Mosaics
Needlework and craft kits
Original prints: engravings, etchings, serigraphs, silk screen prints, woodblock prints
Patterns for sewing, knitting, crochet, needlework
Photographs, photomontages
Posters
Record jacket artwork or photography
Relief and intaglio prints
Reproductions: lithographs, collotypes
Sculpture: carvings, ceramics, figurines, maquettes, molds, relief sculptures
Stained glass designs
Stencils, cut-outs
Technical drawings, architectural drawings, blueprints, diagrams, mechanical drawings
Weaving designs, lace designs, tapestries

Types of Works Not Protected

Copyright protection for an original work of authorship does not extend to the following:

- Ideas, concepts, discoveries, principles;
- Formulas, processes, systems, methods, procedures;
- Words and short phrases such as names, titles, and slogans;
- Familiar symbols or designs;
- Mere variations of typographic ornamentation, lettering or coloring.
- The mechanical or utilitarian aspects of a useful article that may also have a visual design that is copyrightable. See following section.

Useful Articles

A "useful article" is an article having an intrinsic utilitarian function that is not merely to portray the appearance of the article or to convey information. Examples are clothing, furniture, machinery, dinnerware, and lighting fixtures. An article that is normally part of a useful article may itself be a useful article; for example, an ornamental wheel cover on an automobile.

Copyright does not protect the mechanical or utilitarian aspects of such works of craftsmanship. It may, however, protect any pictorial, graphic, or sculptural authorship that can be identified separately from the utilitarian aspects of an object. Thus, a useful article may have both copyrightable and uncopyrightable features. For example, a carving on the back of a chair or a floral relief design on silver flatware could be protected by copyright, but the design of the chair or flatware itself could not. Some designs of useful articles may qualify for protection under federal trademark or patent law. *(See Parts II and III of this book, beginning on pp. 106 and 130.)*

Publication

The copyright law defines "publication" as: the distribution of copies of a work to the public by sale or other transfer of ownership or by rental, lease, or lending. Offering to distribute copies to a group of persons for purposes of further distribution or public display also constitutes publication. A public display does not of itself constitute publication.

A work of art that exists in only one copy, such as a painting or statue, is not regarded as published when the single existing copy is sold or offered for sale in the traditional way—for example, through an art dealer, gallery, or auction house.

When the work is reproduced in multiple copies (such as reproductions of a painting or castings of a statue), the work is published when copies of the reproductions are publicly distributed or offered to a group for further distribution or public display.

All works distributed to the public should bear a notice of copyright, and a work published in the United States with a notice of copyright becomes subject to mandatory deposit in the Library of Congress.

For information about the copyright notice, see Chapter 2, p. 15. For information about mandatory deposit, see Chapter 3, p. 22.

Form of Notice

A proper copyright notice for works of the visual arts consists of the following three elements:

1. *The symbol* © (the letter C in a circle), or the word "Copyright," or the abbreviation "Copr.";
2. *The year of first publication* of the work; and
3. *The name of the copyright owner,* or an abbreviation by which the name can be recognized, or a generally known

alternative designation of the owner. Example:

© 1987 John Doe

The year may be omitted where a pictorial, graphic, or sculptural work, with accompanying text, if any, is reproduced in or on greeting cards, postcards, stationery, jewelry, dolls, toys, or any useful article. In the case of a compilation or derivative work incorporating previously published material, the year date of first publication of the compilation or derivative work is sufficient.

The notice should be permanently attached to the copies, legible to the ordinary user, and placed in such manner and location that it gives reasonable notice of the claim to copyright. It must not be concealed from view upon reasonable examination.

What To Send

Works of the visual arts may be registered in published or unpublished form. Registration may be made at any time during the life of the copyright. To register a copyright claim in a work of the visual arts, send the following material for each claim **in the same envelope or package** to the Register of Copyrights, Copyright Office, Library of Congress, Washington, D.C. 20559:

1. A properly completed application Form VA;
2. A nonreturnable deposit of the work to be registered; and
3. A nonrefundable filing fee of $10 in the form of a check or money order, payable to the **Register of Copyrights.** Do not send cash.

Mandatory Deposit

Whether or not copyright registration is sought, the copyright law contains a mandatory deposit requirement for works published with a notice of copyright in the United States. The owner of copyright, or the owner of the exclusive right of publication in the work, is required to deposit two complete copies of the best edition (see p. 22) for the use of the Library of Congress within three months of publication in the United States. Failure to deposit does not affect copyright protection, but it can result in fines and other penalties.

Some categories of pictorial, graphic, and sculptural works are exempt from this requirement, and the obligation is reduced for other categories. The following works are **exempt** from the mandatory deposit requirement:

- Scientific and technical drawings and models;
- Greeting cards, picture postcards, and stationery;
- 3-dimensional sculptural works (but not including globes, relief models, and similar cartographic works);
- Works published only as reproduced in or on jewelry, toys, games, textiles, packaging material, and any useful article;
- Advertising material published in connection with articles of merchandise, works of authorship, or services;

- Works first published as individual contributions to collective works (but not the collective work as a whole);
- Works first published outside the United States and later published without change in the United States, under certain conditions. (For more information, write to the Register of Copyrights and request Circular 96, Sections 202.19, 20, and 21.)

Deposit Requirements for Registration

This section presents a simplified version of the deposit requirements for registration of claims to copyright in visual arts material. It should be viewed only as a basic guide. The items listed in the tables are only examples and are not meant to be restrictive. For more detailed information, write for a copy of ML–347 "Deposit Regulations of the Copyright Office." Mail to:

Publications Section, LM–455
Copyright Office
Library of Congress
Washington, D.C. 20559

SPECIFICATIONS FOR VISUAL ARTS IDENTIFYING MATERIAL

Copyright Office regulations require the deposit of identifying material instead of copies for three-dimensional works and for works that have been applied to three-dimensional objects. Examples of such works include sculpture, toys, jewelry, artwork on plates, and fabric or textile attached to or part of a three-dimensional object such as furniture. Identifying material must also be submitted for any pictorial, graphic, or sculptural work that exceeds 96" in any dimension.

Identifying material is permitted but not required for registration of certain unpublished two-dimensional works, for example, fabric emblems, decals, greeting cards and picture postcards, maps, drawings, and paintings. Identifying material is permitted but not required for registration of the following unpublished or published works: artwork applied to T-shirts or other wearing apparel; bed, bath, and table linens; and jewelry cast only in base metal.

If you either choose or are required to deposit identifying material to register your claim, you should make sure the identifying material meets the following specifications:

- *Type of identifying material:* The material should consist of photographic prints, transparencies, photocopies, drawings, or similar two-dimensional reproductions or renderings of the work, in a form visually perceivable without the aid of a machine or device.
- *Color or black and white:* If the work is a pictorial or graphic work, the material should reproduce the actual colors employed in the work. In all other cases, the material may be in black and white or may consist of a reproduction of the actual colors.
- *Completeness:* As many pieces of identifying material should

39

be submitted as are necessary to show clearly the entire copyrightable content of the work for which registration is being sought.

- *Number of sets:* Only one set of complete identifying material is required. **NOTE:** With respect to three-dimensional holograms, please write the Copyright Office for additional information.
- *Size:* Photographic transparencies must be at least 35 mm in size and, if 3 × 3 inches or less, must be fixed in cardboard, plastic, or similar mounts; transparencies larger than 3 × 3 inches should be mounted. All types of identifying material other than photographic transparencies must be not less than 3 × 3 inches and not more than 9 × 12 inches, but preferably 8 × 10 inches. The image of the work should show clearly the entire copyrightable content of the work.
- *Title and dimension:* At least one piece of identifying material must give the title of the work on its front, back, or mount, and should include an exact measurement of one or more dimensions of the work.

COPYRIGHT NOTICE

For a work published with notice of copyright, the notice and its position on the work must be clearly shown on at least one piece of identifying material. If necessary because of the size or position of the notice, a separate drawing or similar reproduction may be submitted. Such reproduction should be no smaller than 3 × 3 inches and no larger than 9 × 12 inches, showing the exact appearance and content of the notice and its specific position on the work. For further information about the copyright notice, see Chapter 2.

DEPOSITS FOR TWO-DIMENSIONAL WORKS

Nature of Work	Required Deposit	
	Published	**Unpublished**
Advertisements (pictorial)	1 copy as published or prepublication camera-ready copy	Photocopy, proof, drawing, copy, or layout
Artwork for bed, bath and table linens or for wearing apparel (for example, heat transfers or decals already applied to T-shirts)	1 copy if it can be folded in a form not exceeding 4" in thickness; otherwise, I.D. material	same as published
Blueprints, architectural drawings, mechanical drawings, diagrams	1 complete copy	1 copy
Book jackets or record jackets	1 complete copy	1 copy
Commercial print published in newspaper or other periodical	One copy of entire page or pages	
Commercial print or label (for example, flyers, labels, brochures or catalogs used in connection with the sale of goods or services)	1 complete copy	1 copy
Contributions to Collective Works (Photographs, drawings, cartoons, etc., published as part of a periodical or anthology)	1 complete copy of the best edition of entire collective work, complete section containing contribution if published in newspaper, entire page containing contribution, contribution cut from the newspaper, or photocopy of contribution as it was published	
Fabric, textile, wallpaper, carpeting, floor tile, wrapping paper, yard goods	1 complete copy (or swatch) showing the design repeat and copyright notice	1 complete copy (or I.D. material if the work has not been fixed in repeat
Fabric emblems or patches, decals or heat transfers (not applied to clothing), bumper stickers, campaign buttons.	1 complete copy	1 copy or I.D. material
Greeting cards, picture postcards, stationery, business cards, calendars	1 complete copy	1 copy or I.D. material
Holograms (2-dimensional)	1 actual copy if image is visible without the aid of a machine or device; otherwise 2 sets of display instructions and 2 sets of I.D. material showing the displayed image	1 copy or display instructions and I.D. material of image
Maps or cartographic material	2 complete copies	1 copy or I.D. material
Patterns, cross-stitch graphs, stitchery brochures, needlework and craft kits	1 complete copy	1 copy or I.D. material
Pictorial or graphic works (for example, artwork, drawings, illustrations, paintings)	2 complete copies	1 copy or I.D. material
Pictorial or graphic works fixed only in machine readable form	I.D. material	I.D. material

DEPOSITS FOR TWO-DIMENSIONAL WORKS, CONTINUED

Nature of Work	Required Deposit	
	Published	Unpublished
Posters, photographs, prints, brochures, exhibition catalogs, calendars	2 complete copies	Copy or proofs, photocopy, contact sheets
"Limited edition" posters, prints or etchings (published in quantities of fewer than 5 copies, or 300 or fewer numbered copies if individual author is owner of copyright)	1 copy or I.D. material	
Oversize material (exceeding 96" in any dimension	I.D. material	I.D. material
Artwork or illustrations on 3-D objects (for example, artwork on plates, mugs)	I.D. material	I.D. material
Fabric or textile attached to or part of a 3-D object (such as furniture)	I.D. material	I.D. material
Games	1 complete copy if container is no larger than 12"×24"×6"; otherwise, I.D. material	1 copy if container is no larger than 12"×24"×6" or I.D. material
Globes, relief models, or relief maps	1 complete copy including the stand (I.D. material *not* acceptable)	1 complete copy or I.D. material
Jewelry	I.D. material or 1 copy if fixed only in the form of jewelry cast in base metal not exceeding 4" in any dimension	same as published
Pictorial matter and/or text on a box or container that can be flattened (contents of container are not claimed)	1 copy of box or container if it can be flattened or 1 paper label	1 copy or I.D. material
Prints or labels inseparable from a 3-dimensional object (for example, silk screen label on a bottle)	I.D. material	I.D. material
Sculptures, toys, dolls, molds, relief plaques, statues	I.D. material	I.D. material
Sculpture (for example, doll) in a box with copyrightable pictorial and/or textual material; claim in sculpture and artwork/text	I.D. material for sculpture plus 1 copy of box and any other printed material	I.D. material for sculpture plus copy of box or I.D. material
Oversize material (exceeding 96" in any dimension)	I.D. material	I.D. material

MULTIMEDIA WORKS

To register a multimedia work, use Form PA, SR, or TX (See pp. 76, 80, or 72), depending upon the content of your work (see below, "Choosing the Right Form").

The information in this section supplements, but does not replace, the basic information on copyright procedures and regulations contained in Chapters 1–3.

Definition

A multimedia work is a work, often instructional, which, excluding its container, combines authorship in two or more media. The authorship may include:

- text;
- artwork;
- sculpture;
- cinematography;
- photography;
- sounds;
- music; or
- choreography.

The media may include two or more of the following:

- printed matter, such as a book, charts or posters, or sheet music;
- audiovisual material, such as a filmstrip, slides, videotape, or videodisk;
- a phonorecord, such as an audiodisk or audiotape; or
- a machine-readable copy, such as a computer-read disk, tape, or chip.

For the purpose of copyright registration, it is important to identify the copyrightable elements contained in the multimedia work. Identifying the elements will help you to determine which application form to use and what type of material to deposit.

Choosing the Right Form

Generally, select the applicable form on the following bases:

1. **Use Form PA** if the work contains an audiovisual element, such as a filmstrip, slides, film, or videotape, **regardless of whether there are any sounds.**
2. **Use Form SR** if the work does not contain an audiovisual element, but contains an audiotape or disk in which sound-recording authorship is claimed.
3. **Use Form TX** if the work contains only text, such as a manual and a computer program that produces a textual screen display.

Choosing the Right Form for Multimedia Works

The following are examples of typical multimedia deposits showing the appropriate form and authorship statements for registration. The fact situations pertaining to a particular claim will determine the correct way to complete the form.

Form to Use	Nature of Deposit	Suggested Nature of Authorship Statement
PA	Slides and booklet	(1) Entire work *or* (2) Text and photography
PA	Slides (or filmstrips), booklet, and audiocassettes	(1) Entire work *or* (2) Text as printed and recorded; photography, and sounds
PA	Videocassette, manual with text and pictorial illustrations	(1) Entire work *or* (2) Cinematography, text, and illustrations
PA	Filmstrip, pamphlets, poster, and music soundsheet	(1) Entire work *or* (2) Photography, text, artwork, lyrics, music, and sounds
PA	Manuals, container with artwork, and identifying material (computer program listing, videotape) for machine-readable diskette which produces pictorial screen display	Printed text and artwork, text of computer program, and audiovisual work
PA	Manual, videodisk, and identifying material for computer program on machine-readable diskette (or cassette)	Printed text, cinematography, and text of computer program
SR	Audiocassettes and manual	**Do Not Use "Entire Work" on Form SR.** Text as printed and recorded, and sound recording
SR	Music soundsheets, booklets, and posters	Text, artwork, lyrics, music, and sound recording
SR	Audiocassettes, manual, and identifying material for computer program on machine-readable diskette (or cassette)	Text of manual and computer program, recorded text, and sound recording
TX	Manuals and identifying material for computer program on machine-readable diskette (or cassette) which produces textual screen display	Text of manuals and computer program

Deposit Requirements

The application must be accompanied by a deposit of the work to be registered. The deposit requirement varies according to the type of work being registered, and whether the work has been published. Copies or phonorecords deposited will not be returned.

UNPUBLISHED WORKS

Deposit one complete multimedia kit, containing all elements covered by the registration. (All elements should bear the title of the work. If the work contains color, the copy sent as a deposit should be in color.)

PUBLISHED WORKS (SEE P. 12 FOR THE DEFINITION OF PUBLICATION.)

For a multimedia kit first published in the United States, deposit one "complete copy" of the best published edition. A "complete copy" includes all elements in the unit of publication. (See Chapter 3, p. 22, for information on the best edition criteria.)

For a multimedia kit first published outside the United States, deposit one complete copy as first published.

WORKS CONTAINING A MOTION-PICTURE ELEMENT

If the multimedia kit contains a motion-picture element, deposit a description of the motion picture in addition to the normal deposit requirements. The Library of Congress prefers the most detailed description possible, such as a shooting script, but will accept a synopsis or other general description. (See copyright registraton for motion pictures, p. 32.)

WORKS FIXED OR PUBLISHED IN MACHINE-READABLE COPIES

When the multimedia kit contains authorship that is fixed or published only in machine-readable form, such as a computer tape or disk, or a semiconductor chip, deposit the appropriate identifying material for the machine-readable copy.

• **Pictorial Images.** If the machine-readable copy produces a series of pictorial images (such as a videogame or instructional work), deposit the following material for this kind of audiovisual work:

1. A written synopsis or outline of the content of the audiovisual work; and
2. A reproduction of the audiovisual elements, in the form of:
   a. A videotape, depicting representative portions of the copyrightable content, or
   b. A series of photographs or drawings depicting representative portions of the work; and
3. The container and any instructional guide, if either contains authorship in which copyright is being claimed.

NOTE: If the pictorial images exist in color, they should be reproduced in color.

If the work is published with a copyright notice, the notice and its position on the work must be clearly shown on the identifying material.

• **Textual Images.** If the machine-readable copy produces only a series of textual images, deposit one copy in visually perceptible form of the first and last 25 pages or the equivalent and five or more pages of the remainder, including the copyright notice, if any.

• **Musical Compositions.** If the machine-readable copy produces a musical composition, deposit a notated transcription or recording (audiotape or audiodisk) of the entire work.

• **Sound Recordings.** If the machine-readable copy produces a sound recording, deposit a recording of the entire work on an audiotape or audiodisk.

DERIVATIVE WORKS

To register a creative work based upon another work, use Form PA, TX, or SR (see pp. 76, 72, and 80), depending upon the medium of the work you wish to register (see p. 28 for details).

The information in this section supplements, but does not replace, the basic information on copyright procedures and regulations contained in Chapters 1–3.

Definition

A "derivative work"—that is, a work that is based on (or derived from) one or more already existing works—is copyrightable if it includes what the copyright law calls an "original work of authorship." Derivative works, also known as "new versions," include such works as translations, musical arrangements, dramatizations, fictionalizations, art reproductions, and condensations. Any work in which the editorial revisions, annotations, elaborations, or other modifications represent, as a whole, an original work of authorship is a "derivative work" or "new version."

A typical example of a derivative work received for registration in the Copyright Office is one that is primarily a new work but incorporates some previously published material. This previously published material makes the work a derivative work under the copyright law.

To be copyrightable, a derivative work must be different enough from the original to be regarded as a "new work" or must contain a substantial amount of new material. Making minor changes or additions of little substance to a preexisting work will not qualify the work as a new version for copyright purposes. The new material must be original and copyrightable in itself. Titles, short phrases, and format, for example, are not copyrightable.

Examples of Derivative Works

The following examples show some of the many different types of derivative works:

Television drama (based on a novel)
Motion picture (based on a play)
Novel in English (a translation of a book originally published in Russian)
Sound recording (long-playing record in which two of the 10 selections were previously published on a 45 rpm single)
Sound recording (long-playing record in which several of the previously released tracks have been remixed with new instrumentation)

Sculpture (based on a drawing)
Drawing (based on a photograph)
Book of maps (based on public domain maps with some new
    maps)
Lithograph (based on a painting)
Biography of John Doe (which contains journal entries and
    letters by John Doe)
Drama about John Doe (based on the letters and journal
    entries of John Doe)
Words and music (some of the words are from the Bible)
Words and musical arrangement (arrangement is based on a
    piece by Bach)
Musical arrangement (based on a work by Bach)

Compilations and Abridgments

Compilations and abridgments may also be copyrightable if they contain new work of authorship. When the collecting of the preexisting material that makes up the compilation is a purely mechanical task with no element of editorial selection, or when only a few minor deletions constitute an abridgment, copyright protection for the compilation or abridgment as a new version is not available.

Some examples of copyrightable compilations are:

Book of "Best Short Stories of 1988" (selected from stories
    published in magazines and literary journals in 1988)
Sound recording of "Biggest Pop Hits of 1988" (selected from
    recordings released in 1988)
Book of "Great News Photos of 1988" (selected from
    newspapers and newsmagazines published in 1988)

In the above examples, original authorship was involved in deciding which were the best stories, the biggest hits, or greatest photos and in what order to present the respective works within the compilation.

Copyright Protection

The copyright in a derivative work covers only the additions, changes, or other new material appearing for the first time in the work. It does not extend to any preexisting material and does not imply a copyright in that material.

One cannot extend the length of protection for a copyrighted work by creating a derivative work. A work that has fallen in the public domain—that is, which is no longer protected by copyright—may be used for a derivative work, but the copyright in the derivative work will not restore the copyright of the public domain material. Neither will it prevent anyone else from using the same public domain work for another derivative work.

In any case where a protected work is used unlawfully—that is, without the permission of the owner of copyright—copyright will not be extended to the illegally used part.

Copyright Notice

See Chapter 2, beginning on p. 15, for information on the copyright notice.

In the case of a derivative work or a compilation, the information in the notice should relate to the new work.

Although not required by law, it is perfectly acceptable (and often helpful) for a work to contain a notice for the original material as well as for the new work. For example, if a previously registered book contains only a new introduction, the notice might be:

© 1937 John Doe; introduction © 1988 Mary Smith

Application Forms

The appropriate application form to use to register a claim to copyright in a derivative work depends upon the type of work for which registration is sought. It does *not* depend upon the preexisting or public domain material that may have been used to create the derivative work.

For example, to register a claim for a screenplay based on a novel, use Form PA (for performing arts), not Form TX (for original novels). To register a sound recording based on previously registered words and music, use Form SR (for sound recordings), not Form PA (for original words and music).

AUTOMATED DATABASES

To register your original database, use Form TX (see p. 72).

The information in this section supplements, but does not replace, the basic information on copyright procedures and regulations contained in Chapters 1–3.

Definition

An automated database is a body of facts, data, or other information assembled into an organized format suitable for use in a computer and comprising one or more files.

The copyright law does not specifically enumerate databases as copyrightable subject matter but the legislative history indicates that Congress considered computer databases and compilations of data as "literary works" subject to copyright protection. Databases may be considered copyrightable as a form of compilation, which is defined in the law as a work "formed by the collection and assembling of preexisting materials or of data that are selected, coordinated, or arranged in such a way that the resulting work as a whole constitutes an original work of authorship."

Extent of Copyright Protection

Copyright protection extends to the compilation of facts. Thus, the compilation aspect of a database is generally copyrightable if it represents original authorship. In some instances some or all of the contents of a database, new or revised, may also be copyrightable, as in the case of a full-text bibliographic database.

Copyright protection is not available for the selection and ordering of data in a database where the collection and arrangement of the material is a mechanical task only, and represents no original authorship; e.g., merely transferring data from hard copy to computer storage.

What Constitutes Publication of a Database?

The copyright law defines publication as "the distribution of copies or phonorecords of a work to the public by sale or other transfer of ownership, or by rental, lease, or lending. The offering to distribute copies or phonorecords to a group of persons for purposes of further distribution, public performance, or public display, constitutes publication." It is unclear whether on-line availability with or without printers for the user constitutes publication of the work under the copyright law. The Copyright Office does not determine whether a particular database is published or not. Instead, that decision is made by the copyright owner.

Registration for Published and Unpublished Databases

Since automated databases are typically revised or updated more frequently than other types of works, it is important to be aware of the scope of each registration. Registration for a *published* database extends only to the material first published as a unit, i.e., that which is published on the date given in the application as the "date of publication." Subsequent revisions or updates published together on a given date are considered another single published unit. Several separately published units (for example, updates published on three different dates) cannot be grouped together and registered using a single application and fee. Instead, each unit of publication is subject to separate registration, requiring a separate application, fee, and deposit.

Registration for an *unpublished* database extends to the database as it exists at the time it is submitted for registration. Subsequent additions or revisions to an unpublished database may be grouped together and registered either as a single claim or separately using separate applications and fees.

What to Send
- A completed Form TX
- A $10.00 nonrefundable filing fee payable to the Register of Copyrights
- Appropriate deposit

Deposit Requirements

For databases fixed and/or published only in machine-readable copies, the deposit requirements are the same for published and unpublished databases except that, if the database is published, the deposit must also include a representation of or the page containing the copyright notice, if any.

The deposit for published and unpublished databases should consist of one copy of identifying portions of the work reproduced in a form visually perceptible without the aid of a machine or device, either on paper or in microform.

SPECIFIC REQUIREMENTS

- *Single-file Database* (data records pertaining to a single common subject matter):
  —identifying portions (first and last 25 pages).

- *Multiple-file Database* (separate and distinct groups of data records):
  —representative portions of each file (50 data records or the entire file, whichever is less).

- *Revised Database* (either single or multiple file):
  —representative portions of the added or modified material (50 pages or the entire revised portions, whichever is less).

NOTE: For multiple-file databases (new or revised), the deposit must also include a **descriptive statement** containing: title of the database; name and address of copyright claimant; name and content of each separate file within the database, including subject matter, origin of data and number of separate records within each file. For published multiple-file databases, also include a description of the exact contents of any machine-readable copyright notice used in or with the database (plus manner and frequency of display); and sample of any visually perceptible copyright notice affixed to the copies or container.

SPECIAL DEPOSIT FOR ENCODED DATABASES

Database deposits should be humanly intelligible, preferably printouts written in a natural language. If the deposit is encoded, it should include a key or explanation of the code so that a copyright examiner can determine the presence of copyrightable material. When no key or explanation is provided with an unintelligible database, registration will be made under the rule of doubt upon receipt of the copyright owner's written confirmation that the work as deposited represents copyrightable authorship.

Rule-of-doubt registrations occur when there is a reasonable doubt about the ultimate action which might be taken under the same circumstances by an appropriate court with respect to whether the material deposited for registration constitutes copyrightable subject matter or whether the other legal and formal requirements of the statute have been met. The doubt concerning encoded databases results from the examiner's inability to determine the presence of copyrightable material.

Special Relief and Trade Secrets

When a database contains trade secrets or other confidential material that the applicant is unwilling to disclose through deposit for registration, the Copyright Office is willing to consider special relief requests, permitting the deposit of less than or other than the required deposit. Special relief requests are granted at the discretion of the Chief, Examining Division, upon receipt of the applicant's written request, setting forth specific reasons why the request should be granted and indicating what deposit the applicant is able to make.

SERIALS

To register your newsletter, magazine, and other serial publications, use Form SE (see p. 88).

The information in this section supplements, but does not replace, the basic information on copyright procedures and regulations contained in Chapters 1–3.

Definition

For copyright purposes, serials are defined as works issued or intended to be issued in successive parts bearing numerical or chronological designations and intended to be continued indefinitely. The classification "serial" includes periodicals, newspapers, magazines, bulletins, newsletters, annuals, journals, and proceedings of societies, as well as other similar works.

> **NOTE:** A claim to copyright in a serial issue does not give blanket protection for other issues published under the same serial title. Each serial issue is considered a separate work for copyright purposes and should be registered separately. For example, registration of "vol. 1, no. 1" of *Country Doctor* applies only to that issue, and *not* to "vol. 1, no. 2."

What to Send

To register a serial issue, send the following three elements together in the same envelope or package to:

Register of Copyrights
Copyright Office
Library of Congress
Washington, D.C. 20559

1. A properly completed and signed application Form SE (use typewriter or black ink); be sure that the date on which the application is signed is the same as or later than the date the serial issue was published.
2. A non-returnable filing fee of $10 (check, money order, or bank draft, not cash) payable to: Register of Copyrights.

3. Two copies of the serial issue to be registered. (Send only one copy of the serial issue if the issue is unpublished, or if the issue was first published outside of the United States.)

If you plan to register many successive claims to copyright, you may wish to open a Deposit Account in the Copyright Office from which the $10 fee for each registration and other services may be paid. For further information about Deposit Accounts, write to the Register of Copyrights and request Circular 5.

Authorship: Work Made for Hire

Ordinarily, the person who actually creates the work is considered the author. However, the copyright law provides that in the case of a "work made for hire," the **employer** is the "author" of the work, and is therefore the initial owner of copyright unless the parties have expressly agreed otherwise. A "work made for hire" is either

- "A work prepared by an employee within the scope of his or her employment," or
- Under certain conditions as defined by the copyright law (section 101), a "specially ordered or commissioned work" where the parties have agreed in writing that the commissioned work shall be considered a "work made for hire."

"Made for hire" serials which fall into the first kind of "work made for hire" definition are characterized by employer-employee relationships in which the employees prepare the work within the scope of their employment, and the employer has the power to control or supervise the employees' work. This "work for hire" concept inherently requires that the employer be the initiating or motivating factor in causing the work to be created, and that the employer bear the expense of bringing the work into being. In those cases where an organization uses the efforts of volunteers in the creation of a work, the work may still be considered a "work made for hire" even though those volunteers were not specifically paid by the organization.

For the purpose of copyright registration, the author of a work is either the individual who, independently and in his/her own right, actually created the work, or in the case of a "work made for hire," the organization or individual who caused the work to be created.

For further clarification of this law by a recent U.S. Supreme Court decision, see p. 11.

Authorship: Collective Works

Most serials are collective works in which a number of contributions, constituting separate and independent works in themselves, are assembled into a collective whole. Two categories of authorship are inherent in the creation of collective works:

- Authorship of the collective work as a whole, and
- Authorship of the individual contributions to the collective work.

Authorship of the collective work as a whole includes the elements of revising, editing, compiling, and similar authorship that went into putting the work into final form.

The author of a serial issue as a whole is sometimes an individual person. More typical, however, the author is the organization (corporation, society, club) that directed the preparation of the serial issue as a whole. If so, the serial issue is a "work made for hire." In this case, the employer's authorship includes not only the collective authorship (described above) but also any individual contributions which employees of the employer prepare while working within the scope of their employment.

The Claimant and the Extent of the Claim

The copyright claimant in a serial issue is generally the person, organization, or legal entity authorized to claim copyright in the serial issue. The claimant in a serial issue is the author (often the "employer for hire") if the serial issue is a "work made for hire" as described in the previous paragraphs or the person or organization to whom all rights have been transferred.

The claimant registering a serial is entitled to claim copyright not only in the collective-work authorship for which the claimant is responsible (for example, the editing and compiling of the issue as a whole plus any individual contributions written by employees-for-hire of the author), but also in any independently authored contributions in which all rights have been transferred by the contributors to the serial issue claimant.

INDEPENDENTLY AUTHORED CONTRIBUTIONS WITHOUT THE TRANSFER OF RIGHTS

If the serial issue includes any independently authored contributions in which all rights have *not* been transferred by the contributor to the claimant for the serial issue as a whole, those contributions are not included in the claim being registered. The claimant in the contribution is different from the claimant in the serial issue as a whole.

A separately authored contribution *can*, however, be registered for copyright independently. To register such a contribution, the contributor would need to file a separate claim using Form TX or other appropriate application form.

A Group of Contributions to Periodicals

To register a group of works that qualify for a single registration (see below), use Form GR/CP (see p. 92). This form must be submitted with Form TX, PA, or VA (see pp. 72, 76, and 84).

The information in this section supplements, but does not replace, the basic information on copyright procedures and regulations contained in Chapters 1–3.

When Does a Group of Works Qualify for a Single Registration?

Form GR/CP is the appropriate adjunct application form to use when you are submitting a basic application on Form TX, Form PA, or Form VA, for a group of works that qualify for a single registration under section 408(c)(2) of the copyright statute.

A single copyright registration for a group of works can be made if **all** of the following conditions are met:

1. All of the works are by the same author, who is an individual (not an employer for hire); and
2. All of the works were first published as contributions to periodicals (including newspapers) within a twelve-month period; and
3. Each of the contributions as first published bore a separate copyright notice, and the name of the owner of copyright in the work (or an abbreviation or alternative designation of the owner) was the same in each notice; and
4. One copy of the entire periodical issue or newspaper section in which each contribution was first published must be deposited with the application; and
5. The application must identify each contribution separately, including the periodical containing it and the date of its first publication.

How To Apply for Group Registration

1. Make sure that all of the works you want to register together as a group qualify for a single registration.
2. Read through the following detailed instructions for group registration. Decide which form you should use for the basic registration (Form TX for non-dramatic literary works; or Form PA for musical, dramatic, and other works of the performing arts; or Form VA for pictorial and graphic works). Be sure that you have all of the information you need before you start filling out both the basic and the adjunct application forms.
3. Complete the basic application form, following the detailed instructions accompanying it **and the special instructions below.**
4. Complete the adjunct application on Form GR/CP and mail it, together with the basic application form and the required copy of each contribution, to:

   Register of Copyrights
   Library of Congress
   Washington, D.C. 20559

   Unless you have a deposit account in the Copyright Office, your application and copies must be accompanied by a check or money order for $10, payable to *Register of Copyrights.*

TWO APPLICATION FORMS MUST BE FILED

When you apply for a single registration to cover a group of contributions to periodicals, you must submit two application forms:

1. A basic application on either Form TX, or Form PA, or Form VA. It must contain all of the information required for copyright registration except the titles and information concerning publication of the contributions.
2. An adjunct application on Form GR/CP. The purpose of this form is to provide separate identification for each of the contributions and to give information about their first publication, as required by the statute.

WHICH BASIC APPLICATION FORM TO USE

The basic application form you choose to submit should be determined by the nature of the contributions you are registering. As long as they meet the statutory qualifications for group registration, the contributions can be registered together even if they are entirely different in nature, type, or content. However, you must choose which of three forms is generally the most appropriate on which to submit your basic application:

Form TX: for non-dramatic literary works consisting primarily of text. Examples are fiction, verse, articles, news stories, features, essays, reviews, editorials, columns, quizzes, puzzles, and advertising copy.

Form PA: for works of the performing arts. Examples are music, drama, choreography, and pantomimes.

Form VA: for works of the visual arts. Examples are photographs, drawings, paintings, prints, art reproductions, cartoons, comic strips, charts, diagrams, maps, pictorial ornamentation, and pictorial or graphic material published as advertising.

If your contributions differ in nature, choose the form most suitable for the majority of them. However, if any of the contributions consists preponderantly of non-dramatic text matter in English, you should file Form TX for the entire group.

For instructions to fill out application Form TX, see p. 72; for Form PA, see p. 76; for Form VA, see p. 84.

DEPOSIT REQUIREMENTS

The application forms you file for group registration must be accompanied by one complete copy of each contribution listed in Form GR/CP, exactly as the contribution was first published in a periodical. The deposit must consist of the entire issue of the periodical containing the contribution; or, if the contribution was first published in a newspaper, the deposit should consist of the entire section in which the contribution appeared. Tear sheets or proof copies are not acceptable for deposit.

COPYRIGHT NOTICE REQUIREMENTS

For published works, the law provides that a copyright notice in a specified form "shall be placed on all publicly distributed copies from which the work can be visually perceived." The required form of the notice generally consists of three elements:

1. the symbol "©", or the word "Copyright", or the abbreviation "Copr.";
2. the year of first publication of the work; and
3. the name of the owner of copyright in the work, or an abbreviation or alternative form of the name. For example:

© 1978 Samuel Craig.

Among the conditions for group registration of contributions to periodicals, the statute establishes two requirements involving the copyright notice:

1. Each of the contributions as first published must have borne a separate copyright notice; and
2. "The name of the owner of copyright in the work, or an abbreviation by which the name can be recognized, or a generally known alternative designation of the owner" must have been the same in each notice.

SUPPLEMENTARY REGISTRATION

To correct or amplify information in an earlier copyright registration, use Form CA (see p. 96).

As a general rule, only one basic copyright registration can be made for the same version of a particular work. Once a registration has been made for a work in the Copyright Office, that basic registration will ordinarily stand as the fundamental copyright record on which other, later, records relating to the particular work can be built.

To take care of cases where information in the basic registration turns out to be incorrect or incomplete, the law provides for "the filing of an application for supplementary registration, to correct an error in a copyright registration or to amplify the information given in a registration." The statute also declares: "The information contained in a supplementary registration augments but does not supersede that contained in the earlier registration."

A supplementary registration can be made either to "correct" or to "amplify" information in a basic registration.

Corrections

A "correction" is appropriate if information in a basic registration was incorrect at the time that basic registration was made. Examples: the basic registration identified someone incorrectly as an author of the work; or the work was registered as published when publication had not actually taken place.

Amplifications

"Amplifications" fall into three general categories:

1. Additional information that could have been given but was omitted at the time of basic registration (example: a co-author was omitted);
2. Changes in facts that have occurred since the basic registration (example: change of title); and
3. Explanations clarifying information given in the basic registration (example: statement of changes or additions in the version being registered was not sufficiently explicit).

The application for supplementary registration should be submitted on **Form CA**.

5 DURATION AND RENEWAL OF COPYRIGHT

On January 1, 1978, a completely new copyright statute (Title 17 of the United States Code) came into effect in the United States.

For purposes of computing the duration of copyright protection, the new law divides copyrighted works into three categories, depending on when they were originally copyrighted:

- **Works originally copyrighted before 1950 and renewed before 1978**

  These older works have automatically been given a longer copyright term. Under the new statute, copyrights that had already been renewed and were in their second term at any time between December 31, 1976, and December 31, 1977, inclusive, do not need to be renewed again. They were automatically extended to last for a total term of 75 years (a first term of 28 years plus a renewal term of 47 years) from the end of the year in which they were originally secured.

- **Works originally copyrighted between January 1, 1950, and December 31, 1977**

  Copyrights in their first 28-year term on January 1, 1978, will **still have to be renewed** in order to be protected for a second term. If a valid renewal registration is made at the proper time, the second term will last for 47 years (19 years longer than the 28-year renewal term under the old law). However, if renewal registration is not made within the statutory time limits, a copyright of this sort will expire on December 31st of its 28th year, and protection will be lost permanently.

- **Works created on or after January 1, 1978**

  The U.S. copyright law, for works created after its effective date, adopts the basic "life-plus-50" system already in effect in most other countries. A work that is created (fixed in tangible form for the first time) after January 1, 1978, is automatically protected from the moment of its creation, and is given a term lasting for the author's life, plus an additional 50 years after the author's death. In the case of "a joint work prepared by two or more authors who did not work for hire," the term lasts for 50 years after the last surviving author's death. For works made for hire, and for anonymous and pseudonymous works (unless the author's identity is revealed in Copyright Office records), the duration of copyright will be 75 years from first publication or 100 years from creation, whichever is shorter.

For works created on or after January 1, 1978, copyrights will not be renewable after their "life-plus-50" expiration.

Works that had been created before the current law came into effect but had neither been published nor registered for copyright before January 1, 1978, automatically are given federal copyright protection. The duration of copyright in these works will generally be computed in the same way as for new works: the life-plus-50 or 75/100-year terms will apply to them as well. However, all works in this category are guaranteed at least 25 years of statutory protection. The law specifies that in no case will copyright in a work of this sort expire before December 31, 2002, and if the work is published before that date the term may be extended by another 25 years, through the end of 2027.

YEAR-END EXPIRATION OF COPYRIGHT TERMS

The law provides that all terms of copyright will run through the end of the calendar year in which they would otherwise expire. This affects not only the duration of copyrights, but also the time limits for renewal registrations. From now on, the last day of a copyright will be December 31st of that copyright's last year; and for works originally copyrighted between 1950 and 1977, all periods for renewal registration will run from December 31 of the 27th year of the copyright and will end on December 31 of the following year.

WHO MAY CLAIM RENEWAL

Renewal copyright may be claimed only by those persons specified in the law. The statutory provisions on this point are essentially the same in the new law as those contained in the law in effect before 1978:

A. The following persons may claim renewal in all types of works except those enumerated in Paragraph B, below:

1. The author, if living, may claim as **the author.**
2. If the author is dead, the widow or widower of the author, or the child or children of the author, or both, may claim as **the widow of the author** or **the widower of the author** and/or **the child of the deceased author** or **the children of the deceased author.**
3. If there is no surviving widow, widower, or child, and the author left a will, the author's executors may claim as **the executors of the author.**
4. If there is no surviving widow, widower, or child, and the author left no will, the next of kin may claim as **the next of kin of the deceased author, there being no will.**

59

B. Only in the case of the following four types of works may the copyright proprietor (owner of the copyright at the time of renewal registration) claim renewal:

1. Posthumous work (a work as to which no copyright assignment or other contract for exploitation has occurred during the author's lifetime). Renewal may be claimed as **proprietor of copyright in a posthumous work**.
2. Periodical, cyclopedic, or other composite work. Renewal may be claimed as **proprietor of copyright in a composite work.**
3. Work copyrighted by a corporate body otherwise than as assignee or licensee of the individual author. Renewal may be claimed as **proprietor of copyright in a work copyrighted by a corporate body otherwise than as assignee of licensee of the individual author.** (This type of claim is considered appropriate in relatively few cases.)
4. Work copyrighted by an employer for whom such work was made for hire. Renewal may be claimed as **proprietor of copyright in a work made for hire.**

How to Compute the Renewal Time Limits

To determine the time limits for renewal in a particular case:

1. First, find out the date of original copyright for the work. (In the case of works originally registered in unpublished form, copyright begins on the date of registration; for published works, copyright begins on the date of first publication.)
2. Then add 28 years to the year the work was originally copyrighted.

Your answer will be the calendar year during which the copyright will be eligible for renewal, and December 31st of that year will be the renewal deadline.

Notice of Renewal Copyright

The Copyright Office is frequently asked whether the notice of copyright should be changed on copies of a work issued during the renewal term. The copyright law is silent on this point, and the continued use of the original form of notice may therefore be considered appropriate. However, a notice which also refers to the fact of renewal might be regarded as more informative and hence preferable; for example:

Copyright 1951 Katherine Mason
Copyright renewed 1979 by Richard Mason

NEW VERSIONS

Copyright in a new version of a previous work (such as an arrangement, translation, dramatization, compilation, or work republished with new matter) covers only the additions, changes, or other new material appearing for the first time in that version.

The copyright secured in a new version is independent of any copyright protection in material published or copyrighted earlier, and the only "authors" of a new version are those who contributed copyrightable matter to it. Thus, for renewal purposes, the person who wrote the original version upon which the new work is based cannot be regarded as an "author" of the new version, unless that person also contributed to the new matter.

HOW TO REGISTER A RENEWAL CLAIM

Application for renewal registration should be filed on Form RE (see p. 100). It is not necessary to send copies of the copyrighted work with the renewal application.

Renewal Fee

Each renewal application requires a separate registration fee of $6, which should be made payable to the Register of Copyrights. If several applications are submitted at the same time, a single check or other remittance for the total amount of the registration fees should accompany them.

Original Registration

A renewal claim cannot be registered unless there has already been an original registration for the first 28-year term of copyright in the work. However, as long as the necessary applications, copies, and fees are all received in the Copyright Office before the end of the first term, it is possible to make simultaneous original and renewal registrations.

RENEWALS FOR CONTRIBUTIONS TO PERIODICALS OR OTHER COMPOSITE WORKS

Separate Renewal for a Single Contribution

Separate renewal registration is possible for a work published as a contribution to a periodical, serial, or other composite work, whether the contribution was copyrighted independently or as part of the larger work in which it appeared. Except in the cases described in the next paragraph, each contribution published in a separate issue requires a separate renewal registration.

61

Renewal for a Group of Contributions

A single renewal registration can be made for a group of periodical contributions if all of the following five statutory conditions are met:

1. All of the works were written by the same author, who is or was an individual (not an employer. . .for hire);
2. All of the works were first published as contributions to periodicals (including newspapers) and were copyrighted on their first publication;
3. The renewal claimant or claimants, and the basis of the claim or claims, is the same for all of the works;
4. As explained in more detail below, the renewal application and fee are "received not more than 28 or less than 27 years after the 31st day of December of the calendar year in which all of the works were first published"; and
5. The renewal application identifies each work separately, including the periodical containing it and the date of first publication.

To be renewed as a group, all of the contributions must have been first published during the same calendar year. For example, suppose six contributions by the same author were published on April 1, 1960, July 1, 1960, November 1, 1960, February 1, 1961, July 1, 1961, and March 1, 1962. The three 1960 copyrights can be combined and renewed at any time during 1988, and the two 1961 copyrights can be renewed as a group during 1989, but the 1962 copyright must be renewed by itself, in 1990.

6 RECORDATION OF TRANSFERS AND OTHER DOCUMENTS

The initial owner of copyright generally has the exclusive right:

- **To reproduce the copyrighted work** in copies or phonorecords;
- **To prepare derivative works** based upon the copyrighted work;
- **To distribute copies or phonorecords** of the copyrighted work to the public by sale or other transfer of ownership, or by rental, lease, or lending;
- In the case of literary, musical, dramatic, and choreographic works, pantomimes, and motion pictures and other audiovisual works, **to perform the copyrighted work publicly;**
- In the case of literary, musical, dramatic, and choreographic works, pantomimes, and pictorial, graphic, or sculptural works, including the individual images of a motion picture, or other audiovisual work, **to display the copyrighted work publicly.**

DIVISIBILITY OF COPYRIGHT

Any or all of the exclusive rights of the copyright owner, or any subdivision of those rights, may be transferred. However, the transfer of exclusive rights is not valid unless the transfer is in **writing** and **signed** by the owner of the rights conveyed (or the owner's duly authorized agent). Transfer of a right on a nonexclusive basis does not require a written document, but a written document **is** required for all other transfers.

A copyright may also be conveyed by operation of law and may be bequeathed by will or pass at the death of the copyright owner as personal property by the applicable laws of intestate succession.

WHAT MAY BE RECORDED

A document which transfers copyright ownership or any other document pertaining to a copyright may be recorded in the Copyright

Office, providing the requirements of the copyright statute (title 17 of the United States Code) are met.

Transfers

A "transfer of copyright ownership" is an assignment, mortgage, grant of an exclusive license, transfer by will or intestate succession, or any other change in the ownership of any or all of the exclusive rights in a copyright whether or not it is limited in time or place of effect, but not including a nonexclusive license. A transfer of exclusive rights, other than by operation of law, is not valid unless an instrument of conveyance (for example, contract, bond, deed), or a note or memorandum of the transfer, is in **writing** and **signed** by the owner of the rights conveyed or the owner's duly authorized agent. The Copyright Office does not **make** or in any way participate in the making of transfers of copyright ownership, but rather only **records** a document of transfer after it has been executed by the parties. Special forms for documents and notarization are not essential to recordation. The Copyright Office does not provide forms for the use of persons recording transfers or documents. Documents submitted for recordation should *not* be in the form of a letter to the Copyright Office because this Office cannot make transfers of copyright ownership, but rather, serves as an office of public record of transfers.

Documents Pertaining to a Copyright

A document is considered to "pertain to a copyright" if it has a direct or indirect relationship to the existence, scope, duration, or identification of a copyright or to the ownership, division, allocation, licensing, transfer, or exercise of rights under a copyright. That relationship may be past, present, future, or potential. Examples:

Exclusive and nonexclusive licenses, contracts, mortgages, powers of attorney, certificates of change of corporate title, wills, and decrees of distribution.

The work to which the document pertains may be either published or unpublished, and registration for the work need not have been made before recordation.

ADVANTAGES OF RECORDATION

Recordation of a transfer or document pertaining to a copyright is not mandatory, nor is it necessary before any infringement suit may be filed in a court by a transferee.

However, recordation of a document in the Copyright Office provides the advantage of "constructive notice"—a legal concept implying, in this instance, that the public could have had actual knowledge of the facts stated in a properly recorded document.

WHAT TO SUBMIT FOR RECORDATION

Any transfer of copyright ownership or other document pertaining to a copyright may be recorded in the Copyright Office if the document filed for recordation is accompanied by the appropriate fee and it meets the following requirements:

1. The document must bear the actual signature or signatures of the person or persons who executed (signed) the document. Or, if a photocopy of the original signed document is submitted, it must be accompanied by a sworn or official certification. The certification must state that the attached reproduction is a true copy of the original signed document.

The certification must be:

a. a sworn certification signed by at least one of the parties to the signed document or by an authorized representative of that person and must contain a notarization or a statement made under penalty of perjury. Example:
   "I certify under penalty of perjury under the laws of the United States of America that the foregoing is a true copy of the original document"; **and**

b. an official certification; **and**

2. The document must be complete by its own terms, that is, a document which contains a reference to any schedule, appendix, exhibit, addendum, or other material as being attached or made a part of it, is recordable only if the attachment is submitted for recordation with the document; **and**

3. The document must be legible and capable of being reproduced in legible microform copies.

RECORDING FEE

Before the Copyright Office can record a document, it must receive the full recording fee prescribed in the law. The proper fee may be computed from the following schedule:

- The basic recording fee for a document consisting of six pages or less covering no more than one title is $10.
- An additional charge of 50 cents is made for each page over six.
- An additional charge of 50 cents is made for each title over one listed in the document, including former titles and alternate titles. Examples:

   A document consisting of two pages and containing two titles. Fee is $10.50.

A document consisting of 10 pages and containing six titles. Fee is $14.50.

NOTE: The fee for each transfer is $10 regardless of how many transfers are on a single page.

Recordations, transfers of copyright and other documents pertaining to a copyright should be submitted to:

Documents Unit, LM-462
Cataloging Division
Copyright Office
Library of Congress
Washington, D.C. 20559

7 HIGHLIGHTS OF U.S. ADHERENCE TO THE BERNE CONVENTION

A few areas of copyright law changed when the U.S. entered into the Berne Convention on March 1, 1989. This international treaty (the Berne Convention for the Protection of Literary and Artistic Works) gives copyright protection to individuals in all participating nations.

In order to fulfill its obligations to the Berne Union, the United States amended some of its copyright law. This chapter explains these changes.

EFFECT OF U.S. MEMBERSHIP IN THE BERNE UNION

As of March 1, 1989, copyright in the works of U.S. authors is protected automatically in all member nations of the Berne Union. (As of September 1989, there are a total of 80 member nations in the Berne Union, including the United States.)

Since members of the Berne Union agree to a certain minimum level of copyright protection, each Berne Union country will provide at least that guaranteed level for U.S. authors.

Members of the Berne Union agree to treat nationals of other member countries like their own nationals for purposes of copyright. Therefore, U.S. authors will often receive higher levels of protection than the guaranteed minimum.

Overall, piracy of U.S. works abroad can be fought more effectively.

As of March 1, 1989, works of foreign authors who are nationals of a Berne Union country and works first published in a Berne Union country are automatically protected in the United States.

U.S. LAW AMENDED

In order to fulfill its Berne Convention obligations, the United States made certain changes in its copyright law by passing the Berne Convention Implementation Act of 1988. These changes are not retroactive and are effective only on and after March 1, 1989.

Mandatory Notice of Copyright Is Abolished

Mandatory notice of copyright has been abolished for works published for the first time on or after March 1, 1989. Failure to place a notice of copyright on copies or phonorecords of such works can no longer result in the loss of copyright.

Voluntary Use of Notice Is Encouraged

Placing a notice of copyright on published works is still strongly recommended. One of the benefits is that an infringer will not be able to claim that he or she "innocently infringed" a work. (A successful innocent infringement claim may result in a reduction in damages for infringement that the copyright owner would otherwise receive.)

A sample notice of copyright is: © 1989 John Brown.

The notice requirement for works incorporating a predominant portion of U.S. government work has been eliminated as of March 1, 1989. For these works to receive the evidentiary benefit of voluntary notice, in addition to the notice, a statement is required on the copies identifying what is copyrighted.

A sample is: © 1989 Jane Brown. Copyright claimed in Chapters 7–10, exclusive of U.S. government maps.

Notice Unchanged for Works Published Before March 1, 1989

The Berne Convention Implementation Act is not retroactive. Thus, the notice requirements that were in place before March 1, 1989, govern all works first published during that period (regardless of national origin).

- Works first published between January 1, 1978, and February 28, 1989: If a work was first published without notice during this period, it is still necessary to register the work before or within five years after publication and add the notice to copies distributed in the United States after discovery of the omission.
- Works first published before January 1, 1978: If a work was first published without the required notice before 1978, copyright was lost immediately (except for works seeking "ad interim" protection). Once copyright is lost, it can never be restored in the United States, except by special legislation.

Mandatory Deposit

Copyright owners must deposit in the Copyright Office two complete copies or phonorecords of the best edition (see p. 22) of all works subject to copyright that are publicly distributed (published, see p. 12) in the United States, whether or not the work contains a notice of copyright. In general, this deposit requirement may be satisfied by registration. For more information about mandatory deposit, see p. 22.

Registration as a Prerequisite to Suit

Before a copyright infringement suit is brought for a work of U.S. origin, it must be submitted to the Copyright Office for registration.

When is the United States the country of origin of a work? The United States is the country of origin if:

- Publication first occurred in the United States.
- Publication occurred simultaneously in the United States and a non-Berne Union country. "Simultaneous publication" means within the first 30 days of publication.
- Publication occurred simultaneously in the United States and another Berne Union country that provides the same term as or a longer term of protection than the United States.
- The work is unpublished and all of the authors are nationals of the United States. (U.S. domiciliaries and habitual residents are treated the same as nationals.) In the case of an unpublished audiovisual work, all the authors are legal entities with headquarters in the United States.
- The work is a pictorial, graphic, or sculptural work that is incorporated in a permanent structure located in the United States.
- The work is first published in a non-Berne Union country and all of the authors are U.S. nationals. In the case of a published audiovisual work, all the authors are legal entities with headquarters in the United States.

Although Berne Convention works whose origin is **not** the United States are exempt from the requirement to register before suit can be brought, a person seeking the exemption bears the burden of proving to the court that the work is not subject to the registration requirement.

Benefits of Registration

Berne Convention works whose country of origin is not the United States need not be registered with the Copyright Office in order to bring an infringement suit. However, registration is still strongly recommended.

Presumption of Copyright Validity

The copyright owner who registers before or within five years of first publication receives the benefit of a legal presumption in court, called prima facie evidentiary weight. This means that the court will presume:

- that the facts stated in the copyright certificate of registration are true; and
- that the copyright is valid.

Statutory Damages and Attorney's Fees

Another benefit of timely registration is that the copyright owner of works registered for copyright protection within three months of publication, or before infringement, is eligible for an award of attorney's fees and statutory damages. These damages are now double the amounts previously provided. A copyright owner may elect to receive either actual damages or statutory damages. Where statutory damages are elected, the court determines the amount of the award, within a certain range. The Berne Convention Implementation Act doubles statutory damages to:

- A range between $500 and $20,000 for ordinary infringement;
- A maximum of $100,000 for willful infringement; and
- A minimum of $200 for innocent infringement.

Renewal Is Still Required

Works first federally copyrighted before 1978 must still be renewed in the 28th year in order to receive the second term of 47 years. If such a work is not timely renewed, it will fall into the public domain in the United States at the end of the 28th year.

Recordation

The copyright owner no longer has to record a transfer before bringing a copyright lawsuit in that owner's name.

Benefits of Recordation

The benefits of recordation in the Copyright Office are unchanged:

- Under certain conditions, recordation establishes priorities between conflicting transfers and nonexclusive licenses;
- Under certain conditions, recordation establishes priority between conflicting transfers; and,
- Recordation establishes a public record of the contents of the transfer or document.

Jukebox Licenses

Section 116 of the 1976 Copyright Act provides for a compulsory license to publicly perform nondramatic musical works by means of coin-operated phonorecord players (jukeboxes). The Berne Convention Implementation Act amends the law to provide for negotiated licenses between the user (the jukebox operator) and the copyright owner. If necessary, the parties are encouraged to submit to arbitration to facilitate negotiated licenses. Such licenses take precedence over the compulsory license.

MEMBERS OF THE BERNE UNION

The following are members of the Berne Union:

Argentina, Australia, Austria, The Bahamas, Barbados, Belgium, Benin (formerly Dahomey), Brazil, Bulgaria, Burkina Faso (formerly Upper Volta), Cameroon, Canada, Central African Republic, Chad, Chile, Colombia, Congo, Costa Rica, Côte d'Ivoire (Ivory Coast), Cyprus, Czechoslovakia, Denmark, Egypt, Fiji, Finland, France, Gabon, German Democratic Republic, Federal Republic of Germany, Greece, Guinea, Hungary, Iceland, India, Ireland, Israel, Italy, Japan, Lebanon, Liberia, Libya, Liechtenstein, Luxembourg, Madagascar (Malagasy Republic), Mali, Malta, Mauritania, Mexico, Monaco, Morocco, Netherlands, New Zealand, Niger, Norway, Pakistan, Peru, Philippines, Poland, Portugal, Romania, Rwanda, Senegal, South Africa, Spain, Sri Lanka (formerly Ceylon), Suriname, Sweden, Switzerland, Thailand, Togo, Trinidad and Tobago, Tunisia, Turkey, United Kingdom, United States, Uruguay, Vatican City (Holy See), Venezuela, Yugoslavia, Zaire, Zimbabwe.

8 FORMS AND INSTRUCTIONS FOR COPYRIGHT REGISTRATION

This section contains the following forms with instructions for completing them:

Form TX
Form PA
Form SR
Form VA
Form SE
Form GR/CP: Adjunct Application
Form CA
Form RE: Application for Renewal Registration

ⓔ Filling Out Application Form TX

Detach and read these instructions before completing this form. Make sure all applicable spaces have been filled in before you return this form.

BASIC INFORMATION

When to Use This Form: Use Form TX for registration of published or unpublished non-dramatic literary works, excluding periodicals or serial issues. This class includes a wide variety of works: fiction, non-fiction, poetry, textbooks, reference works, directories, catalogs, advertising copy, compilations of information, and computer programs. For periodicals and serials, use Form SE.

Deposit to Accompany Application: An application for copyright registration must be accompanied by a deposit consisting of copies or phonorecords representing the entire work for which registration is to be made. The following are the general deposit requirements as set forth in the statute:

Unpublished Work: Deposit one complete copy (or phonorecord).

Published Work: Deposit two complete copies (or phonorecords) of the best edition.

Work First Published Outside the United States: Deposit one complete copy (or phonorecord) of the first foreign edition.

Contribution to a Collective Work: Deposit one complete copy (or phonorecord) of the best edition of the collective work.

The Copyright Notice: For works first published on or after March 1, 1989, the law provides that a copyright notice on a specified form "may be placed on all publicly distributed copies from which the work can be visually perceived." Use of the copyright notice is the responsibility of the copyright owner and does not require advance permission from the Copyright Office. The required form of the notice for copies generally consists of three elements: (1) the symbol "©", or the word "Copyright," or the abbreviation "Copr."; (2) the year of first publication; and (3) the name of the owner of copyright. For example: "© 1989 Jane Cole." The notice is to be affixed to the copies "in such manner and location as to give reasonable notice of the claim of copyright." Works first published prior to March 1, 1989, **must** carry the notice or risk loss of copyright protection.

For information about notice requirements for works published before March 1, 1989, or other copyright information, write: Information Section, LM-401, Copyright Office, Library of Congress, Washington, D.C. 20559.

LINE-BY-LINE INSTRUCTIONS

1 SPACE 1: Title

Title of This Work: Every work submitted for copyright registration must be given a title to identify that particular work. If the copies or phonorecords of the work bear a title (or an identifying phrase that could serve as a title), transcribe that wording *completely* and *exactly* on the application. Indexing of the registration and future identification of the work will depend on the information you give here.

Previous or Alternative Titles: Complete this space if there are any additional titles for the work under which someone searching for the registration might be likely to look, or under which a document pertaining to the work might be recorded.

Publication as a Contribution: If the work being registered is a contribution to a periodical, serial, or collection, give the title of the contribution in the "Title of this Work" space. Then, in the line headed "Publication as a Contribution," give information about the collective work in which the contribution appeared.

2 SPACE 2: Author(s)

General Instructions: After reading these instructions, decide who are the "authors" of this work for copyright purposes. Then, unless the work is a "collective work," give the requested information about every "author" who contributed any appreciable amount of copyrightable matter to this version of the work. If you need further space, request additional Continuation sheets. In the case of a collective work, such as an anthology, collection of essays, or encyclopedia, give information about the author of the collective work as a whole.

Name of Author: The fullest form of the author's name should be given. Unless the work was "made for hire," the individual who actually created the work is its "author." In the case of a work made for hire, the statute provides that "the employer or other person for whom the work was prepared is considered the author."

What is a "Work Made for Hire"? A "work made for hire" is defined as: (1) "a work prepared by an employee within the scope of his or her employment"; or (2) "a work specially ordered or commissioned for use as a contribution to a collective work, as a part of a motion picture or other audiovisual work, as a translation, as a supplementary work, as a compilation, as an instructional text, as a test, as answer material for a test, or as an atlas, if the parties expressly agree in a written instrument signed by them that the work shall be considered a work made for hire." If you have checked "Yes" to indicate that the work was "made for hire," you must give the full legal name of the employer (or other person for whom the work was prepared). You may also include the name of the employee along with the name of the employer (for example: "Elster Publishing Co., employer for hire of John Ferguson").

"Anonymous" or "Pseudonymous" Work: An author's contribution to a work is "anonymous" if that author is not identified on the copies or phonorecords of the work. An author's contribution to a work is "pseudonymous" if that author is identified on the copies or phonorecords under a fictitious name. If the work is "anonymous" you may: (1) leave the line blank; or (2) state "anonymous" on the line; or (3) reveal the author's identity. If the work is "pseudonymous" you may: (1) leave the line blank; or (2) give the pseudonym and identify it as such (for example: "Huntley Haverstock, pseudonym"); or (3) reveal the author's name, making clear which is the real name and which is the pseudonym (for example: "Judith Barton, whose pseudonym is Madeline Elster"). However, the citizenship or domicile of the author **must** be given in all cases.

Dates of Birth and Death: If the author is dead, the statute requires that the year of death be included in the application unless the work is anonymous or pseudonymous. The author's birth date is optional, but is useful as a form of identification. Leave this space blank if the author's contribution was a "work made for hire."

Author's Nationality or Domicile: Give the country of which the author is a citizen, or the country in which the author is domiciled. Nationality or domicile **must** be given in all cases.

Nature of Authorship: After the words "Nature of Authorship" give a brief general statement of the nature of this particular author's contribution to the work. Examples: "Entire text"; "Coauthor of entire text"; "Chapters 11-14"; "Editorial revisions"; "Compilation and English translation"; "New text."

3 SPACE 3: Creation and Publication

General Instructions: Do not confuse "creation" with "publication." Every application for copyright registration must state "the year in which creation of the work was completed." Give the date and nation of first publication only if the work has been published.

Creation: Under the statute, a work is "created" when it is fixed in a copy or phonorecord for the first time. Where a work has been prepared over a period of time, the part of the work existing in fixed form on a particular date constitutes the created work on that date. The date you give here should be the year in which the author completed the particular version for which registration is now being sought, even if other versions exist or if further changes or additions are planned.

Publication: The statute defines "publication" as "the distribution of copies or phonorecords of a work to the public by sale or other transfer of ownership, or by rental, lease, or lending"; a work is also "published" if there has been an "offering to distribute copies or phonorecords to a group of persons for purposes of further distribution, public performance, or public display." Give the full date (month, day, year) when, and the country where, publication first occurred. If first publication took place simultaneously in the United States and other countries, it is sufficient to state "U.S.A."

4 SPACE 4: Claimant(s)

Name(s) and Address(es) of Copyright Claimant(s): Give the name(s) and address(es) of the copyright claimant(s) in this work even if the claimant is the same as the author. Copyright in a work belongs initially to the author of the work (including, in the case of a work made for hire, the employer or other person for whom the work was prepared). The copyright claimant is either the author of the work or a person or organization to whom the copyright initially belonging to the author has been transferred.

Transfer: The statute provides that, if the copyright claimant is not the author, the application for registration must contain "a brief statement of how the claimant obtained ownership of the copyright." If any copyright claimant named in space 4 is not an author named in space 2, give a brief, general statement summarizing the means by which that claimant obtained ownership of the copyright. Examples: "By written contract"; "Transfer of all rights by author"; "Assignment"; "By will." Do not attach transfer documents or other attachments or riders.

5 SPACE 5: Previous Registration

General Instructions: The questions in space 5 are intended to find out whether an earlier registration has been made for this work and, if so, whether there is any basis for a new registration. As a general rule, only one basic copyright registration can be made for the same version of a particular work.

Same Version: If this version is substantially the same as the work covered by a previous registration, a second registration is not generally possible unless: (1) the work has been registered in unpublished form and a second registration is now being sought to cover this first published edition; or (2) someone other than the author is identified as copyright claimant in the earlier registration, and the author is now seeking registration in his or her own name. If either of these two exceptions apply, check the appropriate box and give the earlier registration number and date. Otherwise, do not submit Form TX; instead, write the Copyright Office for information about supplementary registration or recordation of transfers of copyright ownership.

Changed Version: If the work has been changed, and you are now seeking registration to cover the additions or revisions, check the last box in space 5, give the earlier registration number and date, and complete both parts of space 6 in accordance with the instructions below.

Previous Registration Number and Date: If more than one previous registration has been made for the work, give the number and date of the latest registration.

6 SPACE 6: Derivative Work or Compilation

General Instructions: Complete space 6 if this work is a "changed version," "compilation," or "derivative work," and if it incorporates one or more earlier works that have already been published or registered for copyright, or that have fallen into the public domain. A "compilation" is defined as "a work formed by the collection and assembling of preexisting materials or of data that are selected, coordinated, or arranged in such a way that the resulting work as a whole constitutes an original work of authorship." A "derivative work" is "a work based on one or more preexisting works." Examples of derivative works include translations, fictionalizations, abridgments, condensations, or "any other form in which a work may be recast, transformed, or adapted." Derivative works also include works "consisting of editorial revisions, annotations, or other modifications" if these changes, as a whole, represent an original work of authorship.

Preexisting Material (space 6a): For derivative works, complete this space **and** space 6b. In space 6a identify the preexisting work that has been recast, transformed, or adapted. An example of preexisting material might be: "Russian version of Goncharov's 'Oblomov'." Do not complete space 6a for compilations.

Material Added to This Work (space 6b): Give a brief, general statement of the new material covered by the copyright claim for which registration is sought. **Derivative work** examples include: "Foreword, editing, critical annotations"; "Translation"; "Chapters 11-17." If the work is a **compilation**, describe both the compilation itself and the material that has been compiled. Example: "Compilation of certain 1917 Speeches by Woodrow Wilson." A work may be both a derivative work and compilation, in which case a sample statement might be: "Compilation and additional new material."

7 SPACE 7: Manufacturing Provisions

Due to the expiration of the Manufacturing Clause of the copyright law on June 30, 1986, this space has been deleted.

8 SPACE 8: Reproduction for Use of Blind or Physically Handicapped Individuals

General Instructions: One of the major programs of the Library of Congress is to provide Braille editions and special recordings of works for the exclusive use of the blind and physically handicapped. In an effort to simplify and speed up the copyright licensing procedures that are a necessary part of this program, section 710 of the copyright statute provides for the establishment of a voluntary licensing system to be tied in with copyright registration. Copyright Office regulations provide that you may grant a license for such reproduction and distribution solely for the use of persons who are certified by competent authority as unable to read normal printed material as a result of physical limitations. The license is entirely voluntary, nonexclusive, and may be terminated upon 90 days notice.

How to Grant the License: If you wish to grant it, check one of the three boxes in space 8. Your check in one of these boxes, together with your signature in space 10, will mean that the Library of Congress can proceed to reproduce and distribute under the license without further paperwork. For further information, write for Circular R63.

9,10,11 SPACE 9, 10, 11: Fee, Correspondence, Certification, Return Address

Deposit Account: If you maintain a Deposit Account in the Copyright Office, identify it in space 9. Otherwise leave the space blank and send the fee of $10 with your application and deposit.

Correspondence (space 9): This space should contain the name, address, area code, and telephone number of the person to be consulted if correspondence about this application becomes necessary.

Certification (space 10): The application can not be accepted unless it bears the date and the **handwritten signature** of the author or other copyright claimant, or of the owner of exclusive right(s), or of the duly authorized agent of author, claimant, or owner of exclusive right(s).

Address for Return of Certificate (space 11): The address box must be completed legibly since the certificate will be returned in a window envelope.

FORM TX

UNITED STATES COPYRIGHT OFFICE

REGISTRATION NUMBER

_____

TX	TXU

EFFECTIVE DATE OF REGISTRATION

_____

Month	Day	Year

DO NOT WRITE ABOVE THIS LINE. IF YOU NEED MORE SPACE, USE A SEPARATE CONTINUATION SHEET.

1

TITLE OF THIS WORK ▼

PREVIOUS OR ALTERNATIVE TITLES ▼

PUBLICATION AS A CONTRIBUTION If this work was published as a contribution to a periodical, serial, or collection, give information about the collective work in which the contribution appeared.   **Title of Collective Work ▼**

If published in a periodical or serial give: **Volume ▼**   **Number ▼**   **Issue Date ▼**   **On Pages ▼**

2

a

NAME OF AUTHOR ▼

DATES OF BIRTH AND DEATH
Year Born ▼   Year Died ▼

Was this contribution to the work a "work made for hire"?
☐ Yes
☐ No

AUTHOR'S NATIONALITY OR DOMICILE
Name of Country
OR { Citizen of ▶_____
Domiciled in ▶_____

WAS THIS AUTHOR'S CONTRIBUTION TO THE WORK
Anonymous?   ☐ Yes ☐ No
Pseudonymous? ☐ Yes ☐ No

If the answer to either of these questions is "Yes," see detailed instructions.

NATURE OF AUTHORSHIP   Briefly describe nature of the material created by this author in which copyright is claimed. ▼

NOTE

Under the law, the "author" of a "work made for hire" is generally the employer, not the employee (see instructions). For any part of this work that was "made for hire" check "Yes" in the space provided, give the employer (or other person for whom the work was prepared) as "Author" of that part, and leave the space for dates of birth and death blank.

b

NAME OF AUTHOR ▼

DATES OF BIRTH AND DEATH
Year Born ▼   Year Died ▼

Was this contribution to the work a "work made for hire"?
☐ Yes
☐ No

AUTHOR'S NATIONALITY OR DOMICILE
Name of country
OR { Citizen of ▶_____
Domiciled in ▶_____

WAS THIS AUTHOR'S CONTRIBUTION TO THE WORK
Anonymous?   ☐ Yes ☐ No
Pseudonymous? ☐ Yes ☐ No

If the answer to either of these questions is "Yes," see detailed instructions.

NATURE OF AUTHORSHIP   Briefly describe nature of the material created by this author in which copyright is claimed. ▼

c

NAME OF AUTHOR ▼

DATES OF BIRTH AND DEATH
Year Born ▼   Year Died ▼

Was this contribution to the work a "work made for hire"?
☐ Yes
☐ No

AUTHOR'S NATIONALITY OR DOMICILE
Name of Country
OR { Citizen of ▶_____
Domiciled in ▶_____

WAS THIS AUTHOR'S CONTRIBUTION TO THE WORK
Anonymous?   ☐ Yes ☐ No
Pseudonymous? ☐ Yes ☐ No

If the answer to either of these questions is "Yes," see detailed instructions.

NATURE OF AUTHORSHIP   Briefly describe nature of the material created by this author in which copyright is claimed. ▼

3

YEAR IN WHICH CREATION OF THIS WORK WAS COMPLETED This information must be given in all cases.
◀ Year

DATE AND NATION OF FIRST PUBLICATION OF THIS PARTICULAR WORK
Complete this information ONLY if this work has been published.
Month ▶ _____ Day ▶ _____ Year ▶ _____
◀ Nation

4

COPYRIGHT CLAIMANT(S) Name and address must be given even if the claimant is the same as the author given in space 2.▼

See instructions before completing this space.

TRANSFER If the claimant(s) named here in space 4 are different from the author(s) named in space 2, give a brief statement of how the claimant(s) obtained ownership of the copyright.▼

DO NOT WRITE HERE
OFFICE USE ONLY

APPLICATION RECEIVED

ONE DEPOSIT RECEIVED

TWO DEPOSITS RECEIVED

REMITTANCE NUMBER AND DATE

MORE ON BACK ▶ • Complete all applicable spaces (numbers 5-11) on the reverse side of this page.
• See detailed instructions.   • Sign the form at line 10.

DO NOT WRITE HERE

Page 1 of _____ pages

DO NOT WRITE ABOVE THIS LINE. IF YOU NEED MORE SPACE, USE A SEPARATE CONTINUATION SHEET.

PREVIOUS REGISTRATION Has registration for this work, or for an earlier version of this work, already been made in the Copyright Office?

☐ Yes   ☐ No   If your answer is "Yes," why is another registration being sought? (Check appropriate box) ▼

☐ This is the first published edition of a work previously registered in unpublished form.

☐ This is the first application submitted by this author as copyright claimant.

☐ This is a changed version of the work, as shown by space 6 on this application.

If your answer is "Yes," give: **Previous Registration Number** ▼   **Year of Registration** ▼

5

DERIVATIVE WORK OR COMPILATION   Complete both space 6a & 6b for a derivative work; complete only 6b for a compilation.

a. Preexisting Material   Identify any preexisting work or works that this work is based on or incorporates. ▼

b. Material Added to This Work   Give a brief, general statement of the material that has been added to this work and in which copyright is claimed. ▼

See instructions
before completing
this space

6

—space deleted—

7

REPRODUCTION FOR USE OF BLIND OR PHYSICALLY HANDICAPPED INDIVIDUALS   A signature on this form at space 10, and a check in one of the boxes here in space 8, constitutes a non-exclusive grant of permission to the Library of Congress to reproduce and distribute solely for the blind and physically handicapped and under the conditions and limitations prescribed by the regulations of the Copyright Office: (1) copies of the work identified in space 1 of this application in Braille (or similar tactile symbols); or (2) phonorecords embodying a fixation of a reading of that work; or (3) both.

a ☐ Copies and Phonorecords   b ☐ Copies Only   c ☐ Phonorecords Only

See instructions

8

DEPOSIT ACCOUNT   If the registration fee is to be charged to a Deposit Account established in the Copyright Office, give name and number of Account.

Name ▼   **Account Number** ▼

9

CORRESPONDENCE   Give name and address to which correspondence about this application should be sent.   Name/Address/Apt/City/State/Zip ▼

Area Code & Telephone Number ▶

Be sure to
give your
daytime phone
◀ number

CERTIFICATION*   I, the undersigned, hereby certify that I am the

Check one ▶

☐ author
☐ other copyright claimant
☐ owner of exclusive right(s)
☐ authorized agent of

of the work identified in this application and that the statements made by me in this application are correct to the best of my knowledge.

Name of author or other copyright claimant, or owner of exclusive right(s) ▲

10

Typed or printed name and date ▼ If this is a published work, this date must be the same as or later than the date of publication given in space 3.

_____ date ▶ _____

☞ Handwritten signature (X) ▼

11

⊚ Filling Out Application Form PA

Detach and read these instructions before completing this form. Make sure all applicable spaces have been filled in before you return this form.

BASIC INFORMATION

When to Use This Form: Use Form PA for registration of published or unpublished works of the performing arts. This class includes works prepared for the purpose of being "performed" directly before an audience or indirectly "by means of any device or process." Works of the performing arts include: (1) musical works, including any accompanying words; (2) dramatic works, including any accompanying music; (3) pantomimes and choreographic works; and (4) motion pictures and other audiovisual works.

Deposit to Accompany Application: An application for copyright registration must be accompanied by a deposit consisting of copies or phonorecords representing the entire work for which registration is to be made. The following are the general deposit requirements as set forth in the statute:

Unpublished Work: Deposit one complete copy (or phonorecord).

Published Work: Deposit two complete copies (or phonorecords) of the best edition.

Work First Published Outside the United States: Deposit one complete copy (or phonorecord) of the first foreign edition.

Contribution to a Collective Work: Deposit one complete copy (or phonorecord) of the best edition of the collective work.

Motion Pictures: Deposit *both* of the following: (1) a separate written description of the contents of the motion picture; and (2) for a published work, one complete copy of the best edition of the motion picture; or, for an unpublished work, one complete copy of the motion picture or identifying material. Identifying material may be either an audiorecording of the entire soundtrack or one frame enlargement or similar visual print from each 10-minute segment.

The Copyright Notice: For works first published on or after March 1, 1989, the law provides that a copyright notice in a specified form "may be placed on all publicly distributed copies from which the work can be visually perceived." Use of the copyright notice is the responsibility of the copyright owner and does not require advance permission from the Copyright Office. The required form of the notice for copies generally consists of three elements: (1) the symbol "©", or the word "Copyright," or the abbreviation "Copr."; (2) the year of first publication; and (3) the name of the owner of copyright. For example: "© 1989 Jane Cole." The notice is to be affixed to the copies "in such manner and location as to give reasonable notice of the claim of copyright." Works first published prior to March 1, 1989, **must** carry the notice or risk loss of copyright protection.

For information about notice requirements for works published before March 1, 1989, or other copyright information, write: Information Section, LM-401, Copyright Office, Library of Congress, Washington, D.C. 20559.

LINE-BY-LINE INSTRUCTIONS

1 SPACE 1: Title

Title of This Work: Every work submitted for copyright registration must be given a title to identify that particular work. If the copies or phonorecords of the work bear a title (or an identifying phrase that could serve as a title), transcribe that wording *completely* and *exactly* on the application. Indexing of the registration and future identification of the work will depend on the information you give here. If the work you are registering is an entire "collective work" (such as a collection of plays or songs), give the overall title of the collection. If you are registering one or more individual contributions to a collective work, give the title of each contribution, followed by the title of the collection. Example: "'A Song for Elinda' in *Old and New Ballads for Old and New People*."

Previous or Alternative Titles: Complete this space if there are any additional titles for the work under which someone searching for the registration might be likely to look, or under which a document pertaining to the work might be recorded.

Nature of This Work: Briefly describe the general nature or character of the work being registered for copyright. Examples: "Music"; "Song Lyrics"; "Words and Music"; "Drama"; "Musical Play"; "Choreography"; "Pantomime"; "Motion Picture"; "Audiovisual Work."

2 SPACE 2: Author(s)

General Instructions: After reading these instructions, decide who are the "authors" of this work for copyright purposes. Then, unless the work is a "collective work," give the requested information about every "author" who contributed any appreciable amount of copyrightable matter to this version of the work. If you need further space, request additional Continuation Sheets. In the case of a collective work, such as a songbook or a collection of plays, give information about the author of the collective work as a whole.

Name of Author: The fullest form of the author's name should be given. Unless the work was "made for hire," the individual who actually created the work is its "author." In the case of a work made for hire, the statute provides that "the employer or other person for whom the work was prepared is considered the author."

What is a "Work Made for Hire"? A "work made for hire" is defined as: (1) "a work prepared by an employee within the scope of his or her employment"; or (2) "a work specially ordered or commissioned for use as a contribution to a collective work, as a part of a motion picture or other audiovisual work, as a translation, as a supplementary work, as a compilation, as an instructional text, as a test, as answer material for a test, or as an atlas, if the parties expressly agree in a written instrument signed by them that the work shall be considered a work made for hire." If you have checked "Yes" to indicate that the work was "made for hire," you must give the full legal name of the employer (or other person for whom the work was prepared). You may also include the name of the employee along with the name of the employer (for example: "Elster Music Co., employer for hire of John Ferguson").

"Anonymous" or "Pseudonymous" Work: An author's contribution to a work is "anonymous" if that author is not identified on the copies or phonorecords of the work. An author's contribution to a work is "pseudonymous" if that author is identified on the copies or phonorecords under a fictitious name. If the work is "anonymous" you may: (1) leave the line blank; or (2) state "anonymous" on the line; or (3) reveal the author's identity. If the work is "pseudonymous" you may: (1) leave the line blank; or (2) give the pseudonym and identify it as such (for example: "Huntley Haverstock, pseudonym"); or (3) reveal the author's name, making clear which is the real name and which is the pseudonym (for example: "Judith Barton, whose pseudonym is Madeline Elster"). However, the citizenship or domicile of the author **must** be given in all cases.

Dates of Birth and Death: If the author is dead, the statute requires that the year of death be included in the application unless the work is anonymous or pseudonymous. The author's birth date is optional, but is useful as a form of identification. Leave this space blank if the author's contribution was a "work made for hire."

Author's Nationality or Domicile: Give the country of which the author is a citizen, or the country in which the author is domiciled. Nationality or domicile **must** be given in all cases.

Nature of Authorship: Give a brief general statement of the nature of this particular author's contribution to the work. Examples: "Words"; "Co-Author of Music"; "Words and Music"; "Arrangement"; "Co-Author of Book and Lyrics"; "Dramatization"; "Screen Play"; "Compilation and English Translation"; "Editorial Revisions."

3 SPACE 3: Creation and Publication

General Instructions: Do not confuse "creation" with "publication." Every application for copyright registration must state "the year in which creation of the work was completed." Give the date and nation of first publication only if the work has been published.

Creation: Under the statute, a work is "created" when it is fixed in a copy or phonorecord for the first time. Where a work has been prepared over a period of time, the part of the work existing in fixed form on a particular date constitutes the created work on that date. The date you give here should be the year in which the author completed the particular version for which registration is now being sought, even if other versions exist or if further changes or additions are planned.

Publication: The statute defines "publication" as "the distribution of copies or phonorecords of a work to the public by sale or other transfer of ownership, or by rental, lease, or lending"; a work is also "published" if there has been an "offering to distribute copies or phonorecords to a group of persons for purposes of further distribution, public performance, or public display." Give the full date (month, day, year) when, and the country where, publication first occurred. If first publication took place simultaneously in the United States and other countries, it is sufficient to state "U.S.A."

4 SPACE 4: Claimant(s)

Name(s) and Address(es) of Copyright Claimant(s): Give the name(s) and address(es) of the copyright claimant(s) in this work even if the claimant is the same as the author. Copyright in a work belongs initially to the author of the work (including, in the case of a work made for hire, the employer or other person for whom the work was prepared). The copyright claimant is either the author of the work or a person or organization to whom the copyright initially belonging to the author has been transferred.

Transfer: The statute provides that, if the copyright claimant is not the author, the application for registration must contain "a brief statement of how the claimant obtained ownership of the copyright." If any copyright claimant named in space 4 is not an author named in space 2, give a brief, general statement summarizing the means by which that claimant obtained ownership of the copyright. Examples: "By written contract"; "Transfer of all rights by author"; "Assignment"; "By will." Do not attach transfer documents or other attachments or riders.

5 SPACE 5: Previous Registration

General Instructions: The questions in space 5 are intended to find out whether an earlier registration has been made for this work and, if so, whether there is any basis for a new registration. As a general rule, only one basic copyright registration can be made for the same version of a particular work.

Same Version: If this version is substantially the same as the work covered by a previous registration, a second registration is not generally possible unless: (1) the work has been registered in unpublished form and a second registration is now being sought to cover this first published edition; or (2) someone other than the author is identified as copyright claimant in the earlier registration, and the author is now seeking registration in his or her own name. If either of these two exceptions apply, check the appropriate box and give the earlier registration number and date. Otherwise, do not submit Form PA; instead, write the Copyright Office for information about supplementary registration or recordation of transfers of copyright ownership.

Changed Version: If the work has been changed, and you are now seeking registration to cover the additions or revisions, check the last box in space 5, give the earlier registration number and date, and complete both parts of space 6 in accordance with the instructions below.

Previous Registration Number and Date: If more than one previous registration has been made for the work, give the number and date of the latest registration.

6 SPACE 6: Derivative Work or Compilation

General Instructions: Complete space 6 if this work is a "changed version," "compilation," or "derivative work," and if it incorporates one or more earlier works that have already been published or registered for copyright, or that have fallen into the public domain. A "compilation" is defined as "a work formed by the collection and assembling of preexisting materials or of data that are selected, coordinated, or arranged in such a way that the resulting work as a whole constitutes an original work of authorship." A "derivative work" is "a work based on one or more preexisting works." Examples of derivative works include musical arrangements, dramatizations, translations, abridgments, condensations, motion picture versions, or "any other form in which a work may be recast, transformed, or adapted." Derivative works also include works "consisting of editorial revisions, annotations, or other modifications" if these changes, as a whole, represent an original work of authorship.

Preexisting Material (space 6a): Complete this space **and** space 6b for derivative works. In this space identify the preexisting work that has been recast, transformed, or adapted. For example, the preexisting material might be: "French version of Hugo's 'Le Roi s'amuse'." Do not complete this space for compilations.

Material Added to This Work (space 6b): Give a brief, general statement of the **additional** new material covered by the copyright claim for which registration is sought. In the case of a derivative work, identify this new material. Examples: "Arrangement for piano and orchestra"; "Dramatization for television"; "New film version"; "Revisions throughout"; "Act III completely new." If the work is a compilation, give a brief, general statement describing both the material that has been compiled **and** the compilation itself. Example: "Compilation of 19th Century Military Songs."

7,8,9 SPACE 7, 8, 9: Fee, Correspondence, Certification, Return Address

Deposit Account: If you maintain a Deposit Account in the Copyright Office, identify it in space 7. Otherwise leave the space blank and send the fee of $10 with your application and deposit.

Correspondence (space 7): This space should contain the name, address, area code, and telephone number of the person to be consulted if correspondence about this application becomes necessary.

Certification (space 8): The application cannot be accepted unless it bears the date and the **handwritten signature** of the author or other copyright claimant, or of the owner of exclusive right(s), or of the duly authorized agent of the author, claimant, or owner of exclusive right(s).

Address for Return of Certificate (space 9): The address box must be completed legibly since the certificate will be returned in a window envelope.

MORE INFORMATION

How To Register a Recorded Work: If the musical or dramatic work that you are registering has been recorded (as a tape, disk, or cassette), you may choose either copyright application Form PA or Form SR, Performing Arts or Sound Recordings, depending on the purpose of the registration.

Form PA should be used to register the underlying musical composition or dramatic work. Form SR has been developed specifically to register a "sound recording" as defined by the Copyright Act—a work resulting from the "fixation of a series of sounds," separate and distinct from the underlying musical or dramatic work. Form SR should be used when the copyright claim is limited to the sound recording itself. (In one instance, Form SR may also be used to file for a copyright registration for both kinds of works—see (4) below.) Therefore:

(1) File Form PA if you are seeking to register the musical or dramatic work, not the "sound recording," even though what you deposit for copyright purposes may be in the form of a phonorecord.

(2) File Form PA if you are seeking to register the audio portion of an audiovisual work, such as a motion picture soundtrack; these are considered integral parts of the audiovisual work.

(3) File Form SR if you are seeking to register the "sound recording" itself, that is, the work that results from the fixation of a series of musical, spoken, or other sounds, but not the underlying musical or dramatic work.

(4) File Form SR if you are the copyright claimant for both the underlying musical or dramatic work and the sound recording, *and* you prefer to register both on the same form.

(5) File both forms PA and SR if the copyright claimant for the underlying work and sound recording differ, or you prefer to have separate registration for them.

"Copies" and "Phonorecords": To register for copyright, you are required to deposit "copies" or "phonorecords." These are defined as follows:

Musical compositions may be embodied (fixed) in "copies," objects from which a work can be read or visually perceived, directly or with the aid of a machine or device, such as manuscripts, books, sheet music, film, and videotape. They may also be fixed in "phonorecords," objects embodying fixations of sounds, such as tapes and phonograph disks, commonly known as phonograph records. For example, a song (the work to be registered) can be reproduced in sheet music ("copies") or phonograph records ("phonorecords"), or both.

FORM PA

UNITED STATES COPYRIGHT OFFICE

REGISTRATION NUMBER

_____

	PA	PAU

EFFECTIVE DATE OF REGISTRATION

_____

Month	Day	Year

DO NOT WRITE ABOVE THIS LINE. IF YOU NEED MORE SPACE, USE A SEPARATE CONTINUATION SHEET.

1

TITLE OF THIS WORK ▼

PREVIOUS OR ALTERNATIVE TITLES ▼

NATURE OF THIS WORK ▼ See instructions

2

a

NAME OF AUTHOR ▼

DATES OF BIRTH AND DEATH
Year Born ▼   Year Died ▼

NOTE

Under the law,
the "author" of a
"work made for
hire" is generally
the employer,
not the em-
ployee (see in-
structions). For
any part of this
work that was
"made for hire"
check "Yes" in
the space pro-
vided, give the
employer (or
other person for
whom the work
was prepared)
as "Author" of
that part, and
leave the space
for dates of birth
and death blank

Was this contribution to the work a "work made for hire"?
☐ Yes
☐ No

AUTHOR'S NATIONALITY OR DOMICILE
Name of Country
OR { Citizen of ▶_____
     { Domiciled in ▶_____

WAS THIS AUTHOR'S CONTRIBUTION TO THE WORK
Anonymous?   ☐ Yes ☐ No
Pseudonymous? ☐ Yes ☐ No
If the answer to either of these questions is "Yes," see detailed instructions.

NATURE OF AUTHORSHIP Briefly describe nature of the material created by this author in which copyright is claimed. ▼

b

NAME OF AUTHOR ▼

DATES OF BIRTH AND DEATH
Year Born ▼   Year Died ▼

Was this contribution to the work a "work made for hire"?
☐ Yes
☐ No

AUTHOR'S NATIONALITY OR DOMICILE
Name of country
OR { Citizen of ▶_____
     { Domiciled in ▶_____

WAS THIS AUTHOR'S CONTRIBUTION TO THE WORK
Anonymous?   ☐ Yes ☐ No
Pseudonymous? ☐ Yes ☐ No
If the answer to either of these questions is "Yes," see detailed instructions.

NATURE OF AUTHORSHIP Briefly describe nature of the material created by this author in which copyright is claimed. ▼

c

NAME OF AUTHOR ▼

DATES OF BIRTH AND DEATH
Year Born ▼   Year Died ▼

Was this contribution to the work a "work made for hire"?
☐ Yes
☐ No

AUTHOR'S NATIONALITY OR DOMICILE
Name of Country
OR { Citizen of ▶_____
     { Domiciled in ▶_____

WAS THIS AUTHOR'S CONTRIBUTION TO THE WORK
Anonymous?   ☐ Yes ☐ No
Pseudonymous? ☐ Yes ☐ No
If the answer to either of these questions is "Yes," see detailed instructions

NATURE OF AUTHORSHIP Briefly describe nature of the material created by this author in which copyright is claimed. ▼

3

a **YEAR IN WHICH CREATION OF THIS WORK WAS COMPLETED** This information must be given in all cases.
_____ ◄ Year

b **DATE AND NATION OF FIRST PUBLICATION OF THIS PARTICULAR WORK** Complete this information ONLY if this work has been published.
Month ▶_____ Day ▶_____ Year ▶_____
_____ ◄ Nation

4

See instructions
before completing
this space

COPYRIGHT CLAIMANT(S) Name and address must be given even if the claimant is the same as the author given in space 2.▼

TRANSFER If the claimant(s) named here in space 4 are different from the author(s) named in space 2, give a brief statement of how the claimant(s) obtained ownership of the copyright.▼

DO NOT WRITE HERE
OFFICE USE ONLY

APPLICATION RECEIVED
_____
ONE DEPOSIT RECEIVED
_____
TWO DEPOSITS RECEIVED
_____
REMITTANCE NUMBER AND DATE

MORE ON BACK ▶ • Complete all applicable spaces (numbers 5-9) on the reverse side of this page
• See detailed instructions   • Sign the form at line 8

DO NOT WRITE HERE

Page 1 of_____pages

DO NOT WRITE ABOVE THIS LINE. IF YOU NEED MORE SPACE, USE A SEPARATE CONTINUATION SHEET.

PREVIOUS REGISTRATION   Has registration for this work, or for an earlier version of this work, already been made in the Copyright Office?

☐ **Yes**   ☐ **No**   If your answer is "Yes," why is another registration being sought? (Check appropriate box) ▼

☐ This is the first published edition of a work previously registered in unpublished form.

☐ This is the first application submitted by this author as copyright claimant.

☐ This is a changed version of the work, as shown by space 6 on this application.

If your answer is "Yes," give: **Previous Registration Number** ▼   **Year of Registration** ▼

5

DERIVATIVE WORK OR COMPILATION   Complete both space 6a & 6b for a derivative work; complete only 6b for a compilation.

a.   Preexisting Material   Identify any preexisting work or works that this work is based on or incorporates. ▼

b.   Material Added to This Work   Give a brief, general statement of the material that has been added to this work and in which copyright is claimed.▼

6

See instructions
before completing
this space.

DEPOSIT ACCOUNT   If the registration fee is to be charged to a Deposit Account established in the Copyright Office, give name and number of Account.

Name ▼   **Account Number** ▼

7

CORRESPONDENCE   Give name and address to which correspondence about this application should be sent.   Name/Address/Apt/City/State/Zip ▼

Area Code & Telephone Number ▶

Be sure to
give your
daytime phone
◀ number

CERTIFICATION*   I, the undersigned, hereby certify that I am the

Check only one ▼

☐ author

☐ other copyright claimant

☐ owner of exclusive right(s)

☐ authorized agent of_____
                        Name of author or other copyright claimant, or owner of exclusive right(s) ▲

8

of the work identified in this application and that the statements made
by me in this application are correct to the best of my knowledge.

Typed or printed name and date ▼ If this application gives a date of publication in space 3, do not sign and submit it before that date.

_____ date ▶ _____

👉   Handwritten signature (X) ▼

⊚ Filling Out Application Form SR

Detach and read these instructions before completing this form. Make sure all applicable spaces have been filled in before you return this form.

BASIC INFORMATION

When to Use This Form: Use Form SR for copyright registration of published or unpublished sound recordings. It should be used where the copyright claim is limited to the sound recording itself, and it may also be used where the same copyright claimant is seeking simultaneous registration of the underlying musical, dramatic, or literary work embodied in the phonorecord.

With one exception, "sound recordings" are works that result from the fixation of a series of musical, spoken, or other sounds. The exception is for the audio portions of audiovisual works, such as a motion picture soundtrack or an audio cassette accompanying a filmstrip; these are considered a part of the audiovisual work as a whole.

Deposit to Accompany Application: An application for copyright registration of a sound recording must be accompanied by a deposit consisting of phonorecords representing the entire work for which registration is to be made.

Unpublished Work: Deposit one complete phonorecord.

Published Work: Deposit two complete phonorecords of the best edition, together with "any printed or other visually perceptible material" published with the phonorecords.

Work First Published Outside the United States: Deposit one complete phonorecord of the first foreign edition.

Contribution to a Collective Work: Deposit one complete phonorecord of the best edition of the collective work.

The Copyright Notice: For sound recordings first published on or after March 1, 1989, the law provides that a copyright notice in a specified form "may be placed on all publicly distributed phonorecords of the sound recording." Use of the copyright notice is the responsibility of the copyright owner and does not require advance permission from the Copyright Office. The required form of the notice for phonorecords of sound recordings consists of three elements: (1) the symbol "℗" (the Letter "P" in a circle); (2) the year of first publication of the sound recording; and (3) the name of the owner of copyright. For example: "℗ 1989 XYZ Record Co." The notice is to be "placed on the surface of the phonorecord, or on the label or container, in such manner and location as to give reasonable notice of the claim of copyright." Works first published prior to March 1, 1989, **must** carry the notice or risk loss of copyright protection.

For information about notice requirements for works published before March 1, 1989, or other copyright information, write: Information Section, LM-401, Copyright Office, Library of Congress, Washington, D.C. 20559.

LINE-BY-LINE INSTRUCTIONS

1 SPACE 1: Title

Title of This Work: Every work submitted for copyright registration must be given a title to identify that particular work. If the phonorecords or any accompanying printed material bear a title (or an identifying phrase that could serve as a title), transcribe that wording completely and exactly on the application. Indexing of the registration and future identification of the work may depend on the information you give here.

Nature of Material Recorded: Indicate the general type or character of the works or other material embodied in the recording. The box marked "Literary" should be checked for nondramatic spoken material of all sorts, including narration, interviews, panel discussions, and training material. If the material recorded is not musical, dramatic, or literary in nature, check "Other" and briefly describe the type of sounds fixed in the recording. For example: "Sound Effects"; "Bird Calls"; "Crowd Noises."

Previous or Alternative Titles: Complete this space if there are any additional titles for the work under which someone searching for the registration might be likely to look, or under which a document pertaining to the work might be recorded.

2 SPACE 2: Author(s)

General Instructions: After reading these instructions, decide who are the "authors" of this work for copyright purposes. Then, unless the work is a "collective work," give the requested information about every "author" who contributed any appreciable amount of copyrightable matter to this version of the work. If you need further space, request additional Continuation Sheets. In the case of a collective work, such as a collection of previously published or registered sound recordings, give information about the author of the collective work as a whole. If you are submitting this Form SR to cover the recorded musical, dramatic, or literary work as well as the sound recording itself, it is important for space 2 to include full information about the various authors of all of the material covered by the copyright claim, making clear the nature of each author's contribution.

Name of Author: The fullest form of the author's name should be given. Unless the work was "made for hire," the individual who actually created the work is its "author." In the case of a work made for hire, the statute provides that "the employer or other person for whom the work was prepared is considered the author."

What is a "Work Made for Hire"? A "work made for hire" is defined as: (1) "a work prepared by an employee within the scope of his or her employment"; or (2) "a work specially ordered or commissioned for use as a contribution to a collective work, as a part of a motion picture or other audiovisual work, as a translation, as a supplementary work, as a compilation, as an instructional text, as a test, as answer material for a test, or as an atlas, if the parties expressly agree in a written instrument signed by them that the work shall be considered a work made for hire." If you have checked "Yes" to indicate that the work was "made for hire," you must give the full legal name of the employer (or other person for whom the work was prepared). You may also include the name of the employee along with the name of the employer (for example: "Elster Record Co., employer for hire of John Ferguson").

"Anonymous" or "Pseudonymous" Work: An author's contribution to a work is "anonymous" if that author is not identified on the copies or phonorecords of the work. An author's contribution to a work is "pseudonymous" if that author is identified on the copies or phonorecords under a fictitious name. If the work is "anonymous" you may: (1) leave the line blank; or (2) state "anonymous" on the line; or (3) reveal the author's identity. If the work is "pseudonymous" you may: (1) leave the line blank; or (2) give the pseudonym and identify it as such (for example: "Huntley Haverstock, pseudonym"); or (3) reveal the author's name, making clear which is the real name and which is the pseudonym (for example: "Judith Barton, whose pseudonym is Madeline Elster"). However, the citizenship or domicile of the author **must** be given in all cases.

Dates of Birth and Death: If the author is dead, the statute requires that the year of death be included in the application unless the work is anonymous or pseudonymous. The author's birth date is optional, but is useful as a form of identification. Leave this space blank if the author's contribution was a "work made for hire."

Author's Nationality or Domicile: Give the country of which the author is a citizen, or the country in which the author is domiciled. Nationality or domicile **must** be given in all cases.

Nature of Authorship: Give a brief general statement of the nature of this particular author's contribution to the work. If you are submitting this Form SR to cover both the sound recording and the underlying musical, dramatic, or literary work, make sure that the precise nature of each author's contribution is reflected here. Examples where the authorship pertains to the recording: "Sound Recording"; "Performance and Recording"; "Compilation and Remixing of Sounds." Examples where the authorship pertains to both the recording and the underlying work: "Words, Music, Performance, Recording"; "Arrangement of Music and Recording"; "Compilation of Poems and Reading."

3 SPACE 3: Creation and Publication

General Instructions: Do not confuse "creation" with "publication." Every application for copyright registration must state "the year in which creation of the work was completed." Give the date and nation of first publication only if the work has been published.

Creation: Under the statute, a work is "created" when it is fixed in a copy or phonorecord for the first time. Where a work has been prepared over a period of time, the part of the work existing in fixed form on a particular date constitutes the created work on that date. The date you give here should be the year in which the author completed the particular version for which registration is now being sought, even if other versions exist or if further changes or additions are planned.

Publication: The statute defines "publication" as "the distribution of copies or phonorecords of a work to the public by sale or other transfer of ownership, or by rental, lease, or lending"; a work is also "published" if there has been an "offering to distribute copies or phonorecords to a group of persons for purposes of further distribution, public performance, or public display." Give the full date (month, day, year) when, and the country where, publication first occurred. If first publication took place simultaneously in the United States and other countries, it is sufficient to state "U.S.A."

4 SPACE 4: Claimant(s)

Name(s) and Address(es) of Copyright Claimant(s): Give the name(s) and address(es) of the copyright claimant(s) in this work even if the claimant is the same as the author. Copyright in a work belongs initially to the author of the work (including, in the case of a work made for hire, the employer or other person for whom the work was prepared). The copyright claimant is either the author of the work or a person or organization to whom the copyright initially belonging to the author has been transferred.

Transfer: The statute provides that, if the copyright claimant is not the author, the application for registration must contain "a brief statement of how the claimant obtained ownership of the copyright." If any copyright claimant named in space 4 is not an author named in space 2, give a brief, general statement summarizing the means by which that claimant obtained ownership of the copyright. Examples: "By written contract"; "Transfer of all rights by author"; "Assignment"; "By will." Do not attach transfer documents or other attachments or riders.

5 SPACE 5: Previous Registration

General Instructions: The questions in space 5 are intended to find out whether an earlier registration has been made for this work and, if so, whether there is any basis for a new registration. As a rule, only one basic copyright registration can be made for the same version of a particular work.

Same Version: If this version is substantially the same as the work covered by a previous registration, a second registration is not generally possible unless: (1) the work has been registered in unpublished form and a second registration is now being sought to cover this first published edition; or (2) someone other than the author is identified as copyright claimant in the earlier registration, and the author is now seeking registration in his or her own name. If either of these two exceptions apply, check the appropriate box and give the earlier registration number and date. Otherwise, do not submit Form SR; instead, write the Copyright Office for information about supplementary registration or recordation of transfers of copyright ownership.

Changed Version: If the work has been changed, and you are now seeking registration to cover the additions or revisions, check the last box in space 5, give the earlier registration number and date, and complete both parts of space 6 in accordance with the instructions below.

Previous Registration Number and Date: If more than one previous registration has been made for the work, give the number and date of the latest registration.

6 SPACE 6: Derivative Work or Compilation

General Instructions: Complete space 6 if this work is a "changed version," "compilation," or "derivative work," and if it incorporates one or more earlier works that have already been published or registered for copyright, or that have fallen into the public domain, or sound recordings that were fixed before February 15, 1972. A "compilation" is defined as "a work formed by the collection and assembling of preexisting materials or of data that are selected, coordinated, or arranged in such a way that the resulting work as a whole constitutes an original work of authorship." A "derivative work" is "a work based on one or more preexisting works." Examples of derivative works include recordings reissued with substantial editorial revisions or abridgments of the recorded sounds, and recordings republished with new recorded material, or "any other form in which a work may be recast, transformed, or adapted." Derivative works also include works "consisting of editorial revisions, annotations, or other modifications" if these changes, as a whole, represent an original work of authorship.

Preexisting Material (space 6a): Complete this space **and** space 6b for derivative works. In this space identify the preexisting work that has been recast, transformed, or adapted. For example, the preexisting material might be: "1970 recording by Sperryville Symphony of Bach Double Concerto." Do not complete this space for compilations.

Material Added to This Work (space 6b): Give a brief, general statement of the **additional** new material covered by the copyright claim for which registration is sought. In the case of a derivative work, identify this new material. Examples: "Recorded performances on bands 1 and 3"; "Remixed sounds from original multitrack sound sources"; "New words, arrangement, and additional sounds." If the work is a compilation, give a brief, general statement describing both the material that has been compiled **and** the compilation itself. Example: "Compilation of 1938 Recordings by various swing bands."

7,8,9 SPACE 7, 8, 9: Fee, Correspondence, Certification, Return Address

Deposit Account: If you maintain a Deposit Account in the Copyright Office, identify it in space 7. Otherwise leave the space blank and send the fee of $10 with your application and deposit.

Correspondence (space 7): This space should contain the name, address, area code, and telephone number of the person to be consulted if correspondence about this application becomes necessary.

Certification (space 8): The application cannot be accepted unless it bears the date and the **handwritten signature** of the author or other copyright claimant, or of the owner of exclusive right(s), or of the duly authorized agent of the author, claimant, or owner of exclusive right(s).

Address for Return of Certificate (space 9): The address box must be completed legibly since the certificate will be returned in a window envelope.

MORE INFORMATION

"Works": "Works" are the basic subject matter of copyright; they are what authors create and copyright protects. The statute draws a sharp distinction between the "work" and "any material object in which the work is embodied."

"Copies" and "Phonorecords": These are the two types of material objects in which "works" are embodied. In general, **"copies"** are objects from which a work can be read or visually perceived, directly or with the aid of a machine or device, such as manuscripts, books, sheet music, film, and videotape. **"Phonorecords"** are objects embodying fixations of sounds, such as audio tapes and phonograph disks. For example, a song (the "work") can be reproduced in sheet music ("copies") or phonograph disks ("phonorecords"), or both.

"Sound Recordings": These are "works," not "copies" or "phonorecords." "Sound recordings" are "works that result from the fixation of a series of musical, spoken, or other sounds, but not including the sounds accompanying a motion picture or other audiovisual work." Example: When a record company issues a new release, the release will typically involve two distinct "works": the "musical work" that has been recorded, and the "sound recording" as a separate work in itself. The material objects that the record company sends out are "phonorecords": physical reproductions of both the "musical work" and the "sound recording."

Should You File More Than One Application?
If your work consists of a recorded musical, dramatic, or literary work, and both that "work," and the sound recording as a separate "work," are eligible for registration, the application form you should file depends on the following:

File Only Form SR if: The copyright claimant is the same for both the musical, dramatic, or literary work and for the sound recording, and you are seeking a single registration to cover both of these "works."

File Only Form PA (or Form TX) if: You are seeking to register only the musical, dramatic, or literary work, not the sound recording. Form PA is appropriate for works of the performing arts; Form TX is for nondramatic literary works.

Separate Applications Should Be Filed on Form PA (or Form TX) and on Form SR if: (1) The copyright claimant for the musical, dramatic, or literary work is different from the copyright claimant for the sound recording; or (2) You prefer to have separate registrations for the musical, dramatic, or literary work and for the sound recording.

FORM SR
UNITED STATES COPYRIGHT OFFICE

REGISTRATION NUMBER

_____

SR _____ SRU _____

EFFECTIVE DATE OF REGISTRATION

_____

Month   Day   Year

DO NOT WRITE ABOVE THIS LINE. IF YOU NEED MORE SPACE, USE A SEPARATE CONTINUATION SHEET.

1

TITLE OF THIS WORK ▼

PREVIOUS OR ALTERNATIVE TITLES ▼

NATURE OF MATERIAL RECORDED ▼ See instructions
☐ Musical   ☐ Musical-Dramatic
☐ Dramatic   ☐ Literary
☐ Other _____

2

a

NAME OF AUTHOR ▼

DATES OF BIRTH AND DEATH
Year Born ▼   Year Died ▼

Was this contribution to the work a "work made for hire"?
☐ Yes
☐ No

AUTHOR'S NATIONALITY OR DOMICILE
Name of Country
OR { Citizen of ▶ _____
Domiciled in ▶ _____

WAS THIS AUTHOR'S CONTRIBUTION TO THE WORK
Anonymous? ☐ Yes ☐ No
Pseudonymous? ☐ Yes ☐ No
If the answer to either of these questions is "Yes." see detailed instructions

NATURE OF AUTHORSHIP Briefly describe nature of the material created by this author in which copyright is claimed. ▼

NOTE

Under the law, the "author" of a "work made for hire" is generally the employer, not the employee (see instructions). For any part of this work that was "made for hire" check "Yes" in the space provided, give the employer (or other person for whom the work was prepared) as "Author" of that part, and leave the space for dates of birth and death blank.

b

NAME OF AUTHOR ▼

DATES OF BIRTH AND DEATH
Year Born ▼   Year Died ▼

Was this contribution to the work a "work made for hire"?
☐ Yes
☐ No

AUTHOR'S NATIONALITY OR DOMICILE
Name of country
OR { Citizen of ▶ _____
Domiciled in ▶ _____

WAS THIS AUTHOR'S CONTRIBUTION TO THE WORK
Anonymous? ☐ Yes ☐ No
Pseudonymous? ☐ Yes ☐ No
If the answer to either of these questions is "Yes see detailed instructions

NATURE OF AUTHORSHIP Briefly describe nature of the material created by this author in which copyright is claimed. ▼

c

NAME OF AUTHOR ▼

DATES OF BIRTH AND DEATH
Year Born ▼   Year Died ▼

Was this contribution to the work a "work made for hire"?
☐ Yes
☐ No

AUTHOR'S NATIONALITY OR DOMICILE
Name of Country
OR { Citizen of ▶ _____
Domiciled in ▶ _____

WAS THIS AUTHOR'S CONTRIBUTION TO THE WORK
Anonymous? ☐ Yes ☐ No
Pseudonymous? ☐ Yes ☐ No
If the answer to either of these questions is "Yes. see detailed instructions

NATURE OF AUTHORSHIP Briefly describe nature of the material created by this author in which copyright is claimed. ▼

3

YEAR IN WHICH CREATION OF THIS WORK WAS COMPLETED This information must be given in all cases.
_____ ◀ Year

DATE AND NATION OF FIRST PUBLICATION OF THIS PARTICULAR WORK
Complete this information ONLY if this work has been published.
Month ▶ _____ Day ▶ _____ Year ▶ _____
◀ Nation

4

See instructions before completing this space.

COPYRIGHT CLAIMANT(S) Name and address must be given even if the claimant is the same as the author given in space 2.▼

TRANSFER If the claimant(s) named here in space 4 are different from the author(s) named in space 2, give a brief statement of how the claimant(s) obtained ownership of the copyright.▼

APPLICATION RECEIVED

ONE DEPOSIT RECEIVED

TWO DEPOSITS RECEIVED

REMITTANCE NUMBER AND DATE

DO NOT WRITE HERE
OFFICE USE ONLY

MORE ON BACK ▶   • Complete all applicable spaces (numbers 5-9) on the reverse side of this page
   • See detailed instructions   • Sign the form at line 8

DO NOT WRITE HERE

Page 1 of _____ pages

DO NOT WRITE ABOVE THIS LINE. IF YOU NEED MORE SPACE, USE A SEPARATE CONTINUATION SHEET.

PREVIOUS REGISTRATION Has registration for this work, or for an earlier version of this work, already been made in the Copyright Office?

☐ **Yes** ☐ **No** If your answer is "Yes," why is another registration being sought? (Check appropriate box) ▼

☐ This is the first published edition of a work previously registered in unpublished form.

☐ This is the first application submitted by this author as copyright claimant.

☐ This is a changed version of the work, as shown by space 6 on this application.

If your answer is "Yes," give: **Previous Registration Number** ▼   **Year of Registration** ▼

5

DERIVATIVE WORK OR COMPILATION Complete both space 6a & 6b for a derivative work; complete only 6b for a compilation.

a. Preexisting Material Identify any preexisting work or works that this work is based on or incorporates. ▼

b. Material Added to This Work Give a brief, general statement of the material that has been added to this work and in which copyright is claimed.▼

6

See instructions before completing this space.

DEPOSIT ACCOUNT If the registration fee is to be charged to a Deposit Account established in the Copyright Office, give name and number of Account.

Name ▼   **Account Number** ▼

7

CORRESPONDENCE Give name and address to which correspondence about this application should be sent. Name/Address/Apt/City/State/Zip ▼

Area Code & Telephone Number ▶

Be sure to give your daytime phone ◀ number.

CERTIFICATION* I, the undersigned, hereby certify that I am the

Check one ▼

☐ author

☐ other copyright claimant

☐ owner of exclusive right(s)

☐ authorized agent of _____
Name of author or other copyright claimant, or owner of exclusive right(s) ▲

of the work identified in this application and that the statements made by me in this application are correct to the best of my knowledge.

Typed or printed name and date ▼ If this is a published work, this date must be the same as or later than the date of publication given in space 3.

_____ **date** ▶ _____

Handwritten signature (X) ▼

8

* 17 U.S.C. § 506(e): Any person who knowingly makes a false representation of a material fact in the application for copyright registration provided for by section 409 or in any written statement filed in connection with the application, shall be fined not more than $2,500.

March 1989—30,000   U.S. GOVERNMENT PRINTING OFFICE: 1989—241-428 80,017

⊘Filling Out Application Form VA

Detach and read these instructions before completing this form. Make sure all applicable spaces have been filled in before you return this form.

BASIC INFORMATION

When to Use This Form: Use Form VA for copyright registration of published or unpublished works of the visual arts. This category consists of "pictorial, graphic, or sculptural works," including two-dimensional and three-dimensional works of fine, graphic, and applied art, photographs, prints and art reproductions, maps, globes, charts, technical drawings, diagrams, and models.

What Does Copyright Protect? Copyright in a work of the visual arts protects those pictorial, graphic, or sculptural elements that, either alone or in combination, represent an "original work of authorship." The statute declares: "In no case does copyright protection for an original work of authorship extend to any idea, procedure, process, system, method of operation, concept, principle, or discovery, regardless of the form in which it is described, explained, illustrated, or embodied in such work."

Works of Artistic Craftsmanship and Designs: "Works of artistic craftsmanship" are registrable on Form VA, but the statute makes clear that protection extends to "their form" and not to "their mechanical or utilitarian aspects." The "design of a useful article" is considered copyrightable "only if, and only to the extent that, such design incorporates pictorial, graphic, or sculptural features that can be identified separately from, and are capable of existing independently of, the utilitarian aspects of the article."

Labels and Advertisements: Works prepared for use in connection with the sale or advertisement of goods and services are registrable if they contain "original work of authorship." Use Form VA if the copyrightable material in the work you are registering is mainly pictorial or graphic; use Form TX if it consists mainly of text. **NOTE:** Words and short phrases such as names, titles, and slogans cannot be protected by copyright, and the same is true of standard symbols, emblems, and other commonly used graphic designs that are in the public domain. When used commercially, material of that sort can sometimes be protected under state laws of unfair competition or under the Federal trademark laws. For information about trademark registration, write to the Commissioner of Patents and Trademarks, Washington, D.C. 20231.

Deposit to Accompany Application: An application for copyright registration must be accompanied by a deposit consisting of copies representing the entire work for which registration is to be made.

Unpublished Work: Deposit one complete copy.

Published Work: Deposit two complete copies of the best edition.

Work First Published Outside the United States: Deposit one complete copy of the first foreign edition.

Contribution to a Collective Work: Deposit one complete copy of the best edition of the collective work.

The Copyright Notice: For works first published on or after March 1, 1989, the law provides that a copyright notice on a specified form "may be placed on all publicly distributed copies from which the work can be visually perceived." Use of the copyright notice is the responsibility of the copyright owner and does not require advance permission from the Copyright Office. The required form of the notice for copies generally consists of three elements: (1) the symbol "©", or the word "Copyright," or the abbreviation "Copr."; (2) the year of first publication; and (3) the name of the owner of copyright. For example: "© 1989 Jane Cole." The notice is to be affixed to the copies "in such manner and location as to give reasonable notice of the claim of copyright." Works first published prior to March 1, 1989, **must** carry the notice or risk loss of copyright protection.

For information about notice requirements for works published before March 1, 1989, or other copyright information, write: Information Section, LM-401, Copyright Office, Library of Congress, Washington, D.C. 20559.

LINE-BY-LINE INSTRUCTIONS

1 SPACE 1: Title

Title of This Work: Every work submitted for copyright registration must be given a title to identify that particular work. If the copies of the work bear a title (or an identifying phrase that could serve as a title), transcribe that wording *completely* and *exactly* on the application. Indexing of the registration and future identification of the work will depend on the information you give here.

Previous or Alternative Titles: Complete this space if there are any additional titles for the work under which someone searching for the registration might be likely to look, or under which a document pertaining to the work might be recorded.

Publication as a Contribution: If the work being registered is a contribution to a perodical, serial, or collection, give the title of the contribution in the "Title of This Work" space. Then, in the line headed "Publication as a Contribution," give information about the collective work in which the contribution appeared.

Nature of This Work: Briefly describe the general nature or character of the pictorial, graphic, or sculptural work being registered for copyright. Examples: "Oil Painting"; "Charcoal Drawing"; "Etching"; "Sculpture"; "Map"; "Photograph"; "Scale Model"; "Lithographic Print"; "Jewelry Design"; "Fabric Design."

2 SPACE 2: Author(s)

General Instructions: After reading these instructions, decide who are the "authors" of this work for copyright purposes. Then, unless the work is a "collective work," give the requested information about every "author" who contributed any appreciable amount of copyrightable matter to this version of the work. If you need further space, request additional Continuation Sheets. In the case of a collective work, such as a catalog of paintings or collection of cartoons by various authors, give information about the author of the collective work as a whole.

Name of Author: The fullest form of the author's name should be given. Unless the work was "made for hire," the individual who actually created the work is its "author." In the case of a work made for hire, the statute provides that "the employer or other person for whom the work was prepared is considered the author."

What is a "Work Made for Hire"? A "work made for hire" is defined as: (1) "a work prepared by an employee within the scope of his or her employment"; or (2) "a work specially ordered or commissioned for use as a contribution to a collective work, as a part of a motion picture or other audiovisual work, as a translation, as a supplementary work, as a compilation, as an instructional text, as a test, as answer material for a test, or as an atlas, if the parties expressly agree in a written instrument signed by them that the work shall be considered a work made for hire." If you have checked "Yes" to indicate that the work was "made for hire," you must give the full legal name of the employer (or other person for whom the work was prepared). You may also include the name of the employee along with the name of the employer (for example: "Elster Publishing Co., employer for hire of John Ferguson").

"Anonymous" or "Pseudonymous" Work: An author's contribution to a work is "anonymous" if that author is not identified on the copies or phonorecords of the work. An author's contribution to a work is "pseudonymous" if that author is identified on the copies or phonorecords under a fictitious name. If the work is "anonymous" you may: (1) leave the line blank; or (2) state "anonymous" on the line; or (3) reveal the author's identity. If the work is "pseudonymous" you may: (1) leave the line blank; or (2) give the pseudonym and identify it as such (for example: "Huntley Haverstock, pseudonym"); or (3) reveal the author's name, making clear which is the real name and which is the pseudonym (for example: "Henry Leek, whose pseudonym is Priam Farrel"). However, the citizenship or domicile of the author **must** be given in all cases.

Dates of Birth and Death: If the author is dead, the statute requires that the year of death be included in the application unless the work is anonymous or pseudonymous. The author's birth date is optional, but is useful as a form of identification. Leave this space blank if the author's contribution was a "work made for hire."

Author's Nationality or Domicile: Give the country of which the author is a citizen, or the country in which the author is domiciled. Nationality or domicile **must** be given in all cases.

Nature of Authorship: Give a brief general statement of the nature of this particular author's contribution to the work. Examples: "Painting"; "Photograph"; "Silk Screen Reproduction"; "Co-author of Cartographic Material"; "Technical Drawing"; "Text and Artwork."

3 SPACE 3: Creation and Publication

General Instructions: Do not confuse "creation" with "publication." Every application for copyright registration must state "the year in which creation of the work was completed." Give the date and nation of first publication only if the work has been published.

Creation: Under the statute, a work is "created" when it is fixed in a copy or phonorecord for the first time. Where a work has been prepared over a period of time, the part of the work existing in fixed form on a particular date constitutes the created work on that date. The date you give here should be the year in which the author completed the particular version for which registration is now being sought, even if other versions exist or if further changes or additions are planned.

Publication: The statute defines "publication" as "the distribution of copies or phonorecords of a work to the public by sale or other transfer of ownership, or by rental, lease, or lending"; a work is also "published" if there has been an "offering to distribute copies or phonorecords to a group of persons for purposes of further distribution, public performance, or public display." Give the full date (month, day, year) when, and the country where, publication first occurred. If first publication took place simultaneously in the United States and other countries, it is sufficient to state "U.S.A."

4 SPACE 4: Claimant(s)

Name(s) and Address(es) of Copyright Claimant(s): Give the name(s) and address(es) of the copyright claimant(s) in this work even if the claimant is the same as the author. Copyright in a work belongs initially to the author of the work (including, in the case of a work made for hire, the employer or other person for whom the work was prepared). The copyright claimant is either the author of the work or a person or organization to whom the copyright initially belonging to the author has been transferred.

Transfer: The statute provides that, if the copyright claimant is not the author, the application for registration must contain "a brief statement of how the claimant obtained ownership of the copyright." If any copyright claimant named in space 4 is not an author named in space 2, give a brief, general statement summarizing the means by which that claimant obtained ownership of the copyright. Examples: "By written contract"; "Transfer of all rights by author"; "Assignment"; "By will." Do not attach transfer documents or other attachments or riders.

5 SPACE 5: Previous Registration

General Instructions: The questions in space 5 are intended to find out whether an earlier registration has been made for this work and, if so, whether there is any basis for a new registration. As a rule, only one basic copyright registration can be made for the same version of a particular work.

Same Version: If this version is substantially the same as the work covered by a previous registration, a second registration is not generally possible unless: (1) the work has been registered in unpublished form and a second registration is now being sought to cover this first published edition; or (2) some-

one other than the author is identified as copyright claimant in the earlier registration, and the author is now seeking registration in his or her own name. If either of these two exceptions apply, check the appropriate box and give the earlier registration number and date. Otherwise, do not submit Form VA; instead, write the Copyright Office for information about supplementary registration or recordation of transfers of copyright ownership.

Changed Version: If the work has been changed, and you are now seeking registration to cover the additions or revisions, check the last box in space 5, give the earlier registration number and date, and complete both parts of space 6 in accordance with the instructions below.

Previous Registration Number and Date: If more than one previous registration has been made for the work, give the number and date of the latest registration.

6 SPACE 6: Derivative Work or Compilation

General Instructions: Complete space 6 if this work is a "changed version," "compilation," or "derivative work," and if it incorporates one or more earlier works that have already been published or registered for copyright, or that have fallen into the public domain. A "compilation" is defined as "a work formed by the collection and assembling of preexisting materials or of data that are selected, coordinated, or arranged in such a way that the resulting work as a whole constitutes an original work of authorship." A "derivative work" is "a work based on one or more preexisting works." Examples of derivative works include reproductions of works of art, sculptures based on drawings, lithographs based on paintings, maps based on previously published sources, or "any other form in which a work may be recast, transformed, or adapted." Derivative works also include works "consisting of editorial revisions, annotations, or other modifications" if these changes, as a whole, represent an original work of authorship.

Preexisting Material (space 6a): Complete this space **and** space 6b for derivative works. In this space identify the preexisting work that has been recast, transformed, or adapted. Examples of preexisting material might be "Grunewald Altarpiece"; or "19th century quilt design." Do not complete this space for compilations.

Material Added to This Work (space 6b): Give a brief, general statement of the **additional** new material covered by the copyright claim for which registration is sought. In the case of a derivative work, identify this new material. Examples: "Adaptation of design and additional artistic work"; "Reproduction of painting by photolithography"; "Additional cartographic material"; "Compilation of photographs." If the work is a compilation, give a brief, general statement describing both the material that has been compiled **and** the compilation itself. Example: "Compilation of 19th Century Political Cartoons."

7,8,9 SPACE 7, 8, 9: Fee, Correspondence, Certification, Return Address

Deposit Account: If you maintain a Deposit Account in the Copyright Office, identify it in space 7. Otherwise leave the space blank and send the fee of $10 with your application and deposit.

Correspondence (space 7): This space should contain the name, address, area code, and telephone number of the person to be consulted if correspondence about this application becomes necessary.

Certification (space 8): The application cannot be accepted unless it bears the date and the **handwritten signature** of the author or other copyright claimant, or of the owner of exclusive right(s), or of the duly authorized agent of the author, claimant, or owner of exclusive right(s).

Address for Return of Certificate (space 9): The address box must be completed legibly since the certificate will be returned in a window envelope.

MORE INFORMATION

Form of Deposit for Works of the Visual Arts

Exceptions to General Deposit Requirements: As explained on the reverse side of this page, the statutory deposit requirements (generally one copy for unpublished works and two copies for published works) will vary for particular kinds of works of the visual arts. The copyright law authorizes the Register of Copyrights to issue regulations specifying "the administrative classes into which works are to be placed for purposes of deposit and registration, and the nature of the copies or phonorecords to be deposited in the various classes specified." For particular classes, the regulations may require or permit "the deposit of identifying material instead of copies or phonorecords," or "the deposit of only one copy or phonorecord where two would normally be required."

What Should You Deposit? The detailed requirements with respect to the kind of deposit to accompany an application on Form VA are contained in the Copyright

Office Regulations. The following does not cover all of the deposit requirements, but is intended to give you some general guidance.

For an Unpublished Work, the material deposited should represent the entire copyrightable content of the work for which registration is being sought.

For a Published Work, the material deposited should generally consist of two complete copies of the best edition. Exceptions: (1) For certain types of works, one complete copy may be deposited instead of two. These include greeting cards, postcards, stationery, labels, advertisements, scientific drawings, and globes; (2) For most three-dimensional sculptural works, and for certain two-dimensional works, the Copyright Office Regulations require deposit of identifying material (photographs or drawings in a specified form) rather than copies; and (3) Under certain circumstances, for works published in five copies or less or in limited, numbered editions, the deposit may consist of one copy or of identifying reproductions.

FORM VA
UNITED STATES COPYRIGHT OFFICE

REGISTRATION NUMBER

VA	VAU

EFFECTIVE DATE OF REGISTRATION

Month	Day	Year

DO NOT WRITE ABOVE THIS LINE. IF YOU NEED MORE SPACE, USE A SEPARATE CONTINUATION SHEET.

1

TITLE OF THIS WORK ▼

NATURE OF THIS WORK ▼ See instructions

PREVIOUS OR ALTERNATIVE TITLES ▼

PUBLICATION AS A CONTRIBUTION If this work was published as a contribution to a periodical, serial, or collection, give information about the collective work in which the contribution appeared. **Title of Collective Work ▼**

If published in a periodical or serial give: **Volume ▼**   **Number ▼**   **Issue Date ▼**   **On Pages ▼**

2

a

NAME OF AUTHOR ▼

DATES OF BIRTH AND DEATH
Year Born ▼   Year Died ▼

Was this contribution to the work a "work made for hire"?
☐ Yes
☐ No

AUTHOR'S NATIONALITY OR DOMICILE
Name of Country
OR { Citizen of ▶_____
     Domiciled in ▶_____

WAS THIS AUTHOR'S CONTRIBUTION TO THE WORK
Anonymous?   ☐ Yes ☐ No
Pseudonymous?   ☐ Yes ☐ No
If the answer to either of these questions is "Yes," see detailed instructions.

NATURE OF AUTHORSHIP Briefly describe nature of the material created by this author in which copyright is claimed. ▼

NOTE
Under the law, the "author" of a "work made for hire" is generally the employer, not the employee (see instructions). For any part of this work that was "made for hire" check "Yes" in the space provided, give the employer (or other person for whom the work was prepared) as "Author" of that part, and leave the space for dates of birth and death blank.

b

NAME OF AUTHOR ▼

DATES OF BIRTH AND DEATH
Year Born ▼   Year Died ▼

Was this contribution to the work a "work made for hire"?
☐ Yes
☐ No

AUTHOR'S NATIONALITY OR DOMICILE
Name of country
OR { Citizen of ▶_____
     Domiciled in ▶_____

WAS THIS AUTHOR'S CONTRIBUTION TO THE WORK
Anonymous?   ☐ Yes ☐ No
Pseudonymous?   ☐ Yes ☐ No
If the answer to either of these questions is "Yes," see detailed instructions.

NATURE OF AUTHORSHIP Briefly describe nature of the material created by this author in which copyright is claimed. ▼

c

NAME OF AUTHOR ▼

DATES OF BIRTH AND DEATH
Year Born ▼   Year Died ▼

Was this contribution to the work a "work made for hire"?
☐ Yes
☐ No

AUTHOR'S NATIONALITY OR DOMICILE
Name of Country
OR { Citizen of ▶_____
     Domiciled in ▶_____

WAS THIS AUTHOR'S CONTRIBUTION TO THE WORK
Anonymous?   ☐ Yes ☐ No
Pseudonymous?   ☐ Yes ☐ No
If the answer to either of these questions is "Yes," see detailed instructions.

NATURE OF AUTHORSHIP Briefly describe nature of the material created by this author in which copyright is claimed. ▼

3

a **YEAR IN WHICH CREATION OF THIS WORK WAS COMPLETED** This information must be given in all cases.
◀ Year

b **DATE AND NATION OF FIRST PUBLICATION OF THIS PARTICULAR WORK** Complete this information ONLY if this work has been published.
Month ▶_____ Day ▶_____ Year ▶_____
◀ Nation

4

See instructions before completing this space.

COPYRIGHT CLAIMANT(S) Name and address must be given even if the claimant is the same as the author given in space 2.▼

TRANSFER If the claimant(s) named here in space 4 are different from the author(s) named in space 2, give a brief statement of how the claimant(s) obtained ownership of the copyright.▼

DO NOT WRITE HERE OFFICE USE ONLY

APPLICATION RECEIVED

ONE DEPOSIT RECEIVED

TWO DEPOSITS RECEIVED

REMITTANCE NUMBER AND DATE

MORE ON BACK ▶
• Complete all applicable spaces (numbers 5-9) on the reverse side of this page.
• See detailed instructions.
• Sign the form at line 8.

DO NOT WRITE HERE

Page 1 of_____pages

DO NOT WRITE ABOVE THIS LINE. IF YOU NEED MORE SPACE, USE A SEPARATE CONTINUATION SHEET.

PREVIOUS REGISTRATION Has registration for this work, or for an earlier version of this work, already been made in the Copyright Office?

☐ **Yes** ☐ **No** If your answer is "Yes," why is another registration being sought? (Check appropriate box) ▼

☐ This is the first published edition of a work previously registered in unpublished form.

☐ This is the first application submitted by this author as copyright claimant.

☐ This is a changed version of the work, as shown by space 6 on this application.

If your answer is "Yes," give: **Previous Registration Number** ▼   **Year of Registration** ▼

5

DERIVATIVE WORK OR COMPILATION Complete both space 6a & 6b for a derivative work; complete only 6b for a compilation.

a. Preexisting Material Identify any preexisting work or works that this work is based on or incorporates. ▼

b. Material Added to This Work Give a brief, general statement of the material that has been added to this work and in which copyright is claimed.▼

6

See instructions
before completing
this space

DEPOSIT ACCOUNT If the registration fee is to be charged to a Deposit Account established in the Copyright Office, give name and number of Account.

Name ▼   **Account Number** ▼

7

CORRESPONDENCE Give name and address to which correspondence about this application should be sent.   Name/Address/Apt/City/State/Zip ▼

Area Code & Telephone Number ▶

Be sure to
give your
daytime phone
◀ number.

CERTIFICATION* I, the undersigned, hereby certify that I am the

Check only one ▼

☐ author

☐ other copyright claimant

☐ owner of exclusive right(s)

☐ authorized agent of_____
       Name of author or other copyright claimant, or owner of exclusive right(s) ▲

8

of the work identified in this application and that the statements made
by me in this application are correct to the best of my knowledge.

Typed or printed name and date ▼ If this application gives a date of publication in space 3, do not sign and submit it before that date.

_____ date ▶ _____

Handwritten signature (X) ▼

**MAIL
CERTIFI-
CATE TO**

**Certificate
will be
mailed in
window
envelope**

Name ▼

Number/Street/Apartment Number ▼

City/State/ZIP ▼

YOU MUST:
• Complete all necessary spaces
• Sign your application in space 8
**SEND ALL 3 ELEMENTS
IN THE SAME PACKAGE:**
1. Application form
2. Non-refundable $10 filing fee
   in check or money order
   payable to *Register of Copyrights*
3. Deposit material
MAIL TO:
Register of Copyrights
Library of Congress
Washington, D.C. 20559

9

Filling Out Application Form SE

Detach and read these instructions before completing this form. Make sure all applicable spaces have been filled in before you return this form.

BASIC INFORMATION

When To Use This Form:
Use a separate Form SE for registration of each individual issue of a serial, Class SE. A serial is defined as a work issued or intended to be issued in successive parts bearing numerical or chronological designations and intended to be continued indefinitely. This class includes a variety of works: periodicals; newspapers; annuals; the journals, proceedings, transactions, etc., of societies. Do not use Form SE to register an individual contribution to a serial. Request Form TX for such contributions.

Deposit to Accompany Application:
An application for copyright registration must be accompanied by a deposit consisting of copies or phonorecords representing the entire work for which registration is to be made. The following are the general deposit requirements as set forth in the statute:

Unpublished Work: Deposit one complete copy (or phonorecord).

Published Work: Deposit two complete copies (or phonorecords) of the best edition.

Work First Published Outside the United States: Deposit one complete copy (or phonorecord) of the first foreign edition.

Mailing Requirements:
It is important that you send the application, the deposit copy or copies, and the $10 fee together in the same envelope or package. The Copyright Office cannot process them unless they are received together. Send to: *Register of Copyrights, Library of Congress, Washington, D.C. 20559.*

The Copyright Notice:
For published works, the law provides that a copyright notice in a specified form "shall be placed on all publicly distributed copies from which the work can be visually perceived." Use of the copyright notice is the responsibility of the copyright owner and does not require advance permission from the Copyright Office. The required form of the notice for copies generally consists of three elements: (1) the symbol "©"; or the word "Copyright," or the abbreviation "Copr."; (2) the year of first publication; and (3) the name of the owner of copyright. For example: "© 1981 National News Publishers, Inc." The notice is to be affixed to the copies "in such manner and location as to give reasonable notice of the claim of copyright." For further information about copyright registration, notice, or special questions relating to copyright problems, write:

Information and Publications Section, LM-455
Copyright Office, Library of Congress, Washington, D.C. 20559

LINE-BY-LINE INSTRUCTIONS

1 SPACE 1: Title

Title of This Serial: Every work submitted for copyright registration must be given a title to identify that particular work. If the copies or phonorecords of the work bear a title (or an identifying phrase that could serve as a title), copy that wording *completely* and *exactly* on the application. Give the volume and number of the periodical issue for which you are seeking registration. The "Date on copies" in space 1 should be the date appearing on the actual copies (for example: "June 1981," "Winter 1981"). Indexing of the registration and future identification of the work will depend on the information you give here.

Previous or Alternative Titles: Complete this space only if there are any additional titles for the serial under which someone searching for the registration might be likely to look, or under which a document pertaining to the work might be recorded.

2 SPACE 2: Author(s)

General Instructions: After reading these instructions, decide who are the "authors" of this work for copyright purposes. In the case of a serial issue, the organization which directs the creation of the serial issue as a whole is generally considered the author of the "collective work" (see "Nature of Authorship") whether it employs a staff or uses the efforts of volunteers. Where, however, an individual is independently responsible for the serial issue, name that person as author of the "collective work."

Name of Author: The fullest form of the author's name should be given. In the case of a "work made for hire," the statute provides that "the employer or other person for whom the work was prepared is considered the author." If this issue is a "work made for hire," the author's name will be the full legal name of the hiring organization, corporation, or individual. The title of the periodical should not ordinarily be listed as "author" because the title itself does not usually correspond to a legal entity capable of authorship. When an individual creates an issue of a serial independently and not as an "employee" of an organization or corporation, that individual should be listed as the "author."

Author's Nationality or Domicile: Give the country of which the author is a citizen, or the country in which the author is domiciled. Nationality or domicile **must** be given in all cases. The citizenship of an organization formed under United States Federal or state law should be stated as "U.S.A."

What is a "Work Made for Hire"? A "work made for hire" is defined as: (1) "a work prepared by an employee within the scope of his or her employment"; or (2) "a work specially ordered or commissioned for use as a contribution to a collective work, as a part of a motion picture or other audiovisual work, as a translation, as a supplementary work, as a compilation, as an instructional text, as a test, as answer material for a test, or as an atlas, if the parties expressly agree in a written instrument signed by them that the work shall be considered a work made for hire." An organization that uses the efforts of volunteers in the creation of a "collective work" (see "Nature of Authorship") may also be considered the author of a "work made for hire" even though those volunteers were not specifically paid by the organization. In the case of a "work made for hire," give the full legal name of the employer and check "Yes" to indicate that the work was made for hire. You may also include the name of the employee along with the name of the employer (for example: "Elster Publishing Co., employer for hire of John Ferguson").

"Anonymous" or "Pseudonymous" Work: Leave this space **blank** if the serial is a "work made for hire." An author's contribution to a work is "anonymous" if that author is not identified on the copies or phonorecords of the work. An author's contribution to a work is "pseudonymous" if that author is identified on the copies or phonorecords under a fictitious name. If the work is "anonymous" you may: (1) leave the line blank; or (2) state "anonymous" on the line; or (3) reveal the author's identity. If the work is "pseudonymous" you may: (1) leave the line blank; or (2) give the pseudonym and identify it as such (for example: "Huntley Haverstock, pseudonym"); or (3) reveal the author's name, making clear which is the real name and which is the pseudonym (for example: "Judith Barton, whose pseudonym is Madeline Elster"). However, the citizenship or domicile of the author **must** be given in all cases.

Dates of Birth and Death: Leave this space blank if the author's contribution was a "work made for hire." If the author is dead, the statute requires that the year of death be included in the application unless the work is anonymous or pseudonymous. The author's birth date is optional, but is useful as a form of identification.

Nature of Authorship: Give a brief statement of the nature of the particular author's contribution to the work. If an organization directed, controlled, and supervised the creation of the serial issue as a whole, check the box "collective work." The term "collective work" means that the author is responsible for compilation and editorial revision, and may also be responsible for certain individual contributions to the serial issue. Further examples of "Authorship" which may apply both to organizational and to individual authors are "Entire text"; "Entire text and/or illustrations"; "Editorial revision, compilation, plus additional new material."

3 SPACE 3: Creation and Publication

General Instructions: Do not confuse "creation" with "publication." Every application for copyright registration must state "the year in which creation of the work was completed." Give the date and nation of first publication only if the work has been published.

Creation: Under the statute, a work is "created" when it is fixed in a copy or phonorecord for the first time. Where a work has been prepared over a period of time, the part of the work existing in fixed form on a particular date constitutes the created work on that date. The date you give here should be the year in which this particular issue was completed.

Publication: The statute defines "publication" as "the distribution of copies or phonorecords of a work to the public by sale or other transfer of ownership, or by rental, lease, or lending"; a work is also "published" if there has been an "offering to distribute copies or phonorecords to a group of persons for purposes of further distribution, public performance, or public display." Give the full date (month, day, year) when, and the country where, publication of this particular issue first occurred. If first publication took place simultaneously in the United States and other countries, it is sufficient to state "U.S.A."

4 SPACE 4: Claimant(s)

Name(s) and Address(es) of Copyright Claimant(s): This space must be completed. Give the name(s) and address(es) of the copyright claimant(s) of this work even if the claimant is the same as the author named in space 2. Copyright in a work belongs initially to the author of the work (including, in the case of a work made for hire, the employer or other person for whom the work was prepared). The copyright claimant is either the author of the work or a person or organization to whom the copyright initially belonging to the author has been transferred.

Transfer: The statute provides that, if the copyright claimant is not the author, the application for registration must contain "a brief statement of how the claimant obtained ownership of the copyright." A transfer of copyright ownership (other than one brought about by operation of law) must be in writing. If any copyright claimant named in space 4 is not an author named in space 2, give a brief, general statement describing the means by which that claimant obtained ownership of the copyright from the original author. Examples: "By written contract"; "Written transfer of all rights by author"; "Assignment"; "Inherited by will." Do not attach the actual document of transfer or other attachments or riders.

5 SPACE 5: Previous Registration

General Instructions: This space applies only rarely to serials. Complete space 5 if this particular issue has been registered earlier or if it contains a substantial amount of material that has been previously registered. Do not complete this space if the previous registrations are simply those made for earlier issues.

Previous Registration:
a. Check this box if this issue has been registered in unpublished form and a second registration is now sought to cover the first published edition.
b. Check this box if someone other than the author is identified as copyright claimant in the earlier registration and the author is now seeking registration in his or her own name. If the work in question is a contribution to a collective work, as opposed to the issue as a whole, file Form TX, not Form SE.
c. Check this box (and complete space 6) if this particular issue, or a substantial portion of the material in it, has been previously registered and you are now seeking registration for the additions and revisions which appear in this issue for the first time.

Previous Registration Number and Date: Complete this line if you checked one of the boxes above. If more than one previous registration has been made for the issue or for material in it, give only the number and year date for the latest registration.

6 SPACE 6: Derivative Work or Compilation

General Instructions: Complete space 6 if this issue is a "changed version," "compilation," or "derivative work," which incorporates one or more earlier works that have already been published or registered for copyright, or that have fallen into the public domain. Do not complete space 6 for an issue consisting of entirely new material appearing for the first time, such as a new issue of a continuing serial. A "compilation" is defined as "a work formed by the collection and assembling of preexisting materials or of data that are selected, coordinated, or arranged in such a way that the resulting work as a whole constitutes an original work of authorship." A "derivative work" is "a work based on one or more preexisting works." Examples of derivative works include translations, fictionalizations, abridgments, condensations, or "any other form in which a work may be recast, transformed, or adapted." Derivative works also include works "consisting of editorial revisions, annotations, or other modifications" if these changes, as a whole, represent an original work of authorship.

Preexisting Material (space 6a): For derivative works, complete this space and space 6b. In space 6a identify the preexisting work that has been recast, transformed, adapted, or updated. Example: "1978 Morgan Co. Sales Catalog." Do not complete space 6a for compilations.

Material Added to This Work (space 6b): Give a brief, general statement of the new material covered by the copyright claim for which registration is sought. **Derivative work** examples include: "Editorial revisions and additions to the Catalog"; "Translation"; "Additional material." If a periodical issue is a **compilation**, describe both the compilation itself and the material that has been compiled. Examples: "Compilation of previously published journal articles"; "Compilation of previously published data." An issue may be both a derivative work and a compilation, in which case a sample statement might be: "Compilation of [describe] and additional new material."

7 SPACE 7: Manufacturing Provisions

Due to the expiration of the Manufacturing Clause of the copyright law on June 30, 1986, this space has been deleted.

8 SPACE 8: Reproduction for Use of Blind or Physically Handicapped Individuals

General Instructions: One of the major programs of the Library of Congress is to provide Braille editions and special recordings of works for the exclusive use of the blind and physically handicapped. In an effort to simplify and speed up the copyright licensing procedures that are a necessary part of this program, section 710 of the copyright statute provides for the establishment of a voluntary licensing system to be tied in with copyright registration. Copyright Office regulations provide that you may grant a license for such reproduction and distribution solely for the use of persons who are certified by competent authority as unable to read normal printed material as a result of physical limitations. The license is entirely voluntary, nonexclusive, and may be terminated upon 90 days notice.

How to Grant the License: If you wish to grant it, check one of the three boxes in space 8. Your check in one of these boxes, together with your signature in space 10, will mean that the Library of Congress can proceed to reproduce and distribute under the license without further paperwork. For further information, write for Circular R63.

9,10,11 SPACE 9, 10, 11: Fee, Correspondence, Certification, Return Address

Deposit Account: If you maintain a Deposit Account in the Copyright Office, identify it in space 9. Otherwise leave the space blank and send the fee of $10 with your application and deposit.

Correspondence (space 9): This space should contain the name, address, area code, and telephone number of the person to be consulted if correspondence about this application becomes necessary.

Certification (space 10): The application cannot be accepted unless it bears the date and the **handwritten signature** of the author or other copyright claimant, or of the owner of exclusive right(s), or of the duly authorized agent of the author, claimant, or owner of exclusive right(s).

Address for Return of Certificate (space 11): The address box must be completed legibly since the certificate will be returned in a window envelope.

FORM SE
UNITED STATES COPYRIGHT OFFICE

REGISTRATION NUMBER

U

EFFECTIVE DATE OF REGISTRATION

Month	Day	Year

DO NOT WRITE ABOVE THIS LINE. IF YOU NEED MORE SPACE, USE A SEPARATE CONTINUATION SHEET.

1 TITLE OF THIS SERIAL ▼

Volume ▼   Number ▼   Date on Copies ▼   Frequency of Publication ▼

PREVIOUS OR ALTERNATIVE TITLES ▼

2

NOTE

Under the law, the "author" of a "work made for hire" is generally the employer, not the employee (see instructions). For any part of this work that was "made for hire" check "Yes" in the space provided, give the employer (or other person for whom the work was prepared) as "Author" of that part, and leave the space for dates of birth and death blank.

a

NAME OF AUTHOR ▼

DATES OF BIRTH AND DEATH
Year Born ▼   Year Died ▼

Was this contribution to the work a "work made for hire"?
☐ Yes
☐ No

AUTHOR'S NATIONALITY OR DOMICILE
Name of Country
OR { Citizen of ▶_____
Domiciled in ▶_____

WAS THIS AUTHOR'S CONTRIBUTION TO THE WORK
Anonymous? ☐ Yes ☐ No
Pseudonymous? ☐ Yes ☐ No
If the answer to either of these questions is "Yes," see detailed instructions.

NATURE OF AUTHORSHIP   Briefly describe nature of the material created by this author in which copyright is claimed. ▼
☐ Collective Work   Other:

b

NAME OF AUTHOR ▼

DATES OF BIRTH AND DEATH
Year Born ▼   Year Died ▼

Was this contribution to the work a "work made for hire"?
☐ Yes
☐ No

AUTHOR'S NATIONALITY OR DOMICILE
Name of country
OR { Citizen of ▶_____
Domiciled in ▶_____

WAS THIS AUTHOR'S CONTRIBUTION TO THE WORK
Anonymous? ☐ Yes ☐ No
Pseudonymous? ☐ Yes ☐ No
If the answer to either of these questions is "Yes," see detailed instructions.

NATURE OF AUTHORSHIP   Briefly describe nature of the material created by this author in which copyright is claimed. ▼
☐ Collective Work   Other:

c

NAME OF AUTHOR ▼

DATES OF BIRTH AND DEATH
Year Born ▼   Year Died ▼

Was this contribution to the work a "work made for hire"?
☐ Yes
☐ No

AUTHOR'S NATIONALITY OR DOMICILE
Name of Country
OR { Citizen of ▶_____
Domiciled in ▶_____

WAS THIS AUTHOR'S CONTRIBUTION TO THE WORK
Anonymous? ☐ Yes ☐ No
Pseudonymous? ☐ Yes ☐ No
If the answer to either of these questions is "Yes," see detailed instructions.

NATURE OF AUTHORSHIP   Briefly describe nature of the material created by this author in which copyright is claimed. ▼
☐ Collective Work   Other:

3

YEAR IN WHICH CREATION OF THIS ISSUE WAS COMPLETED   This information must be given in all cases.
◀ Year

DATE AND NATION OF FIRST PUBLICATION OF THIS PARTICULAR ISSUE
Complete this information ONLY if this work has been published.
Month ▶ _____ Day ▶ _____ Year ▶ _____
◀ Nation

4

See instructions before completing this space.

COPYRIGHT CLAIMANT(S) Name and address must be given even if the claimant is the same as the author given in space 2.▼

TRANSFER If the claimant(s) named here in space 4 are different from the author(s) named in space 2, give a brief statement of how the claimant(s) obtained ownership of the copyright.▼

DO NOT WRITE HERE / OFFICE USE ONLY

APPLICATION RECEIVED

ONE DEPOSIT RECEIVED

TWO DEPOSITS RECEIVED

REMITTANCE NUMBER AND DATE

MORE ON BACK ▶
• Complete all applicable spaces (numbers 5-11) on the reverse side of this page.
• See detailed instructions.   • Sign the form at line 10.

DO NOT WRITE HERE

Page 1 of_____pages

DO NOT WRITE ABOVE THIS LINE. IF YOU NEED MORE SPACE, USE A SEPARATE CONTINUATION SHEET.

PREVIOUS REGISTRATION   Has registration for this issue, or for an earlier version of this particular issue, already been made in the Copyright Office?

☐ **Yes** ☐ **No** If your answer is "Yes," why is another registration being sought? (Check appropriate box) ▼

a. ☐ This is the first published version of an issue previously registered in unpublished form.

b. ☐ This is the first application submitted by this author as copyright claimant.

c. ☐ This is a changed version of this issue, as shown by space 6 on this application.

If your answer is "Yes," give: **Previous Registration Number** ▼   **Year of Registration** ▼

5

DERIVATIVE WORK OR COMPILATION   Complete both space 6a & 6b for a derivative work; complete only 6b for a compilation.
a. Preexisting Material   Identify any preexisting work or works that this work is based on or incorporates. ▼

b.   Material Added to This Work   Give a brief, general statement of the material that has been added to this work and in which copyright is claimed.▼

6

See instructions
before completing
this space.

—space deleted—

7

REPRODUCTION FOR USE OF BLIND OR PHYSICALLY HANDICAPPED INDIVIDUALS   A signature on this form at space 10, and a check in one of the boxes here in space 8, constitutes a non-exclusive grant of permission to the Library of Congress to reproduce and distribute solely for the blind and physically handicapped and under the conditions and limitations prescribed by the regulations of the Copyright Office: (1) copies of the work identified in space 1 of this application in Braille (or similar tactile symbols); or (2) phonorecords embodying a fixation of a reading of that work; or (3) both.

a ☐ Copies and Phonorecords   **b** ☐ Copies Only   **c** ☐ Phonorecords Only

8

See instructions.

DEPOSIT ACCOUNT   If the registration fee is to be charged to a Deposit Account established in the Copyright Office, give name and number of Account.
Name ▼   **Account Number** ▼

9

CORRESPONDENCE   Give name and address to which correspondence about this application should be sent.   Name/Address/Apt/City/State/Zip ▼

Area Code & Telephone Number ▶

Be sure to
give your
daytime phone
◀ number.

CERTIFICATION*   I, the undersigned, hereby certify that I am the
Check one ▶
☐ author
☐ other copyright claimant
☐ owner of exclusive right(s)
☐ authorized agent of _____
of the work identified in this application and that the statements made
by me in this application are correct to the best of my knowledge.
Name of author or other copyright claimant, or owner of exclusive right(s) ▲

10

Typed or printed name and date ▼ If this is a published work, this date must be the same as or later than the date of publication given in space 3.

_____ date ▶ _____

✍ Handwritten signature (X) ▼

* 17 U.S.C. § 506(e): Any person who knowingly makes a false representation of a material fact in the application for copyright registration provided for by section 409, or in any written statement filed in connection with the application, shall be fined not more than $2,500.

☆U.S. GOVERNMENT PRINTING OFFICE: 1988—202-133/80,005

July 1988—30,000

FILLING OUT APPLICATION FORM GR/CP: ADJUNCT APPLICATION FOR COPYRIGHT REGISTRATION FOR A GROUP OF CONTRIBUTIONS TO PERIODICALS

THIS FORM:

- Can be used solely as an adjunct to a basic application for copyright registration.
- Is not acceptable unless submitted together with Form TX, Form PA, or Form VA.
- Is acceptable only if the group of works listed on it all qualify for a single copyright registration under 17 U.S.C. §408 (c)(2).

Part A: Identification of Application

- *Identification of Basic Application:* Indicate, by checking one of the boxes, which of the basic application forms (Form TX, or Form PA, or Form VA) you are filing for registration.
- *Identification of Author and Claimant:* Give the name of the individual author exactly as it appears in line 2 of the basic application, and give the name of the copyright claimant exactly as it appears in line 4. These must be the same for all of the contributions listed in Part B of Form GR/CP.

Part B: Registration for Group of Contributions

- *General Instructions:* Under the statute, a group of contributions to periodicals will qualify for a single registration only if the application "identifies each work separately, including the periodical containing it and its date of first publication." Part B of the Form GR/CP provides lines enough to list 19 separate contributions: if you need more space, use additional Forms GR/CP. If possible, list the contributions in the order of their publication, giving the earliest first. Number each line consecutively.
- *Important:* All of the contributions listed on Form GR/CP must have been published within a single twelve-month period. This does not mean that all of the contributions must have been published during the same calendar year, but it does mean that, to be grouped in a single application, the earliest and latest contributions must not have been published more than twelve months apart. Example: Contributions published on April 1, 1978, July 1, 1978, and March 1, 1979, could be grouped together, but a contribution published on April 15, 1979, could not be registered with them as part of the group.

- *Title of Contribution:* Each contribution must be given a title that is capable of identifying that particular work and of distinguishing it from others. If the contribution as published in the periodical bears a title (or an identifying phrase that could serve as a title), transcribe its wording completely and exactly.
- *Identification of Periodical:* Give the overall title of the periodical in which the contribution was first published, together with the volume and issue number (if any) and the issue date.
- *Pages*: Give the number of the page of the periodical issue on which the contribution appeared. If the contribution covered more than one page, give the inclusive pages, if possible.
- *First Publication:* The statute defines "publication" as "the distribution of copies or phonorecords of a work to the public by sale or other transfer of ownership, or by rental, lease, or lending"; a work is also "published" if there has been an "offering to distribute copies or phonorecords to a group of persons for purposes of further distribution, public performance, or public display." Give the full date (month, day, and year) when, and the country where, publication of the periodical issue containing the contribution first occurred. If first publication took place simultaneously in the United States and other countries, it is sufficient to state "U.S.A."

ADJUNCT APPLICATION
for
Copyright Registration for a Group of Contributions to Periodicals

Ⓔ FORM GR/CP

UNITED STATES COPYRIGHT OFFICE

- Use this adjunct form only if your are making a single registration for a group of contributions to periodicals, and you are also filing a basic application on Form TX, Form PA, or Form VA. Follow the instructions, attached.
- Number each line in Part B consecutively. Use additional Forms GR/CP if you need more space.
- Submit this adjunct form with the basic application form. Clip (do not tape or staple) and fold all sheets together before submitting them.

REGISTRATION NUMBER
TX   PA   VA
EFFECTIVE DATE OF REGISTRATION
. . . .
(Month)   (Day)   (Year)
FORM GR/CP RECEIVED
Page _____ of _____ pages

DO NOT WRITE ABOVE THIS LINE. FOR COPYRIGHT OFFICE USE ONLY

Ⓐ

Identification of Application

IDENTIFICATION OF BASIC APPLICATION:
- This application for copyright registration for a group of contributions to periodicals is submitted as an adjunct to an application filed on: (Check which)

☐ Form TX   ☐ Form PA   ☐ Form VA

IDENTIFICATION OF AUTHOR AND CLAIMANT: (Give the name of the author and the name of the copyright claimant in all of the contributions listed in Part B of this form. The names should be the same as the names given in spaces 2 and 4 of the basic application.)

Name of Author: . . . .

Name of Copyright Claimant: . . . .

Ⓑ

Registration For Group of Contributions

COPYRIGHT REGISTRATION FOR A GROUP OF CONTRIBUTIONS TO PERIODICALS: (To make a single registration for a group of works by the same individual author, all first published as contributions to periodicals within a 12-month period (see instructions), give full information about each contribution. If more space is needed, use additional Forms GR/CP.)

☐ Title of Contribution: . . . .
Title of Periodical: . . . . Vol. . . . . . No. . . . . . Issue Date . . . . Pages . . . .
Date of First Publication: . . . . Nation of First Publication . . . .
(Month)   (Day)   (Year)   (Country)

☐ Title of Contribution: . . . .
Title of Periodical: . . . . Vol. . . . . . No. . . . . . Issue Date . . . . Pages . . . .
Date of First Publication: . . . . Nation of First Publication . . . .
(Month)   (Day)   (Year)   (Country)

☐ Title of Contribution: . . . .
Title of Periodical: . . . . Vol. . . . . . No. . . . . . Issue Date . . . . Pages . . . .
Date of First Publication: . . . . Nation of First Publication . . . .
(Month)   (Day)   (Year)   (Country)

☐ Title of Contribution: . . . .
Title of Periodical: . . . . Vol. . . . . . No. . . . . . Issue Date . . . . Pages . . . .
Date of First Publication: . . . . Nation of First Publication . . . .
(Month)   (Day)   (Year)   (Country)

☐ Title of Contribution: . . . .
Title of Periodical: . . . . Vol. . . . . . No. . . . . . Issue Date . . . . Pages . . . .
Date of First Publication: . . . . Nation of First Publication . . . .
(Month)   (Day)   (Year)   (Country)

☐ Title of Contribution: . . . .
Title of Periodical: . . . . Vol. . . . . . No. . . . . . Issue Date . . . . Pages . . . .
Date of First Publication: . . . . Nation of First Publication . . . .
(Month)   (Day)   (Year)   (Country)

☐ Title of Contribution: . . . .
Title of Periodical: . . . . Vol. . . . . . No. . . . . . Issue Date . . . . Pages . . . .
Date of First Publication: . . . . Nation of First Publication . . . .
(Month)   (Day)   (Year)   (Country)

DO NOT WRITE ABOVE THIS LINE. FOR COPYRIGHT OFFICE USE ONLY

☐ Title of Contribution: . . . .
   Title of Periodical: . . . . Vol. . . . . . No. . . . . Issue Date . . . . Pages . . . .
   Date of First Publication:. . . . . Nation of First Publication . . . .
                      (Month)   (Day)   (Year)   (Country)

Ⓑ **Continued**

☐ Title of Contribution: . . . .
   Title of Periodical: . . . . Vol. . . . . . No. . . . . . Issue Date . . . . Pages . . . .
   Date of First Publication:. . . . . Nation of First Publication . . . .
                      (Month)   (Day)   (Year)   (Country)

☐ Title of Contribution: . . . .
   Title of Periodical: . . . . Vol. . . . . . No. . . . . . Issue Date . . . . Pages . . . .
   Date of First Publication:. . . . . Nation of First Publication . . . .
                      (Month)   (Day)   (Year)   (Country)

☐ Title of Contribution: . . . .
   Title of Periodical: . . . . Vol. . . . . . No. . . . . . Issue Date . . . . Pages . . . .
   Date of First Publication:. . . . . Nation of First Publication . . . .
                      (Month)   (Day)   (Year)   (Country)

☐ Title of Contribution: . . . .
   Title of Periodical: . . . . Vol. . . . . . No. . . . . . Issue Date . . . . Pages . . . .
   Date of First Publication:. . . . . Nation of First Publication . . . .
                      (Month)   (Day)   (Year)   (Country)

☐ Title of Contribution: . . . .
   Title of Periodical: . . . . Vol. . . . . . No. . . . . . Issue Date . . . . Pages . . . .
   Date of First Publication:. . . . . Nation of First Publication . . . .
                      (Month)   (Day)   (Year)   (Country)

☐ Title of Contribution: . . . .
   Title of Periodical: . . . . Vol. . . . . . No. . . . . . Issue Date . . . . Pages . . . .
   Date of First Publication:. . . . . Nation of First Publication . . . .
                      (Month)   (Day)   (Year)   (Country)

☐ Title of Contribution: . . . .
   Title of Periodical: . . . . Vol. . . . . . No. . . . . . Issue Date . . . . Pages . . . .
   Date of First Publication:. . . . . Nation of First Publication . . . .
                      (Month)   (Day)   (Year)   (Country)

☐ Title of Contribution: . . . .
   Title of Periodical: . . . . Vol. . . . . . No. . . . . . Issue Date . . . . Pages . . . .
   Date of First Publication:. . . . . Nation of First Publication . . . .
                      (Month)   (Day)   (Year)   (Country)

☐ Title of Contribution: . . . .
   Title of Periodical: . . . . Vol. . . . . . No. . . . . . Issue Date . . . . Pages . . . .
   Date of First Publication:. . . . . Nation of First Publication . . . .
                      (Month)   (Day)   (Year)   (Country)

☐ Title of Contribution: . . . .
   Title of Periodical: . . . . Vol. . . . . . No. . . . . . Issue Date . . . . Pages . . . .
   Date of First Publication:. . . . . Nation of First Publication . . . .
                      (Month)   (Day)   (Year)   (Country)

FILLING OUT APPLICATION FORM CA: APPLICATION FOR SUPPLEMENTARY COPYRIGHT REGISTRATION TO CORRECT OR AMPLIFY INFORMATION GIVEN IN THE COPYRIGHT OFFICE RECORD OF AN EARLIER REGISTRATION

Part A: Basic Instructions

- *General Instructions:* The information in this part identifies the basic registration to be corrected or amplified. Each item must agree exactly with the information as it already appears in the basic registration (even if the purpose of filing Form CA is to change one of these items).
- *Title of Work:* Give the title as it appears in the basic registration, including previous or alternative titles if they appear.
- *Registration Number:* This is a series of numerical digits, preceded by one or more letters. The registration number appears in the upper right hand corner of the certificate of registration.
- *Registration Date:* Give the year when the basic registration was completed.
- *Name(s) of Author(s) and Name(s) of Copyright Claimant(s):* Give all of the names as they appear in the basic registration.

Part B: Correction

- *General Instructions:* Complete this part **only** if information in the basic registration was incorrect at the time that basic registration was made. Leave this part blank and complete Part C, instead, if your purpose is to add, update, or clarify information rather than to rectify an actual error.
- *Location and Nature of Incorrect Information:* Give the line number and the heading or description of the space in the basic registration where the error occurs (for example: "Line number 3...Citizenship of author").
- *Incorrect Information as it Appears in Basic Registration:* Transcribe the erroneous statement exactly as it appears in the basic registration.
- *Corrected Information:* Give the statement as it should have appeared.
- *Explanation of Correction (Optional):* If you wish, you may add an explanation of the error or its correction.

Part C: Amplification

- *General Instructions:* Complete this part if you want to provide any of the following: (1) additional information that could have been given but was omitted at the time of basic registration; (2) changes in facts, such as changes of title or address of claimant, that have occurred since the basic registration; or (3) explanations clarifying information in the basic registration.
- *Location and Nature of Information to be Amplified:* Give

the line number and the heading or description of the space in the basic registration where the information to be amplified appears.

- *Amplified Information:* Give a statement of the added, updated, or explanatory information as clearly and succinctly as possible.
- *Explanation of Amplification (Optional):* If you wish, you may add an explanation of the amplification.

Parts D, E, F, G: Continuation, Fee, Mailing Instructions and Certification

- *Continuation (Part D):* Use this space if you do not have enough room in Parts B or C.
- *Deposit Account and Mailing Instructions (Part E):* If you maintain a Deposit Account in the Copyright Office, identify it in Part E. Otherwise, you will need to send the non-refundable filing fee of $10 with your form. The space headed "Correspondence" should contain the name and address of the person to be consulted if correspondence about the form becomes necessary.
- *Certification (Part F):* The application is not acceptable unless it bears the handwritten signature of the author, or other copyright claimant, or of the owner of exclusive right(s), or of the duly authorized agent of such author, claimant, or owner.
- *Address for Return of Certificate (Part G):* The address box must be completed legibly, since the certificate will be returned in a window envelope.

FORM CA
UNITED STATES COPYRIGHT OFFICE

REGISTRATION NUMBER

TX	TXU	PA	PAU	VA	VAU	SR	SRU	RE

Effective Date of Supplementary Registration

. . . .
MONTH   DAY   YEAR

DO NOT WRITE ABOVE THIS LINE. FOR COPYRIGHT OFFICE USE ONLY

(A) Basic Instructions

TITLE OF WORK:

REGISTRATION NUMBER OF BASIC REGISTRATION:

YEAR OF BASIC REGISTRATION:

NAME(S) OF AUTHOR(S):

NAME(S) OF COPYRIGHT CLAIMANT(S):

(B) Correction

LOCATION AND NATURE OF INCORRECT INFORMATION IN BASIC REGISTRATION:

Line Number . . . . Line Heading or Description . . . .

INCORRECT INFORMATION AS IT APPEARS IN BASIC REGISTRATION:

CORRECTED INFORMATION:

EXPLANATION OF CORRECTION: (Optional)

(C) Amplification

LOCATION AND NATURE OF INFORMATION IN BASIC REGISTRATION TO BE AMPLIFIED:

Line Number . . . . Line Heading or Description . . . .

AMPLIFIED INFORMATION:

EXPLANATION OF AMPLIFIED INFORMATION: (Optional)

CONTINUATION OF: (Check which) ☐ PART B OR ☐ PART C

D
Continuation

DEPOSIT ACCOUNT: If the registration fee is to be charged to a Deposit Account established in the Copyright Office, give name and number of Account:

Name . . . . Account Number . . . .

CORRESPONDENCE: Give name and address to which correspondence should be sent:

Name . . . . Apt. No. . . . .

Address . . . .
(Number and Street)   (City)   (State)   (ZIP Code)

E
Deposit Account and Mailing Instructions

CERTIFICATION ✱ I, the undersigned, hereby certify that I am the: (Check one)

☐ author ☐ other copyright claimant ☐ owner of exclusive right(s) ☐ authorized agent of: . . . .
(Name of author or other copyright claimant, or owner of exclusive right(s))

of the work identified in this application and that the statements made by me in this application are correct to the best of my knowledge.

Handwritten signature: (X) . . . .

Typed or printed name . . . .

Date: . . . .

✱ 17 USC §506(e): FALSE REPRESENTATION - Any person who knowingly makes a false representation of a material fact in the application for copyright registration provided for by section 409, or in any written statement filed in connection with the application, shall be fined not more than $2,500.

F
Certification (Application must be signed)

. . . .
(Name)

. . . .
(Number, Street and Apartment Number)

. . . .
(City)   (State)   (ZIP code)

MAIL CERTIFICATE TO

(Certificate will be mailed in window envelope)

G
Address for Return of Certificate

■ March 1989—15,000   ☆U.S. GOVERNMENT PRINTING OFFICE: 1989—241-428 80,015

FILLING OUT APPLICATION FORM RE: APPLICATION FOR RENEWAL REGISTRATION

Space 1: Renewal Claim(s)

- *General Instructions:* In order for this application to result in a valid renewal, space 1 must identify one or more of the persons who are entitled to renew the copyright under the statute. Give the full name and address of each claimant, with a statement of the basis of each claim, using the wording given in these instructions.

- *Persons Entitled to Renew:*

  A. The following persons may claim renewal in all types of works except those enumerated in Paragraph B, below:

  1. The author, if living. State the claim as: *the author.*

  2. The widow, widower, and/or children of the author, if the author is not living. State the claim as: *the widow (widower) of the author* . . . . *and/or the* (NAME OF AUTHOR) *child (children) of the deceased author* . . . . (NAME OF AUTHOR)

  3. The author's executor(s), if the author left a will and if there is no surviving widow, widower, or child. State the claim as: *the executor(s) of the author* . . . . (NAME OF AUTHOR)

  4. The next of kin of the author, if the author left no will and if there is no surviving widow, widower, or child. State the claim as: *the next of kin of the deceased author* . . . . , (NAME OF AUTHOR) *there being no will.*

  B. In the case of the following four types of works, the proprietor (owner of the copyright at the time of renewal registration) may claim renewal:

  1. Posthumous work (a work as to which no copyright assignment or other contract for exploitation has occurred during the author's lifetime). State the claim as: *proprietor of copyright in a posthumous work.*

  2. Periodical, cyclopedic, or other composite work. State the claim as: *proprietor of copyright in a composite work.*

  3. "Work copyrighted by a corporate body otherwise than as assignee or licensee of the individual author." State the claim as: *proprietor of copyright in a work copyrighted by a corporate body otherwise than as assignee or licensee of the individual author.* (This type of claim is considered appropriate in relatively few cases.)

  4. Work copyrighted by an employer for whom such work was made for hire. State the claim as: *proprietor of copyright in a work made for hire.*

Space 2: Work Renewed

- *General Instructions:* This space is to identify the particular work being renewed. The information given here should agree with that appearing in the certificate of original registration.

100

- *Title:* Give the full title of the work, together with any subtitles or descriptive wording included with the title in the original registration. In the case of a musical composition, give the specific instrumentation of the work.
- *Renewable Matter:* Copyright in a new version of a previous work (such as an arrangement, translation, dramatization, compilation, or work republished with new matter) covers only the additions, changes, or other new material appearing for the first time in that version. If this work was a new version, state in general the new matter upon which copyright was claimed.
- *Contribution to Periodical, Serial, or other Composite Work:* Separate renewal registration is possible for a work published as a contribution to a periodical, serial, or other composite work, whether the contribution was copyrighted independently or as part of the larger work in which it appeared. Each contribution published in a separate issue ordinarily requires a separate renewal registration. However, the new law provides an alternative, permitting groups of periodical contributions by the same individual author to be combined under a single renewal application and fee in certain cases.

  If this renewal application covers a single contribution, give all of the requested information in space 2. If you are seeking to renew a group of contributions, include a reference such as "See space 5" in space 2 and give the requested information about all of the contributions in space 5.

Space 3: Author(s)

- *General Instructions:* The copyright in a new version of a work is independent of any copyright protection in material published earlier. The only "authors" of a new version are those who contributed copyrightable matter to it. Thus, for renewal purposes, the person who wrote the original version on which the new work is based cannot be regarded as an "author" of the new version unless that person also contributed to the new matter.
- *Authors of Renewable Matter:* Give the full names of all authors who contributed copyrightable matter to this particular version of the work.

Space 4: Facts of Original Registration

- *General Instructions:* Each item in space 4 should agree with the information appearing in the original registration for the work. If the work being renewed is a single contribution to a periodical or composite work that was not separately registered, give information about the particular issue in which the contribution appeared. You may leave this space blank if you are completing space 5.
- *Original Registration Number:* Give the full registration

number, which is a series of numerical digits, preceded by one or more letters. The registration number appears in the upper right hand corner of the certificate of registration.

- *Original Copyright Claimant:* Give the name in which ownership of the copyright was claimed in the original registration.
- *Date of Publication or Registration:* Give only one date. If the original registration gave a publication date, it should be transcribed here; otherwise the registration was for an unpublished work, and the date of registration should be given.

Space 5: Group Renewals

- *General Instructions:* A single renewal registration can be made for a group of works if **all** of the following statutory conditions are met: (1) all of the works were written by the same author, who is named in space 3 and who is or was an individual (not an employer for hire); (2) all of the works were first published as contributions to periodicals (including newspapers) and were copyrighted on their first publication; (3) the renewal claimant or claimants, and the basis of claim or claims, as stated in space 1, is the same for all of the works; (4) the renewal application and fee are "received not more than 28 or less than 27 years after the 31st day of December of the calendar year in which all of the works were first published"; and (5) the renewal application identifies each work separately, including the periodical containing it and the date of first publication.
- *Time Limits for Group Renewals:* To be renewed as a group, all of the contributions must have been first published during the same calendar year. For example, suppose six contributions by the same author were published on April 1, 1960, July 1, 1960, November 1, 1960, February 1, 1961, July 1, 1961, and March 1, 1962. The three 1960 copyrights can be combined and renewed at any time during 1988, and the two 1961 copyrights can be renewed as a group during 1989, but the 1962 copyright must be renewed by itself, in 1990.
- *Identification of Each Work:* Give all of the requested information for each contribution. The registration number should be that for the contribution itself if it was separately registered, and the registration number for the periodical issue if it was not.

Spaces 6, 7, and 8: Fee, Mailing Instructions and Certification

- *Deposit Account and Mailing Instructions (Space 6):* If you maintain a Deposit Account in the Copyright Office, identify it in space 6. Otherwise, you will need to send the renewal registration fee of $6 with your form. The space headed "Correspondence" should contain the name and address of the person to be consulted if correspondence about the form becomes necessary.

- *Certification (Space 7):* The renewal application is not acceptable unless it bears the handwritten signature of the renewal claimant or the duly authorized agent of the renewal claimant.

- *Address for Return of Certificate (Space 8):* The address box must be completed legibly, since the certificate will be returned in a window envelope.

FORM RE

UNITED STATES COPYRIGHT OFFICE

REGISTRATION NUMBER

EFFECTIVE DATE OF RENEWAL REGISTRATION

....
(Month)   (Day)   (Year)

DO NOT WRITE ABOVE THIS LINE.   FOR COPYRIGHT OFFICE USE ONLY

---

① Renewal Claimant(s)

RENEWAL CLAIMANT(S), ADDRESS(ES), AND STATEMENT OF CLAIM: (See Instructions)

1
Name ....
Address ....
Claiming as ....
(Use appropriate statement from instructions)

2
Name ....
Address ....
Claiming as ....
(Use appropriate statement from instructions)

3
Name ....
Address ....
Claiming as ....
(Use appropriate statement from instructions)

---

② Work Renewed

TITLE OF WORK IN WHICH RENEWAL IS CLAIMED:

RENEWABLE MATTER:

CONTRIBUTION TO PERIODICAL OR COMPOSITE WORK:

Title of periodical or composite work: ....

If a periodical or other serial, give: Vol. .... No. .... Issue Date ....

---

③ Author(s)

AUTHOR(S) OF RENEWABLE MATTER:

---

④ Facts of Original Registration

ORIGINAL REGISTRATION NUMBER:

....

ORIGINAL COPYRIGHT CLAIMANT:

ORIGINAL DATE OF COPYRIGHT:

• If the original registration for this work was made in published form, give:

DATE OF PUBLICATION: ....
(Month)   (Day)   (Year)

} OR {

• If the original registration for this work was made in unpublished form, give:

DATE OF REGISTRATION: ....
(Month)   (Day)   (Year)

	EXAMINED BY: . . . . CHECKED BY: . . . . CORRESPONDENCE: ☐ Yes DEPOSIT ACCOUNT FUNDS USED: ☐	RENEWAL APPLICATION RECEIVED: REMITTANCE NUMBER AND DATE:	FOR COPYRIGHT OFFICE USE ONLY

DO NOT WRITE ABOVE THIS LINE. FOR COPYRIGHT OFFICE USE ONLY

RENEWAL FOR GROUP OF WORKS BY SAME AUTHOR: To make a single registration for a group of works by the same individual author published as contributions to periodicals (see instructions), give full information about each contribution. If more space is needed, request continuation sheet (Form RE/CON).

(5) Renewal for Group of Works

1
Title of Contribution: . . . .
Title of Periodical: . . . . Vol. . . . . . . No. . . . . . . Issue Date . . . .
Date of Publication: . . . . Registration Number: . . . .
(Month)   (Day)   (Year)

2
Title of Contribution: . . . .
Title of Periodical: . . . . Vol. . . . . . . No. . . . . . . Issue Date . . . .
Date of Publication: . . . . Registration Number: . . . .
(Month)   (Day)   (Year)

3
Title of Contribution: . . . .
Title of Periodical: . . . . Vol. . . . . . . No. . . . . . . Issue Date . . . .
Date of Publication: . . . . Registration Number: . . . .
(Month)   (Day)   (Year)

4
Title of Contribution: . . . .
Title of Periodical: . . . . Vol. . . . . . . No. . . . . . . Issue Date . . . .
Date of Publication: . . . . Registration Number: . . . .
(Month)   (Day)   (Year)

5
Title of Contribution: . . . .
Title of Periodical: . . . . Vol. . . . . . . No. . . . . . . Issue Date . . . .
Date of Publication: . . . . Registration Number: . . . .
(Month)   (Day)   (Year)

6
Title of Contribution: . . . .
Title of Periodical: . . . . Vol. . . . . . . No. . . . . . . Issue Date . . . .
Date of Publication: . . . . Registration Number: . . . .
(Month)   (Day)   (Year)

7
Title of Contribution: . . . .
Title of Periodical: . . . . Vol. . . . . . . No. . . . . . . Issue Date . . . .
Date of Publication: . . . . Registration Number: . . . .
(Month)   (Day)   (Year)

DEPOSIT ACCOUNT: (If the registration fee is to be charged to a Deposit Account established in the Copyright Office, give name and number of Account.)

Name: . . . .
Account Number: . . . .

CORRESPONDENCE: (Give name and address to which correspondence about this application should be sent.)

Name: . . . .
Address: . . . . (Apt.)
. . . .
(City)   (State)   (ZIP)

(6) Fee and Correspondence

CERTIFICATION: I, the undersigned, hereby certify that I am the: (Check one)
☐ renewal claimant   ☐ duly authorized agent of: . . . .
(Name of renewal claimant)

of the work identified in this application, and that the statements made by me in this application are correct to the best of my knowledge.

☞ Handwritten signature: (X) . . . .
Typed or printed name: . . . .
Date: . . . .

(7) Certification (Application must be signed)

MAIL CERTIFICATE TO

. . . .
(Name)
. . . .
(Number, Street and Apartment Number)
. . . .
(City)   (State)   (ZIP code)

(Certificate will be mailed in window envelope)

(8) Address for Return of Certificate

☆U.S. GOVERNMENT PRINTING OFFICE: 1987—181-531/40,019

March 1987—30,000

PART 2

TRADEMARKS

In this section you'll find basic facts about trademarks and the benefits of registration, how to file an application for registration, and how an application is processed.

Forms for registration and instructions for filing them with the U.S. Patent and Trademark Office (PTO) begin on p. 118.

There are many benefits to registering your trademark (see p. 108), but a trademark need not be registered to be protected. The trademark law will support the rights of the person who has used a trademark first. For this reason, selecting your trademark can involve legal risk. It is wise to seek the advice of an attorney to determine when and how to search records to be sure the trademark you want to use is available and not already being used by another person or organization (see ''Trademark Search Library,'' p. 111).

Registration, on the other hand, can more easily be accomplished by a trademark owner without the help of an attorney.

1 THE BASICS OF TRADEMARKS

Changes in federal trademark law became effective on November 16, 1989. The information in this section includes those changes.

WHAT IS A TRADEMARK?

A trademark may be a word, symbol, design or combination word and design, a slogan or even a distinctive sound which identifies and distinguishes the goods or services of one party from those of another. Used to identify a service, it can be called a service mark. In general, the term trademark refers to both trademarks and service marks. Normally, a trademark for goods appears on the product or on its packaging, while a service mark is usually used in advertising to identify the owner's services.

A trademark is different from a copyright or a patent. A copyright gives protection for an artistic or literary work and a patent gives protection for an invention.

Unlike a copyright or patent, trademark rights can last indefinitely if the mark continues to perform a source-indicating function. The term of the Federal trademark registration is 10 years, with 10-year renewal terms. However, between the fifth and sixth year after the date of the registration, the registrant must file an affidavit stating the mark is currently in use in commerce. If no affidavit is filed, the registration will be cancelled.

Trademark rights arise from either (1) use of the mark, or (2) a bona fide intention to use a mark, along with the filing of an application to Federally register that mark on the Principal Register. A Federal trademark registration is not required in order for a trademark to be protected, and a trademark may be used without obtaining a registration.

Before a trademark owner may file an application for a Federal registration, the owner must either (1) use the mark on goods which are shipped or sold, or services which are rendered, in commerce regulated by Congress (e.g., interstate commerce or commerce between the U.S. and a foreign country), or (2) have a bona fide intention to use the mark in such commerce in relation to specific goods or services.

FUNCTIONS OF THE U.S. PATENT AND TRADEMARK OFFICE

The Patent and Trademark Office is an agency of the U.S. Department of Commerce.

The role of the Patent and Trademark Office is to provide patent protection for inventions and to register trademarks. It serves the interest of inventors and businesses with respect to their inventions and corporate, product, and service identifications. It also advises and assists the bureaus and offices of the Department of Commerce and other agencies of the Government in matters involving "intellectual property" such as trademarks.

The Patent and Trademark Office examines applications and grants patents on inventions when applicants are entitled to them; it publishes and disseminates patent information, records assignments of patents, maintains search files of U.S. and foreign patents and a search room for public use in examining issued patents and records. It supplies copies of patents and official records to the public. Similar functions are performed relating to trademarks.

The Federal registration of trademarks is governed by the Trademark Act of 1946, 15 U.S.C. Sec. 1051 et seq.; the Rules, 37 C.F.R. Part 2; and the Trademark Manual of Examining Procedure.

BENEFITS OF REGISTRATION

While Federal registration is not necessary for trademark protection, registration on the Principal Register does provide certain advantages:

1. The filing date of the application is a constructive date of first use of the mark in commerce. (This first use gives registrant nationwide priority as of that date, except as to certain prior users or prior applicants);
2. The right to sue in Federal court for trademark infringement;
3. Recovery of profits, damages, and costs in a Federal court infringement action and the possibility of treble damages and attorneys' fees;
4. Constructive notice of a claim of ownership (which eliminates a good faith defense for a party adopting the trademark subsequent to the registrant's date of registration);
5. The right to deposit the registration with Customs in order to stop the importation of goods bearing an infringing mark;
6. Prima facie evidence of the validity of the registration, registrant's ownership of the mark and of registrant's exclusive right to use the mark in commerce in connection with the goods or services specified in the certificate;
7. The possibility of incontestability, in which case the

registration constitutes conclusive evidence of the
registrant's exclusive right, with certain limited exceptions,
to use the registered mark in commerce;

8. Limited grounds for attacking a registration once it is five
years old;
9. Availability of criminal penalties and treble damages in an
action for counterfeiting a registered trademark;
10. A basis for filing trademark applications in foreign
countries.

NOTICE

Once a Federal registration is issued, the registrant may give
notice of registration by using the ® symbol, or the phrase
"Registered in U.S. Patent and Trademark Office" or "Reg. U.S. Pat.
& Tm. Off." Although registration symbols may not be lawfully used
prior to registration, many trademark owners use a TM or SM (if the
mark identifies a service) symbol to indicate a claim of ownership,
even if no Federal trademark application is pending.

THE REGISTRATION PROCESS

The Patent and Trademark Office (PTO) is responsible for the
Federal registration of trademarks. When an application is filed, it is
reviewed to determine if it meets the requirements for receiving a
filing date (see "Filing Requirements," p. 112). If the filing
requirements are not met, the entire mailing, including the fee, is
returned to the applicant. If the application meets the filing
requirements, it is assigned a serial number, and the applicant is sent a
filing receipt.

The first part of the registration process is a determination by the
Trademark Examining Attorney as to whether the mark may be
registered. An initial determination of registrability, listing any
statutory grounds for refusal as well as any procedural informalities in
the application, is issued about three months after filing. The applicant
must respond to any objections raised within six months, or the
application will be considered abandoned. If, after reviewing the
applicant's response, the Examining Attorney makes a final refusal of
registration, the applicant may appeal to the Trademark Trial and
Appeal Board, an administrative tribunal within the PTO.

Once the Examining Attorney approves the mark, the mark will
be published in the Trademark Official Gazette, a weekly publication
of the PTO. Any other party then has 30 days to oppose the
registration of the mark, or request an extension of time to oppose. An
opposition is similar to a proceeding in the Federal district courts, but
is held before the Trademark Trial and Appeal Board. If no opposition
is filed, the application enters the next stage of the registration process.

If the mark was published based upon its actual use in commerce, a registration will issue approximately 12 weeks from the date the mark was published.

If, instead, the mark was published based upon applicant's statement of a bona fide intention to use the mark in commerce, a *notice of allowance* will issue approximately 12 weeks from the date the mark was published. The applicant then has six months from the date of the notice of allowance to either (1) use the mark in commerce and submit a *statement of use,* or (2) request a six-month *extension of time* to file a statement of use (see forms and instructions, beginning p. 118). The applicant may request additional extensions of time only as noted in the instructions on the back of the form.

Statutory Grounds for Refusal

The Examining Attorney will refuse registration if the mark or term applied for:

1. Does not function as a trademark to identify the goods or services as coming from a particular source; for example, the matter applied for is merely ornamentation;
2. Is immoral, deceptive or scandalous;
3. May disparage or falsely suggest a connection with persons, institutions, beliefs or national symbols, or bring them into contempt or disrepute;
4. Consists of or simulates the flag or coat of arms or other insignia of the United States, or a State or municipality, or any foreign nation;
5. Is the name, portrait or signature of a particular living individual, unless he has given written consent; or is the name, signature or portrait of a deceased President of the United States during the life of his widow, unless she has given her consent;
6. So resembles a mark already registered in the PTO as to be likely, when applied to the goods of the applicant, to cause confusion, or to cause mistake, or to deceive;
7. Is merely descriptive or deceptively misdescriptive of the goods or services;
8. Is primarily geographically descriptive or deceptively misdescriptive of the goods or services of the applicant;
9. Is primarily merely a surname.

A mark will not be refused registration of the grounds listed in numbers 7, 8, and 9 if the applicant can show that, through use of the mark in commerce, the mark has become distinctive so that it now identifies to the public the applicant's goods or services.

Marks which are refused registration on the grounds listed in numbers 1, 7, 8, and 9 may be registered on the *Supplemental Register,* which contains terms or designs considered capable of distinguishing the owner's goods or services, but that do not yet do so. A term or design cannot be considered for registration on the *Supplemental Register* unless it is in use in commerce in relation to all the goods or services identified in the application, and an acceptable allegation of use has been submitted. If a mark is registered on the *Supplemental Register,* the registrant may bring suit for trademark infringement in the Federal courts, or may use the registration as a basis for filing in some foreign countries. None of the other benefits of Federal registration listed on pp. 108–109 apply.

An applicant may file an application on the *Principal Register* and, if appropriate, amend the application to the *Supplemental Register* for no additional fee.

TRADEMARK SEARCH LIBRARY

A record of all active registrations and pending applications is maintained by the PTO to help determine whether a previously registered mark exists which could prevent the registration of an applicant's mark. (See ground for refusal No. 6, above.) The search library is located near Washington, D.C. at Crystal Plaza 2, 2nd Floor, 2011 Jefferson Davis Highway, Arlington, VA 22202 (703/557–3281), and is open to the public free of charge Monday through Friday, 8:00 AM to 5:30 PM.

The PTO cannot advise prospective applicants of the availability of a particular mark prior to the filing of an application. The applicant may hire a private search company or law firm to perform a search if a search is desired before filing an application and the applicant is unable to visit the search library. The PTO cannot recommend any such companies, but the applicant may wish to consult listings for "Trademark Search Services" in the telephone directories or contact local bar associations for a list of attorneys specializing in trademark law.

The use of a trademark, if not selected carefully, can involve legal risk; it is wise to seek the advice of an attorney.

2 HOW TO FILE AN APPLICATION FOR REGISTRATION

The owners of marks may file and prosecute their own applications for registration, or be represented by an attorney. The Patent and Trademark Office cannot help select an attorney.

FILING REQUIREMENTS

An application consists of (1) a written application form (See "Trademark/Service Mark Application, Principal Register, with Declaration," p. 120. The back page of the form is printed upside down so that it may be affixed to the application file at the top and still be easily read.); (2) a drawing of the mark; (3) the required filing fee (see p. 116); and, *only if the application is filed based upon prior use of the mark in commerce;* (4) three specimens showing actual use of the mark in connection with the goods or services. A separate application must be filed for each mark for which registration is requested.

1. Written Application Form

The application form (p. 120) must be written in English. The form may be used for either a trademark or service mark application. Additional forms may be photocopied. The following explanation covers each blank, beginning at the top.

Heading. Identify (a) the mark (e.g. "ERGO" or "ERGO and design") and (b) the class number(s) of the goods or services for which registration is sought. Classification is part of the PTO's administrative processing. The International Schedule of Goods and Services is used (see p. 119). The class may be left blank if the appropriate class number is not known.

Applicant. The application must be filed in the name of the owner of the mark. Specify, if an individual, applicant's name and citizenship; if a partnership, the names and citizenship of the general partners and the domicile of the partnership; if a corporation or association, the name under which it is incorporated and the state or foreign nation under the laws of which it is organized. Also indicate the applicant's post office address.

Identification of Goods or Services. State briefly the specific goods or services for which the mark is used or intended to be used and for which registration is sought.

Use clear and precise language, for example, "women's clothing namely, blouses and skirts," or "computer programs for use by accountants," or "retail food store services." Note that the identification of goods or services should describe the goods the applicant sells or the services the applicant renders, not the medium in which the mark appears, which is often advertising. "Advertising" in this context identifies a service rendered by advertising agencies. For example, a restaurateur would identify his service as "restaurant services," not "menus, signs, etc." which is the medium through which the mark is communicated.

Basis for Application. The applicant must check at least one of four boxes to specify the basis for filing the application. Usually an application is based upon either (1) prior use of the mark in commerce (the first box), or (2) a bona fide intention to use the mark in commerce (the second box), but not both. If both the first and second boxes are checked, the Patent and Trademark Office will *not* accept the application and will return it to the applicant without processing.

The last two boxes pertain to applications filed in the United States pursuant to international agreements, based upon applications or registrations in foreign countries. These bases are asserted relatively infrequently. For further information about foreign-based applications, the applicant may call the trademark information number listed on p. 7 or contact a private attorney.

If the applicant is using the mark in commerce in relation to all the goods or services listed in the application, check the first box and state each of the following:

- The date the trademark was first used anywhere in the U.S. on the goods, or in connection with the services, specified in the application;
- The date the trademark was first used on the specified goods, or in connection with the specified services, sold or shipped (or rendered) in a type of commerce which may be regulated by Congress;
- The type of commerce in which the goods were sold or shipped or services were rendered; for example, "interstate commerce" or "commerce between the United States and (specify foreign country)"; and
- How the mark is used on the goods, or in connection with the services; for example, "the mark is used on labels which are affixed to the goods," or "the mark is used in advertisements for the services."

If the applicant has a bona fide intention to use the mark in commerce in relation to the goods or services specified in the application, check the second box and supply the requested information. This would include situations where the mark has not

113

been used at all or where the mark has been used on the specified goods or services only within a single state (intrastate commerce).

Execution. The application form must be dated and signed (see back of form). The declaration and signature block appear on the back of the form. The Patent and Trademark Office will *not* accept an unsigned application and will return it to the applicant without processing. By signing the form, the applicant is swearing that all the information in the application is believed to be true. If the applicant is an individual, the individual must execute it; if joint applicants, all must execute; if a partnership, one general partner must execute the application; and if a corporation or association, one officer of the organization must execute the application.

2. Drawing

The drawing is a representation of the mark as actually used or intended to be used on the goods or services. There are two types: (a) typed drawings and (b) special form drawings. All drawings must be made upon pure white durable nonshiny paper 8½″ wide by 11″ long. One of the shorter sides of the sheet should be regarded as its top. There must be a margin of at least one inch on the sides and bottom of the paper and at least one inch between the drawing of the mark and the heading.

The *drawing* is different than the *specimens,* which are the actual tags or labels (for goods) or advertisements (for services) which evidence use of the mark in commerce. The *drawing* is a black and white, or typed, rendition of the mark which is used in printing the mark in the Official Gazette and on the registration certificate. A copy of the drawing is also filed in the paper records of the Trademark Search Library to provide notice of the pending application.

Heading. Across the top of the drawing, beginning one inch from the top edge and not exceeding one third of the sheet, list on separate lines:

- Applicant's name;
- Applicant's post office address;
- The goods or services specified in the application (or typical items of the goods or services if there are many goods or services listed);
- Only in an application based on use in commerce: the date of first use of the mark anywhere in the U.S. and the date of first use of the mark in commerce;
- Only in an application based on a foreign application: the filing date of the foreign application.

Typed Drawing. If the mark is only words, or words and numerals, and the applicant does not wish the registration to be issued for a particular depiction of the words and/or numerals, the mark may be typed in capital letters in the center of the page.

Special Form Drawing. This form must be used if the applicant wishes the registration for the mark to be issued in a particular style, or if the mark contains a design element. The drawing of the mark must be done in black ink, either with an india ink pen or by a process which will give satisfactory reproduction characteristics. Every line and letter, including words, must be black. This applies to all lines, including lines used for shading. Half-tones and gray are not acceptable. All lines must be clean, sharp, and solid, and not be fine or crowded. A photolithographic reproduction, printer's proof or camera ready copy may be used if otherwise suitable. Photographs are not acceptable. Photocopies are acceptable only if they produce an unusually clear and sharp black and white rendering. The use of white pigment to cover lines is not acceptable.

The preferred size of the drawing of the mark is 2½" × 2½", and in no case may it be larger than 4" × 4". The Patent and Trademark Office will not accept an application with a special form drawing depicted larger than 4" by 4" and will return the application without processing. If the amount of detail in the mark precludes clear reduction to the required 4" × 4" size, such detail should not be shown in the drawing but should be verbally described in the body of the application.

Where color is a feature of a mark, the color or colors may be designated in the drawing by the linings shown in the following chart:

RED or PINK **BROWN** **BLUE** **GRAY or SILVER**

VIOLET or PURPLE **GREEN** **ORANGE** **YELLOW or GOLD**

3. Filing Fee

The fee, effective April 17, 1989, is $175 for each class of goods or services for which the application is made. (See International Schedule of Goods and Services, p. 119) At least $175 must be submitted for the application to be given a filing date.

All payments should be made in United States specie, treasury notes, national bank notes, post office money orders, or certified checks. Personal or business checks may be submitted. The Patent and Trademark Office will cancel credit if payment cannot be collected. Money orders and checks should be made payable to the Commissioner of Patents and Trademarks. Money sent by mail to the Patent and Trademark Office will be at the risk of the sender; letters containing cash should be registered. Remittances made from foreign countries must be payable and immediately negotiable in the United States for the full amount of the fee required. Application fees are non-refundable.

4. Specimens (Examples of Use)

Trademarks may be placed on the goods; on the container for the goods; on displays associated with the goods; on tags or labels attached to the goods; or, if the nature of the goods makes such placement impractical, then on documents associated with the goods or their sale. Service marks may appear in advertisements for the services, or in brochures about the services, or on business cards or stationery used in connection with the services.

For an application based on actual use of the mark in commerce, the applicant must furnish three examples of use, as described in the paragraph above, when the application is filed. The Patent and Trademark Office will not accept an application based on use in commerce without at least one "specimen" and will return it to the applicant without processing.

The three "specimens" may be identical or they may be examples of three different types of uses. The three specimens should be actual labels, tags, containers, displays, etc. for goods; and actual advertisements, brochures, store signs or stationery (if the nature of the services is clear from the letterhead or body of the letter), etc. for services. Specimens may not be larger than 8½″ by 11″ and must be capable of being arranged flat. Three-dimensional or bulky material is not acceptable. Photographs or other reproductions clearly and legibly showing the mark on the goods, or on displays associated with the goods, may be submitted if the manner of affixing the mark to the goods, or the nature of the goods, is such that specimens as described above cannot be submitted.

FURTHER REQUIREMENTS FOR INTENT-TO-USE APPLICANTS

An applicant who alleges only a bona fide intention to use a mark in commerce must make use of the mark in commerce before a registration will be issued. After use begins, the applicant must submit, along with specimens evidencing use (see above) and a fee of $100 per class of goods or services in the application, either (1) an Amendment to Allege Use or (2) a Statement of Use. The difference between the two filings is the timing of the filing. These forms appear on pp. 124 and 128. See the instructions and information concerning the filing of these forms on the back of each form.

Also included is a form entitled "Request for Extension of Time under 37 CFR 2.89 to File a Statement of Use, with Declaration." This form is intended for use only when an applicant needs to request an extension of time to file a statement of use. See the instructions and information concerning the use of this form on the back of the form.

FOREIGN APPLICANTS

DOMESTIC REPRESENTATIVE. Applicants not living in the United States must designate by a written document the name and address of some person resident in the United States on whom notices of process in proceedings affecting the mark may be served. This person will also receive all official communications unless the applicant is represented by an attorney in the United States.

3 FORMS AND INSTRUCTIONS FOR TRADEMARK REGISTRATION

The application and all other communications should be addressed to: The Commissioner of Patents and Trademarks, Washington, D.C., 20231. It is preferred that the applicant indicate his or her telephone number on the application form. Once a serial number is assigned to the application, the applicant should refer to this number in all telephone and written communications concerning the application.

For phone numbers and addresses, see p. 7.

International schedule of classes of goods and services

Goods

1 Chemicals used in industry, science, photography, as well as in agriculture, horticulture, and forestry; unprocessed artificial resins; unprocessed plastics; manures; fire extinguishing compositions; tempering and soldering preparations; chemical substances for preserving foodstuffs; tanning substances; adhesives used in industry.

2 Paints, varnishes, lacquers; preservatives against rust and against deterioration of wood; colourants; mordants; raw natural resins; metals in foil and powder form for painters, decorators, printers and artists.

3 Bleaching preparations and other substances for laundry use; cleaning, polishing, scouring and abrasive preparations; soaps; perfumery, essential oils, cosmetics, hair lotions; dentifrices.

4 Industrial oils and greases; lubricants; dust absorbing, wetting and binding compositions; fuels (including motor spirit) and illuminants; candles, wicks.

5 Pharmaceutical, veterinary, and sanitary preparations; dietetic substances adapted for medical use, food for babies; plasters, materials for dressings material for stopping teeth, dental wax, disinfectants; preparations for destroying vermin; fungicides, herbicides.

6 Common metals and their alloys; metal building materials; transportable buildings of metal; materials of metal for railway tracks; non-electric cables and wires of common metal; iron-mongery, small items of metal hardware; pipes and tubes of metal; safes; goods of common metal not included in other classes; ores

7 Machines and machine tools; motors (except for land vehicles); machine coupling and belting (except for land vehicles); agricultural implements; incubators for eggs.

8 Hand tools and implements (hand operated); cutlery; side arms; razors.

9 Scientific, nautical, surveying, electric, photographic, cinematographic, optical, weighing, measuring, signalling, checking (supervision), life-saving and teaching apparatus and instruments; apparatus for recording transmission or reproduction of sound or images; magnetic data carriers, recording discs; automatic vending machines and mechanisms for coin-operated apparatus; cash registers, calculating machines, data processing equipment and computers; fire-extinguishing apparatus.

10 Surgical, medical, dental, and veterinary apparatus and instruments, artificial limbs, eyes and teeth; orthopedic articles; suture materials.

11 Apparatus for lighting, heating, steam generating, cooking, refrigerating, drying, ventilating, water supply, and sanitary purposes.

12 Vehicles; apparatus for locomotion by land, air or water.

13 Firearms; ammunition and projectiles; explosives; fireworks.

14 Precious metals and their alloys and goods in precious metals or coated therewith, not included in other classes; jewelry, precious stones; horological and other chronometric instruments.

15 Musical instruments.

16 Paper and cardboard and goods made from these materials, not included in other classes; printed matter; bookbinding material; photographs; stationery; adhesives for stationery or household purposes; artists' materials; paint brushes; typewriters and office requisites (except furniture); instructional and teaching material (except apparatus); plastic materials for packaging (not included on other classes); playing cards; printers' type; printing blocks.

17 Rubber, gutta-percha, gum, asbestos, mica and goods made from these materials and not included in other classes; plastics in extruded form for use in manufacture; packing, stopping and insulating materials; flexible pipes, not of metal.

18 Leather and imitations of leather, and goods made from these materials and not included in other classes; animal skins, hides; trunks and travelling bags; umbrellas, parasols and walking sticks; whips, harness and saddlery.

19 Building materials (non-metallic); non-metallic rigid pipes for building; asphalt, pitch and bitumen; non-metallic transportable buildings; monuments, not of metal.

20 Furniture, mirrors, picture frames; goods (not included in other classes) of wood, cork, reed, cane, wicker, horn, bone, ivory, whalebone, shell, amber, mother-of-pearl, meerschaum and substitutes for all these materials, or of plastics.

21 Household or kitchen utensils and containers (not of precious metal or coated therewith); combs and sponges; brushes (except paint brushes); brush-making materials; articles for cleaning purposes; steel wool; unworked or semi-worked glass (except glass used in building); glassware, porcelain and earthenware, not included in other classes.

22 Ropes, string, nets, tents, awnings, tarpaulins, sails, sacks; and bags (not included other classes); padding and stuffing materials (except of rubber or plastics); raw fibrous textile materials.

23 Yarns and threads, for textile use.

24 Textile and textile goods, not included in other classes; bed and table covers.

25 Clothing, footwear, headgear.

26 Lace and embroidery, ribbons and braid; buttons, hooks and eyes, pins and needles; artificial flowers.

27 Carpets, rugs, mats and matting; linoleum and other materials for covering existing floors; wall hangings (non-textile).

28 Games and playthings; gymnastic and sporting articles not included in other classes; decorations for Christmas trees.

29 Meats, fish, poultry and game; meat extracts; preserved, dried and cooked fruits and vegetables; jellies, jams; eggs, milk and milk products; edible oils and fats; salad dressings; preserves.

30 Coffee, tea, cocoa, sugar, rice, tapioca, sago, artificial coffee; flour, and preparations made from cereals, bread, pastry and confectionery, ices; honey, treacle; yeast, baking-powder; salt, mustard, vinegar, sauces, (except salad dressings) spices; ice.

31 Agricultural, horticultural and forestry products and grains not included in other classes; living animals; fresh fruits and vegetables; seeds, natural plants and flowers; foodstuffs for animals, malt.

32 Beers; mineral and aerated waters and other non-alcoholic drinks; fruit drinks and fruit juices; syrups and other preparations for making beverages.

33 Alcholic beverages (except beers).

34 Tobacco; smokers' articles; matches.

Services

35 Advertising and business.

36 Insurance and financial.

37 Construction and repair.

38 Communication.

39 Transportation and storage.

40 Material treatment.

41 Education and entertainment.

42 Miscellaneous.

<table>
<tr>
<td>

TRADEMARK/SERVICE MARK APPLICATION, PRINCIPAL REGISTER, WITH DECLARATION

</td>
<td>

MARK (Identify the mark)

CLASS NO. (If known)

</td>
</tr>
</table>

TO THE ASSISTANT SECRETARY AND COMMISSIONER OF PATENTS AND TRADEMARKS:

APPLICANT NAME:

APPLICANT BUSINESS ADDRESS:

APPLICANT ENTITY: (Check one and supply requested information)

☐ Individual - Citizenship: (Country) _____

☐ Partnership - Partnership Domicile: (State and Country) _____
Names and Citizenship (Country) of General Partners: _____

_____

☐ Corporation - State (Country, if appropriate) of Incorporation: _____

☐ Other: (Specify Nature of Entity and Domicile) _____

_____

GOODS AND/OR SERVICES:

Applicant requests registration of the above-identified trademark/service mark shown in the accompanying drawing in the United States Patent and Trademark Office on the Principal Register established by the Act of July 5, 1946 (15 U.S.C. 1051 et. seq., as amended.) for the following goods/services: _____

_____

_____

BASIS FOR APPLICATION: (Check one or more, but NOT both the first AND second boxes, and supply requested information)

☐ Applicant is using the mark in commerce or in connection with the above identified goods/services. (15 U.S.C. 1051(a), as amended.) Three specimens showing the mark as used in commerce are submitted with this application.
- Date of first use of the mark anywhere: _____
- Date of first use of the mark in commerce which the U.S. Congress may regulate: _____
- Specify the type of commerce: _____
  (e.g., interstate, between the U.S. and a specified foreign country)
- Specify manner or mode of use of mark on or in connection with the goods/services: _____
_____
  (e.g., trademark is applied to labels, service mark is used in advertisements)

☐ Applicant has a bona fide intention to use the mark in commerce on or in connection with the above identified goods/services. (15 U.S.C. 1051(b), as amended.)
- Specify intended manner or mode of use of mark on or in connection with the goods/services: _____
_____
  (e.g., trademark will be applied to labels, service mark will be used in advertisements)

☐ Applicant has a bona fide intention to use the mark in commerce on or in connection with the above identified goods/services, and asserts a claim of priority based upon a foreign application in accordance with 15 U.S.C. 1126(d), as amended.
- Country of foreign filing: _____ • Date of foreign filing: _____

☐ Applicant has a bona fide intention to use the mark in commerce on or in connection with the above identified goods/services and, accompanying this application, submits a certification or certified copy of a foreign registration in accordance with 15 U.S.C. 1126(e), as amended.
- Country of registration: _____ • Registration number: _____

Note: Declaration, on Reverse Side, MUST be Signed

DECLARATION

The undersigned being hereby warned that willful false statements and the like so made are punishable by fine or imprisonment, or both, under 18 U.S.C. 1001, and that such willful false statements may jeopardize the validity of the application or any resulting registration, declares that he/she is properly authorized to execute this application on behalf of the applicant; he/she believes the applicant to be the owner of the trademark/service mark sought to be registered, or, if the application is being filed under 15 U.S.C. 1051(b), he/she believes applicant to be entitled to use such mark in commerce; to the best of his/her knowledge and belief no other person, firm, corporation, or association has the right to use the above identified mark in commerce, either in the identical form thereof or in such near resemblance thereto as to be likely, when used on or in connection with the goods/services of such other person, to cause confusion, or to cause mistake, or to deceive; and that all statements made of his/her own knowledge are true and all statements made on information and belief are believed to be true.

_____   _____
Date   Signature

_____   _____
Telephone Number   Print or Type Name and Position

INSTRUCTIONS AND INFORMATION FOR APPLICANT

To receive a filing date, the application must be completed and **signed by the applicant** and submitted along with:

1. The prescribed fee for each class of goods/services listed in the application;
2. A drawing of the mark in conformance with 37 CFR 2.52;
3. If the application is based on use of the mark in commerce, three (3) specimens (evidence) of the mark as used in commerce for each class of goods/services listed in the application. All three specimens may be the same and may be in the nature of: (a) labels showing the mark which are placed on the goods; (b) a photograph of the mark as it appears on the goods, (c) brochures or advertisements showing the mark as used in connection with the services.

Verification of the application - The application must be signed in order for the application to receive a filing date. Only the following person may sign the verification (Declaration) for the application, depending on the applicant's legal entity: (1) the individual applicant; (b) an officer of the corporate applicant; (c) one general partner of a partnership applicant; (d) all joint applicants.

Additional information concerning the requirements for filing an application are available in a booklet entitled **Basic Facts about Trademarks**, which may be obtained by writing:

U.S. DEPARTMENT OF COMMERCE
Patent and Trademark Office
Washington, D.C. 20231

Or by calling: (703) 557-INFO

<table>
<tr><td rowspan="2">

AMENDMENT TO ALLEGE USE UNDER 37 CFR 2.76, WITH DECLARATION

</td><td>MARK (Identify the mark)</td></tr>
<tr><td>SERIAL NO.</td></tr>
</table>

TO THE ASSISTANT SECRETARY AND COMMISSIONER OF PATENTS AND TRADEMARKS:

APPLICANT NAME:

Applicant requests registration of the above-identified trademark/service mark in the United States Patent and Trademark Office on the Principal Register established by the Act of July 5, 1946 (15 U.S.C. 1051 et. seq., as amended). Three specimens showing the mark as used in commerce are submitted with this amendment.

☐   Check here if Request to Divide under 37 CFR 2.87 is being submitted with this amendment.

Applicant is using the mark in commerce on or in connection with the following goods/services:

_____

_____

(NOTE: Goods/services listed above may not be broader than the goods/services identified in the application as filed)

Date of first use of mark anywhere: _____

Date of first use of mark in commerce
which the U.S. Congress may regulate: _____

Specify type of commerce: (e.g., interstate, between the U.S. and a specified foreign country) _____

_____

Specify manner or mode of use of mark on or in connection with the goods/services: (e.g., trademark is applied to labels, service mark is used in advertisements) _____

_____

The undersigned being hereby warned that willful false statements and the like so made are punishable by fine or imprisonment, or both, under 18 U.S.C. 1001, and that such willful false statements may jeopardize the validity of the application or any resulting registration, declares that he/she is properly authorized to execute this Amendment to Allege Use on behalf of the applicant; he/she believes the applicant to be the owner of the trademark/service mark sought to be registered; the trademark/ service mark is now in use in commerce; and all statements made of his/her own knowledge are true and all statements made on information and belief are believed to be true.

_____   _____
Date   Signature

_____   _____
Telephone Number   Print or Type Name and Position

INSTRUCTIONS AND INFORMATION FOR APPLICANT

In an application based upon a bona fide intention to use a mark in commerce, applicant must use its mark in commerce before a registration will be issued. After use begins, the applicant must submit, along with evidence of use (specimens) and the prescribed fee(s), **either**:

(l) an Amendment to Allege Use under 37 CFR 2.76, or
(2) a Statement of Use under 37 CFR 2.88.

The difference between these two filings is the timing of the filing. Applicant may file an Amendment to Allege Use before approval of the mark for publication for opposition in the **Official Gazette**, or, if a final refusal has been issued, prior to the expiration of the six month response period. Otherwise, applicant must file a Statement of Use after the Office issues a Notice of Allowance. The Notice of Allowance will issue after the opposition period is completed if no successful opposition is filed. Neither Amendment to Allege Use or Statement of Use papers will be accepted by the Office during the period of time between approval of the mark for publication for opposition in the **Official Gazette** and the issuance of the Notice of Allowance.

Applicant may call (703) 557-5249 to determine whether the mark has been approved for publication for opposition in the **Official Gazette.**

Before filing an Amendment to Allege Use or a Statement of Use, applicant must use the mark in commerce on or in connection with **all** of the goods/services for which applicant will seek registration, **unless** applicant submits with the papers, a request to divide out from the application the goods or services to which the Amendment to Allege Use or Statement of Use pertains. (See: 37 CFR 2.87, Dividing an application)

Applicant **must** submit with an Amendment to Allege Use or a Statement of Use:

(l) the appropriate fee of $100 per class of goods/services listed in the Amendment to Allege Use or the Statement of Use, and

(2) three (3) specimens or facsimiles of the mark as used in commerce for each class of goods/services asserted (e.g., photograph of mark as it appears on goods, label containing mark which is placed on goods, or brochure or advertisement showing mark as used in connection with services).

Cautions/Notes concerning completion of this Amendment to Allege Use form:

(l) The goods/services identified in the Amendment to Allege Use must be within the scope of the goods/services identified in the application as filed. Applicant may delete goods/services. Deleted goods/services may not be reinstated in the application at a later time.

(2) Applicant **may** list dates of use for only one item in each class of goods/services identified in the Amendment to Allege Use. However, applicant must have used the mark in commerce on all the goods/services in the class. Applicant must identify the particular item to which the dates apply.

(3) Only the following person may sign the verification of the Amendment to Allege Use, depending on the applicant's legal entity: (a) the individual applicant; (b) an officer of corporate applicant; (c) one general partner of partnership applicant; (d) all joint applicants.

<table>
<tr>
<td>

REQUEST FOR EXTENSION OF TIME UNDER 37 CFR 2.89 TO FILE A STATEMENT OF USE, WITH DECLARATION

</td>
<td>

MARK (Identify the mark)

SERIAL NO.

</td>
</tr>
</table>

TO THE ASSISTANT SECRETARY AND COMMISSIONER OF PATENTS AND TRADEMARKS:

APPLICANT NAME:

NOTICE OF ALLOWANCE MAILING DATE:

Applicant requests a six-month extension of time to file the Statement of Use under 37 CFR 2.88 in this application.

☐   Check here if a Request to Divide under 37 CFR 2.87 is being submitted with this request.

Applicant has a continued bona fide intention to use the mark in commerce in connection with the following goods/services: (Check one below)

☐   Those goods/services identified in the Notice of Allowance in this application.

☐   Those goods/services identified in the Notice of Allowance in this application except: (Identify goods/services to be **deleted** from application) _____

_____

This is the _____ request for an Extension of Time following mailing of the Notice of Allowance.
       (Specify first - fifth)

If this is not the first request for an Extension of Time, check one box below. If the first box is checked, explain the circumstance(s) of the non-use in the space provided:

☐   Applicant has not used the mark in commerce yet on all goods/services specified in the Notice of Allowance; however, applicant has made the following ongoing efforts to use the mark in commerce on or in connection with each of the goods/services specified above:

_____

_____

If additional space is needed, please attach a separate sheet to this form

☐   Applicant believes that it has made valid use of the mark in commerce, as evidenced by the Statement of Use submitted with this request; however, if the Statement of Use is found by the Patent and Trademark Office to be fatally defective, applicant will need additional time in which to file a new statement.

The undersigned being hereby warned that willful false statements and the like so made are punishable by fine or imprisonment, or both, under 18 U.S.C. 1001, and that such willful false statements may jeopardize the validity of the application or any resulting registration, declares that he/she is properly authorized to execute this Request for Extension of Time to File a Statement of Use on behalf of the applicant; he/she believes the applicant to be the owner of the trademark/service mark sought to be registered; and all statements made of his/her own knowledge are true and all statements made on information and belief are believed to be true.

_____   _____
Date   Signature

_____   _____
Telephone Number   Print or Type Name and Position

INSTRUCTIONS AND INFORMATION FOR APPLICANT

Applicant must file a Statement of Use within six months after the mailing of the Notice of Allowance in an application based upon a bona fide intention to use a mark in commerce, UNLESS, within that same period, applicant submits a request for a six-month extension of time to file the Statement of Use. The request **must**:

> (l) be in writing,
> (2) include applicant's verified statement of continued bona fide intention to use the mark in commerce,
> (3) specify the goods/services to which the request pertains as they are identified in the Notice of Allowance, and
> (4) include a fee of $100 for each class of goods/services.

Applicant may request four further six-month extensions of time. No extension may extend beyond 36 months from the issue date of the Notice of Allowance. Each request must be filed within the previously granted six-month extension period and must include, in addition to the above requirements, a showing of **GOOD CAUSE**. This good cause showing must include:

> (l) applicant's statement that the mark has not been used in commerce yet on all the goods or services specified in the Notice of Allowance with which applicant has a continued bona fide intention to use the mark in commerce, **and**

> (2) applicant's statement of ongoing efforts to make such use, which may include the following: (a) product or service research or development, (b) market research, (c) promotional activities, (d) steps to acquire distributors, (e) steps to obtain required governmental approval, or (f) similar specified activity .

Applicant may submit one additional six-month extension request during the existing period in which applicant files the Statement of Use, unless the granting of this request would extend beyond 36 months from the issue date of the Notice of Allowance. As a showing of good cause, applicant should state its belief that applicant has made valid use of the mark in commerce, as evidenced by the submitted Statement of Use, but that if the Statement is found by the PTO to be defective, applicant will need additional time in which to file a new statement of use.

Only the following person may sign the verification of the Request for Extentsion of Time, depending on the applicant's legal entity: (a) the individual applicant; (b) an officer of corporate applicant; (c) one general partner of partnership applicant; (d) all joint applicants.

This form is estimated to take 15 minutes to complete. Time will vary depending upon the needs of the individual case. Any comments on the amount of time you require to complete this form should be sent to the Office of Management and Organization, U.S. Patent and Trademark Office, U.S. Department of Commerce, Washington D.C., 20231, and to the Office of Information and Regulatory Affairs, Office of Management and Budget, Washington, D.C. 20503.

STATEMENT OF USE UNDER 37 CFR 2.88, WITH DECLARATION	MARK (Identify the mark)
	SERIAL NO.

TO THE ASSISTANT SECRETARY AND COMMISSIONER OF PATENTS AND TRADEMARKS:

APPLICANT NAME:

NOTICE OF ALLOWANCE ISSUE DATE:

Applicant requests registration of the above-identified trademark/service mark in the United States Patent and Trademark Office on the Principal Register established by the Act of July 5, 1946 (15 U.S.C. 1051 et. seq., as amended). Three (3) specimens showing the mark as used in commerce are submitted with this statement.

☐ Check here only if a Request to Divide under 37 CFR 2.87 is being submitted with this Statement.

Applicant is using the mark in commerce on or in connection with the following goods/services: (Check One)

☐ Those goods/services identified in the Notice of Allowance in this application.

☐ Those goods/services identified in the Notice of Allowance in this application except: (Identify goods/services to be deleted from application) _____

_____

_____

Date of first use of mark anywhere: _____

Date of first use of mark in commerce
which the U.S. Congress may regulate: _____

Specify type of commerce: (e.g., interstate, between the U.S. and a specified foreign country) _____

_____

Specify manner or mode of use of mark on or in connection with the goods/services: (e.g., trademark is applied to labels, service mark is used in advertisements) _____

_____

The undersigned being hereby warned that willful false statements and the like so made are punishable by fine or imprisonment, or both, under 18 U.S.C. 1001, and that such willful false statements may jeopardize the validity of the application or any resulting registration, declares that he/she is properly authorized to execute this Statement of Use on behalf of the applicant; he/she believes the applicant to be the owner of the trademark/service mark sought to be registered; the trademark/ service mark is now in use in commerce; and all statements made of his/her own knowledge are true and all statements made on information and belief are believed to be true.

_____
Date

_____
Signature

_____
Telephone Number

_____
Print or Type Name and Position

PTO Form 1580 (REV. 9/89)
OMB No. 06510023
Exp. 6-30-92

U.S. DEPARTMENT OF COMMERCE/Patent and Trademark Office

INSTRUCTIONS AND INFORMATION FOR APPLICANT

In an application based upon a bona fide intention to use a mark in commerce, applicant must use its mark in commerce before a registration will be issued. After use begins, the applicant must submit, along with evidence of use (specimens) and the prescribed fee(s), **either**:

> (1) an Amendment to Allege Use under 37 CFR 2.76, or
> (2) a Statement of Use under 37 CFR 2.88.

The difference between these two filings is the timing of the filing. Applicant may file an Amendment to Allege Use before approval of the mark for publication for opposition in the **Official Gazette**, or, if a final refusal has been issued, prior to the expiration of the six month response period. Otherwise, applicant must file a Statement of Use after the Office issues a Notice of Allowance. The Notice of Allowance will issue after the opposition period is completed if no successful opposition is filed. Neither Amendment to Allege Use or Statement of Use papers will be accepted by the Office during the period of time between approval of the mark for publication for opposition in the **Official Gazette** and the issuance of the Notice of Allowance.

Applicant may call (703) 557-5249 to determine whether the mark has been approved for publication for opposition in the **Official Gazette.**

Before filing an Amendment to Allege Use or a Statement of Use, applicant must use the mark in commerce on or in connection with **all** of the goods/services for which applicant will seek registration, **unless** applicant submits with the papers, a request to divide out from the application the goods or services to which the Amendment to Allege Use or Statement of Use pertains. (See: 37 CFR 2.87, Dividing an application)

Applicant **must** submit with an Amendment to Allege Use or a Statement of Use:

> (1) the appropriate fee of $100 per class of goods/services listed in the Amendment to Allege Use or the Statement of Use, and

> (2) three (3) specimens or facsimiles of the mark as used in commerce for each class of goods/services asserted (e.g., photograph of mark as it appears on goods, label containing mark which is placed on goods, or brochure or advertisement showing mark as used in connection with services).

Cautions/Notes concerning completion of this Statement of Use form:

> (1) The goods/services identified in the Statement of Use must be identical to the goods/services identified in the Notice of Allowance. Applicant may delete goods/services. Deleted goods/services may not be reinstated in the application at a later time.

> (2) Applicant may list dates of use for only one item in each class of goods/services identified in the Statement of Use. However, applicant must have used the mark in commerce on all the goods/services in the class. Applicant must identify the particular item to which the dates apply.

> (3) Only the following person may sign the verification of the Statement of Use, depending on the applicant's legal entity: (a) the individual applicant; (b) an officer of corporate applicant; (c) one general partner of partnership applicant; (d) all joint applicants.

Applicant or Patentee: _____

Serial or Patent No.: _____

Filed or Issued: _____

Title: _____

Attorney's
Docket No.: _____

VERIFIED STATEMENT (DECLARATION) CLAIMING SMALL ENTITY STATUS
(37 CFR 1.9(f) & 1.27(c))--SMALL BUSINESS CONCERN

I hereby declare that I am

☐ the owner of the small business concern identified below:

☐ an official of the small business concern empowered to act on behalf of the concern identified below:

NAME OF SMALL BUSINESS CONCERN _____

ADDRESS OF SMALL BUSINESS CONCERN _____

_____

I hereby declare that the above identified small business concern qualifies as a small business concern as defined in 13 CFR 121.12, and reproduced in 37 CFR 1.9(d), for purposes of paying reduced fees to the United States Patent and Trademark Office, in that the number of employees of the concern, including those of its affiliates, does not exceed 500 persons. For purposes of this statement, (1) the number of employees of the business concern is the average over the previous fiscal year of the concern of the persons employed on a full-time, part-time or temporary basis during each of the pay periods of the fiscal year, and (2) concerns are affiliates of each other when either, directly or indirectly, one concern controls or has the power to control the other, or a third party or parties controls or has the power to control both.

I hereby declare that rights under contract or law have been conveyed to and remain with the small business concern identified above with regard to the invention, entitled _____ by inventor(s)

_____

described in

☐ the specification filed herewith

☐ application serial no. _____, filed _____.

☐ patent no. _____, issued _____.

If the rights held by the above identified small business concern are not exclusive, each individual, concern or organization having rights in the invention is listed below* and no rights to the invention are held by any person, other than the inventor, who would not qualify as an independent inventor under 37 CFR 1.9(c) if that person made the invention, or by any concern which would not qualify as a small business concern under 37 CFR 1.9(d), or a nonprofit organization under 37 CFR 1.9(e). *NOTE: Separate verified statements are required from each named person, concern or organization having rights to the invention averring to their status as small entities. (37 CFR 1.27)

NAME _____

ADDRESS _____

☐ INDIVIDUAL   ☐ SMALL BUSINESS CONCERN   ☐ NONPROFIT ORGANIZATION

NAME _____

ADDRESS _____

☐ INDIVIDUAL   ☐ SMALL BUSINESS CONCERN   ☐ NONPROFIT ORGANIZATION

I acknowledge the duty to file, in this application or patent, notification of any change in status resulting in loss of entitlement to small entity status prior to paying, or at the time of paying, the earliest of the issue fee or any maintenance fee due after the date on which status as a small entity is no longer appropriate. (37 CFR 1.28(b))

I hereby declare that all statements made herein of my own knowledge are true and that all statements made on information and belief are believed to be true; and further that these statements were made with the knowledge that willful false statements and the like so made are punishable by fine or imprisonment, or both, under section 1001 of Title 18 of the United States Code, and that such willful false statements may jeopardize the validity of the application, any patent issuing thereon, or any patent to which this verified statement is directed.

NAME OF PERSON SIGNING _____

TITLE OF PERSON IF OTHER THAN OWNER _____

ADDRESS OF PERSON SIGNING _____

_____

SIGNATURE _____ DATE _____

Applicant or Patentee: _____ Attorney's
Serial or Patent No. : _____ Docket No.: _____
Filed or Issued: _____
Title: _____

VERIFIED STATEMENT (DECLARATION) CLAIMING SMALL ENTITY STATUS
(37 CFR 1.9(f) & 1.27(d))--NONPROFIT ORGANIZATION

I hereby declare that I am an official empowered to act on behalf of the nonprofit organization identified below:
NAME OF NONPROFIT ORGANIZATION _____
ADDRESS OF NONPROFIT ORGANIZATION _____
_____

TYPE OF NONPROFIT ORGANIZATION
☐ UNIVERSITY OR OTHER INSTITUTION OF HIGHER EDUCATION
☐ TAX EXEMPT UNDER INTERNAL REVENUE SERVICE CODE (26 U.S.C. 501(a) and 501(c)(3))
☐ NONPROFIT SCIENTIFIC OR EDUCATIONAL UNDER STATUTE OF STATE OF THE UNITED STATES OF AMERICA
   (NAME OF STATE _____)
   (CITATION OF STATUTE _____)
☐ WOULD QUALIFY AS TAX EXEMPT UNDER INTERNAL REVENUE SERVICE CODE (26 U.S.C. 501(a) and 501(c)(3)) IF LOCATED IN THE UNITED STATES OF AMERICA
☐ WOULD QUALIFY AS NONPROFIT SCIENTIFIC OR EDUCATIONAL UNDER STATUTE OF STATE OF THE UNITED STATES OF AMERICA IF LOCATED IN THE UNITED STATES OF AMERICA
   (NAME OF STATE _____)
   (CITATION OF STATUTE _____)

I hereby declare that the nonprofit organization identified above qualifies as a nonprofit organization as defined in 37 CFR 1.9(e) for purposes of paying reduced fees to the United States Patent and Trademark Office regarding the invention entitled _____
_____ by inventor(s) _____

described in:
☐ the specification filed herewith.
☐ application serial no. _____, filed _____.
☐ patent no. _____, issued _____.

I hereby declare that rights under contract or law have been conveyed to and remain with the nonprofit organization regarding the above identified invention.

If the rights held by the nonprofit organization are not exclusive, each individual, concern or organization having rights in the invention is listed below* and no rights to the invention are held by any person, other than the inventor, who would not qualify as an independent inventor under 37 CFR 1.9(c) if that person made the invention, or by any concern which would not qualify as a small business concern under 37 CFR 1.9(d) or a nonprofit organization under 37 CFR 1.9(e).

*NOTE: Separate verified statements are required from each named person, concern or organization having rights to the invention averring to their status as small entities. (37 CFR 1.27)

NAME _____
ADDRESS _____
☐ INDIVIDUAL   ☐ SMALL BUSINESS CONCERN   ☐ NONPROFIT ORGANIZATION

NAME _____
ADDRESS _____
☐ INDIVIDUAL   ☐ SMALL BUSINESS CONCERN   ☐ NONPROFIT ORGANIZATION

I acknowledge the duty to file, in this application or patent, notification of any change in status resulting in loss of entitlement to small entity status prior to paying, or at the time of paying, the earliest of the issue fee or any maintenance fee due after the date on which status as a small entity is no longer appropriate. (37 CFR 1.28(b))

I hereby declare that all statements made herein of my own knowledge are true and that all statements made on information and belief are believed to be true; and further that these statements were made with the knowledge that willful false statements and the like so made are punishable by fine or imprisonment, or both, under section 1001 of Title 18 of the United States Code, and that such willful false statements may jeopardize the validity of the application, any patent issuing thereon, or any patent to which this verified statement is directed.

NAME OF PERSON SIGNING _____
TITLE IN ORGANIZATION OF PERSON SIGNING _____
ADDRESS OF PERSON SIGNING _____
_____

SIGNATURE _____ DATE _____

PART 3

PATENTS

Basic information about patents, directions on how to apply for a patent, and patent office proceedings are described in this section.

You'll find patent application forms issued by the U.S. Patent and Trademark Office (PTO) beginning on p. 171.

1 THE BASICS OF PATENTS

A patent gives protection for an invention. This chapter explains the basic patent laws that give you protection.

WHAT IS A PATENT

A patent for an invention is a grant of a property right by the Government to the inventor (or his or her heirs or assigns), acting through the Patent and Trademark Office. The term of the patent is 17 years from the date the patent is granted, subject to the payment of maintenance fees.

The right conferred by the patent grant extends throughout the United States and its territories and possessions.

The right conferred by the patent grant is, in the language of the statute and of the grant itself, "the right to exclude others from making, using, or selling" the invention. What is granted is not the right to make, use, or sell, but the right to exclude others from making, using, or selling the invention.

WHO MAY APPLY FOR A PATENT

According to the law, only the inventor may apply for a patent, with certain exceptions. If a person who is not the inventor should apply for a patent, the patent, if it were obtained, would be invalid. The person applying in such a case who falsely states that he/she is the inventor would also be subject to criminal penalties. If the inventor is dead, the application may be made by legal representatives, that is, the administrator or executor of the estate. If the inventor is insane, the application for patent may be made by a guardian. If an inventor refuses to apply for a patent or cannot be found, a joint inventor or person having a proprietary interest in the invention may apply on behalf of the missing inventor.

If two or more persons make an invention jointly, they apply for a patent as joint inventors. A person who makes a financial contribution is not a joint inventor and cannot be joined in the application as an inventor. It is possible to correct an innocent mistake in erroneously omitting an inventor or in erroneously naming a person as an inventor.

Officers and employees of the Patent and Trademark Office are prohibited by law from applying for a patent or acquiring, directly or

131

indirectly, except by inheritance or bequest, any patent or any right or interest in any patent.

ANSWERS TO QUESTIONS FREQUENTLY ASKED

1. Q. What do the terms "patent pending" and "patent applied for" mean?

A. They are used by a manufacturer or seller of an article to inform the public that an application for patent on that article is on file in the Patent and Trademark Office. The law imposes a fine on those who use these terms falsely to deceive the public.

2. Q. Is there any danger that the Patent and Trademark Office will give others information contained in my application while it is pending?

A. No. All patent applications are maintained in the strictest secrecy until the patent is issued. After the patent is issued, however, the Office file containing the application and all correspondence leading up to issuance of the patent is made available in the Files Information Room for inspection by anyone, and copies of these files may be purchased from the Office.

3. Q. May I write to the Patent and Trademark Office directly about my application after it is filed?

A. The Office will answer an applicant's inquiries as to the status of the application, and inform you whether your application has been rejected, allowed, or is awaiting action. However, if you have a patent attorney or agent the Office will not correspond with both you and the attorney concerning the merits of your application. All comments concerning your application should be forwarded through your attorney or agent.

4. Q. Is it necessary to go to the Patent and Trademark Office to transact business concerning patent matters?

A. No; most business with the Office is conducted by correspondence. Interviews regarding pending applications can be arranged with examiners if necessary, however, and are often helpful.

5. Q. If two or more persons work together to make an invention, to whom will the patent be granted?

A. If each had a share in the ideas forming the invention, they are joint inventors and a patent will be issued to them jointly on the basis of a proper patent application. If on the other hand one of these persons has provided all of the ideas of the invention, and the other has only followed instructions in making it, the person who contributed the ideas is the sole inventor and the patent application and patent shall be in his name alone.

6. Q. If one person furnishes all of the ideas to make an invention and another employs him or furnishes the money for building and testing the invention, should the patent application be filed by them jointly?

A. No. The application must be signed by the true inventor, and filed in the Patent and Trademark Office, in the inventor's name. This is the person who furnishes the ideas, not the employer or the person who furnishes the money.

7. Q. Does the Patent and Trademark Office control the fees charged by patent attorneys and agents for their services?

A. No. This is a matter between you and your patent attorney or agent in which the Office takes no part. To avoid misunderstanding you may wish to ask for estimate charges for: (a) the search, (b) preparation of the patent application, (c) Patent and Trademark Office prosecution.

8. Q. Will the Patent and Trademark Office help me to select a patent attorney or agent to make my patent search or to prepare and prosecute my patent application?

A. No. The Office cannot make this choice for you. However, your own friends or general attorney may help you in making a selection from among those listed as registered practitioners on the Office roster. Also, some bar associations operate lawyer referral services that maintain lists of patent lawyers available to accept new clients.

9. Q. Will the Patent and Trademark Office advise me as to whether a certain patent promotion organization is reliable and trustworthy?

A. No. The Office has no control over such organizations and does not supply information about them. *It is advisable, however, to check on the reputation of invention promotion firms before making any commitments.* It is suggested that you obtain this information by inquiring of the Better Business Bureau of the city in which the organization is located, or of the bureau of commerce and industry or bureau of consumer affairs of the state in which the organization has its place of business. You may also undertake to make sure that you are dealing with reliable people by asking your own patent attorney or agent or by inquiry of others who may know them.

10. Q. Are there any organizations in my area which can tell me how and where I may be able to obtain assistance in developing and marketing my invention?

A. Yes. In your own or neighboring communities you may inquire of such organizations as chambers of commerce, and banks. Many communities have locally financed industrial development organizations which can help you locate manufacturers and individuals who might be interested in promoting your idea.

FUNCTIONS OF THE U.S. PATENT AND TRADEMARK OFFICE

The Patent and Trademark Office is an agency of the U.S. Department of Commerce.

The role of the Patent and Trademark Office is to provide patent protection for inventions and to register trademarks. It serves the interest of inventors and businesses with respect to their inventions and corporate, product, and service identifications. It also advises and assists the bureaus and offices of the Department of Commerce and other agencies of the Government in matters involving "intellectual property" such as patents. Through the preservation, classification, and dissemination of patent information, the Office aids and encourages innovation and the scientific and technical advancement of the Nation.

In discharging its duties, the Patent and Trademark Office examines applications and grants patents on inventions when applicants are entitled to them; it publishes and disseminates patent information, records assignments of patents, maintains search files to U.S. and foreign patents and a search room for public use in examining issued patents and records. It supplies copies of patents and official records to the public. Patent applications are received at the rate of over 100,000 per year. Over 4,700,000 patents have been issued.

PATENT LAWS

The patent laws specify the subject matter for which a patent may be obtained and the conditions for patentability. The laws establish the Patent and Trademark Office for administering the law relating to the granting of patents, and contains various other provisions relating to patents.

WHAT CAN BE PATENTED

In the language of the statute, any person who "invents or discovers any new and useful process, machine, manufacture, or composition of matter, or any new and useful improvements thereof, may obtain a patent," subject to the conditions and requirements of the law. By the word "process" is meant a process or method, and new processes, primarily industrial or technical processes, may be patented. The term "machine" used in the statute needs no explanation. The term "manufacture" refers to articles which are made, and includes all manufactured articles. The term "composition of matter" relates to chemical compositions and may include mixtures of ingredients as well as new chemical compounds. These classes of subject matter taken together include practically everything which is made by man and the processes for making them.

The Atomic Energy Act of 1954 excludes the patenting of inventions useful solely in the utilization of special nuclear material or atomic energy for atomic weapons.

The patent law specifies that the subject matter must be "useful." The term "useful" in this connection refers to the condition that the subject matter has a useful purpose and also includes operativeness, that is, a machine which will not operate to perform the intended purpose would not be called useful, and therefore would not be granted a patent.

Interpretations of the statute by the courts have defined the limits of the field of subject matter which can be patented, thus it has been held that methods of doing business and printed matter cannot be patented.

In the case of mixtures of ingredients, such as medicines, a patent cannot be granted unless there is more to the mixture than the effect of its components. A patent cannot be obtained upon a mere idea or suggestion. The patent is granted upon the new machine, manufacture, etc., as has been said, and not upon the idea or suggestion of the new machine. A complete description of the actual machine or other subject matter sought to be patented is required.

NOVELTY AND OTHER CONDITIONS FOR OBTAINING A PATENT

In order for an invention to be patentable it must be new as defined in the patent law, which provides that an invention cannot be patented if—

(a) The invention was known or used by others in this country, or patented or described in a printed publication in this or a foreign country, before the invention thereof by the applicant for patent, or

(b) The invention was patented or described in a printed publication in this or a foreign country or in public use or on sale in this country more than one year prior to the application for patent in the United States. . . .

If the invention has been described in a printed publication anywhere in the world, or if it has been in public use or on sale in this country before the date that the applicant made his invention, a patent cannot be obtained. If the invention has been described in a printed publication anywhere, or has been in public use or on sale in this country more than one year before the date on which an application for patent is filed in this country, a valid patent cannot be obtained. In this connection it is immaterial when the invention was made, or whether the printed publication or public use was by the inventor himself or by someone else. If the inventor describes the invention in a printed publication or uses the invention publicly, or places it on sale, he must apply for a patent before one year has gone by, otherwise any right to a patent will be lost.

Even if the subject matter sought to be patented is not exactly shown by the prior art, and involves one or more differences over the most nearly similar thing already known, a patent may still be refused if the differences would be obvious. The subject matter sought to be patented must by sufficiently different from what has been used or described before so that it may be said to be unobvious to a person having ordinary skill in the area of technology related to the invention. For example, the substitution of one material for another, or mere changes in shape or size, are ordinarily not patentable.

ATTORNEYS AND AGENTS

The preparation of an application for patent and the conducting of the proceedings in the Patent and Trademark Office to obtain the patent is an undertaking requiring the knowledge of patent law and Patent and Trademark Office practice as well as knowledge of the scientific or technical matters involved in the particular invention.

Inventors may prepare their own applications and file them in the Patent and Trademark Office and conduct the proceedings themselves, but unless they are familiar with these matters or study them in detail, they may get into considerable difficulty. While a patent may be obtained in many cases by persons not skilled in this work, there would be no assurance that the patent obtained would adequately protect the particular invention.

Most inventors employ the services of registered patent attorneys or patent agents. The law gives the Patent and Trademark Office the power to make rules and regulations governing conduct and the recognition of patent attorneys and agents to practice before the Patent and Trademark Office. Persons who are not recognized by the Patent and Trademark Office for this practice are not permitted by law to represent inventors. The Patent and Trademark Office maintains a register of attorneys and agents.

The Patent and Trademark Office registers both attorneys at law and persons who are not attorneys at law. The former persons are now referred to as "patent attorneys" and the latter persons are referred to as "patent agents." Insofar as the work of preparing an application for patent and conducting the prosecution in the Patent and Trademark Office is concerned, patent agents are usually just as well qualified as patent attorneys, although patent agents cannot conduct patent litigation in the courts or perform various services which the local jurisdiction considers as practicing law.

The Patent and Trademark Office cannot recommend any particular attorney or agent, or aid in the selection of an attorney or agent, as by stating, in response to inquiry that a named patent attorney, agent, or firm, is "reliable" or "capable." The Patent and Trademark Office publishes a directory of all registered patent attorneys and agents who have indicated their availability to accept new clients, arranged by states, cities, and foreign countries. The Directory must be purchased from the Government Printing Office.

The telephone directories of most large cities have, in the classified section, a heading for patent attorneys under which those in that area are listed. Many large cities have associations of patent attorneys.

In employing a patent attorney or agent, the inventor executes a power of attorney or authorization of agent which must be filed in the Patent and Trademark Office and is usually a part of the application papers. When an attorney has been appointed, the Office does not communicate with the inventor directly but conducts the correspondence with the attorney since he is acting for the inventor thereafter, although the inventor is free to contact the Patent and Trademark Office concerning the status of his application. The inventor may remove the attorney or agent by revoking the power or authorization.

The Patent and Trademark Office has the power to disbar, or suspend from practicing before it, persons guilty of gross misconduct, etc., but this can only be done after a full hearing with the presentation of clear and convincing evidence concerning the misconduct. The Patent and Trademark Office will receive and, in appropriate cases, act upon complaints against attorneys and agents. The fees charged to inventors by patent attorneys and agents for their professional services are not subject to regulation by the Patent and Trademark Office. Definite evidence of overcharging may afford basis for Patent and Trademark Office action, but the Office rarely intervenes in disputes concerning fees.

DISCLOSURE DOCUMENT

One of the services provided for inventors by the Patent and Trademark Office is the acceptance and preservation for a two-year period of papers disclosing an invention. This disclosure is accepted as evidence of the dates of conception of the invention.

It will be retained for two years at which time it will be destroyed unless it is referred to in a separate letter in a related patent application.

A fee of $6 must accompany the disclosure. The disclosure is limited to written matter or drawings on paper or other thin, flexible material, such as linen or plastic drafting material, having dimensions or being folded to dimensions not to exceed 8½ x 13 inches. Photographs are acceptable. Each page should be numbered. Text and drawings should be of such quality as to permit reproduction.

The disclosure must be accompanied by a stamped, self-addressed envelope and a separate paper in duplicate also signed by the inventor. The papers will be stamped with an identifying number and returned with the reminder that the Disclosure Document may be relied upon only as evidence and that an application must be filed in order to provide patent protection.

2 HOW TO APPLY FOR A PATENT

An application for a patent is made to the Commissioner of Patents and Trademarks and includes:

(1) A letter of transmittal (see form on p. 171);
(2) A specification (description and claims, see p. 139);
(3) An oath or declaration (see form on p. 140);
(4) A drawing in those cases in which a drawing is necessary (see p. 141);
(5) The filing fee (see p. 145).

The specification and oath or declaration must be legibly written or printed in permanent ink on one side of the paper. The Office prefers typewriting on legal size paper, 8 to 8½ by 10½ to 13 inches, 1½ or double spaced, with margins of 1 inch on the left-hand side and at the top. If the papers filed are not correctly, legibly, and clearly written, The Patent and Trademark Office may require typewritten or printed papers.

The application for patent is not forwarded for examination until all its required parts, complying with the rules relating thereto, are received. If the papers and parts are incomplete, or so defective that they cannot be accepted as a complete application for examination, the applicant will be notified about the deficiencies and be given a time period in which to remedy them. A surcharge may be required. If the applicant does not respond within the prescribed time period, the application will be returned or otherwise disposed of. The filing fee may be refunded when an application is refused acceptance as incomplete; however, a handling fee will be charged.

It is desirable that all parts of the complete application be deposited in the Office together; otherwise each part must be signed and a letter must accompany each part, accurately and clearly connecting it with the other parts of the application.

All applications are numbered in serial order, and the applicant is informed of the serial number and filing date of the application by a filing receipt. The filing date of the application is the date on which a specification (including claims) and any required drawings are received in the Patent and Trademark Office; or the date on which the last part completing the application is received in the case of a previously incomplete or defective application.

SPECIFICATION (DESCRIPTION AND CLAIMS)

The specification must include a written description of the invention and of the manner and process of making and using it, and is required to be in such full, clear, concise, and exact terms as to enable any person skilled in the technological area to which the invention pertains, or with which it is most nearly connected, to make and use the same.

The specification must set forth the precise invention for which a patent is solicited, in such manner as to distinguish it from other inventions and from what is old. It must describe completely a specific embodiment of the process, machine, manufacture, composition of matter or improvement invented, and must explain the mode of operation or principle whenever applicable. The best mode contemplated by the inventor of carrying out his invention must be set forth.

In the case of an improvement, the specification must particularly point out the part or parts of the process, machine, manufacture, or composition of matter to which the improvement relates, and the description should be confined to the specific improvement and to such parts as necessarily cooperate with it or as may be necessary to a complete understanding or description of it.

The title of the invention, which should be as short and specific as possible, should appear as a heading on the first page of the specification, if it does not otherwise appear at the beginning of the application.

A brief abstract of the technical disclosure in the specification must be set forth in a separate page immediately following the claims in a separate paragraph under the heading "Abstract of the Disclosure."

A brief summary of the invention indicating its nature and substance, which may include a statement of the object of the invention, commensurate with the invention as claimed and any object recited should precede the detailed description. Such summary should be that of the invention as claimed.

When there are drawings, there shall be a brief description of the several views of the drawings, and the detailed description of the invention shall refer to the different views by specifying the numbers of the figures, and to the different parts by use of reference numerals.

The specification must conclude with one or more claims particularly pointing out and distinctly claiming the subject matter which the applicant regards as the invention.

The claims are brief descriptions of the subject matter of the invention, eliminating unnecessary details and reciting all essential features necessary to distinguish the invention from what is old. The claims are the operative part of the patent. Novelty and patentability are judged by the claims, and, when a patent is granted, questions of infringement are judged by the courts on the basis of the claims.

When more than one claim is presented, they may be placed in dependent form in which a claim may refer back to and further restrict one or more preceding claims.

A claim in multiple dependent form shall contain a reference, in the alternative only, to more than one claim previously set forth and then specify a further limitation of the subject matter claimed. A multiple dependent claim shall not serve as a basis for any other multiple dependent claim. A multiple dependent claim shall be construed to incorporate by reference all the limitations of the particular claim in relation to which it is being considered.

The claim or claims must conform to the invention as set forth in the remainder of the specification and the terms and phrases used in the claims must find clear support or antecedent basis in the description so that the meaning of the terms in the claims may be ascertainable by reference to the description.

The following order of arrangement should be observed in framing the specification:

(a) Title of the invention; or a preamble stating the name, citizenship, and residence of the applicant and the title of the invention may be used.
(b) Cross-references to related applications, if any.
(c) Brief summary of the invention.
(d) Brief description of the several views of the drawing, if there are drawings.
(e) Detailed Description.
(f) Claim or claims.
(g) Abstract of the disclosure.

OATH OR DECLARATION, SIGNATURE

The oath or declaration of the applicant is required by law. The inventor must make an oath or declaration that he/she believes himself/herself to be the original and first inventor of the subject matter of the application, and he/she must make various other allegations required by law and various allegations required by the Patent and Trademark Office rules. The oath must be sworn to by the inventor before a notary public or other officer authorized to administer oaths. A declaration may be used in lieu of an oath as part of the original application for a patent involving designs, plants, and other patentable inventions; for reissue patents; when claiming matter originally shown or described but not originally claimed; or when filing a divisional or continuing application. A declaration does not need to be notarized (see form 2 on p. 172).

The application, oath or declaration must be signed by the inventor(s) in person, or by the person entitled by law to make application on the inventor's behalf. A full first or middle name of each inventor without abbreviation and a middle or first initial, if any, are required. The post-office address of each inventor is also required.

Blank forms for applications or certain other papers are not supplied by the Patent and Trademark Office.

The papers in a complete application will not be returned for any purpose whatever, nor will the filing fee be returned. If applicants have not preserved copies of the papers, the Office will furnish copies for a fee.

DRAWING

The applicant for a patent will be required by law to furnish a drawing of the invention whenever the nature of the case admits of it; this drawing must be filed with the application. This includes practically all inventions except compositions of matter or processes, but a drawing may also be useful in the case of many processes.

The drawing must show every feature of the invention specified in the claims and is required by the Office rules to be in a particular form. The Office specifies the size of the sheet on which the drawing is made, the type of paper, the margins, and other details relating to the making of the drawing. The reason for specifying the standards in detail is that the drawings are printed and published in a uniform style when the patent issues, and the drawings must also be such that they can be readily understood by persons using the patent descriptions.

No names or other identification will be permitted within the "sight" of the drawing, and applicants are expected to use the space above and between the hole locations to identify each sheet of drawings. This identification may consist of the attorney's name and docket number or the inventor's name and case number and may include the sheet number and the total number of sheets filed (for example, "sheet 2 of 4"). The following rule, reproduced from title 37 of the Code of Federal Regulations, relates to the standards for drawings:

1.84 Standards for drawings:

(a) *Paper and ink.* Drawings must be made upon paper which is flexible, strong, white, smooth, non-shiny and durable. Two-ply or three-ply bristol board is preferred. The surface of the paper should be calendered and of a quality which will permit erasure and correction with India ink. India ink, or its equivalent in quality, is preferred for pen drawings to secure perfectly black solid lines. The use of white pigment to cover lines is not normally acceptable.

(b) *Size of sheet and margins.* The size of the sheets on which drawings are made may either be exactly 8½ by 14 inches (21.6 by 35.6 cm.) or exactly 21.0 by 29.7 cm. (DIN size A4). All drawing sheets in a particular application must be the same size. One of the shorter sides of the sheet is regarded as its top.

  (1) On 8½ by 14 inch drawing sheets, the drawings must include a top margin of 2 inches (5.1 cm.) and bottom and side margins of ¼ inch (6.4 mm.) from the edges, thereby leaving a "sight" precisely 8 by 11¾ inches

(20.3 × 29.8 cm.). Margin border lines are not permitted. All work must be included within the "sight". The sheets may be provided with two ¼ inch (6.4 mm.) diameter holes having their centerlines spaced 11/16 inch (17.5 mm.) below the top edge and 2¾ inches (7.0 cm.) apart, said holes being equally spaced from the respective side edges.

    (2) On 21.0 by 29.7 cm. drawing sheets, the drawing must include a top margin of at least 2.5 cm., a left side margin of 2.5 cm., a right side margin of 1.5 cm., and a bottom margin of 1.0 cm. Margin border lines are not permitted. All work must be contained within a sight size not to exceed 17 by 26.2 cm.

(c) Character of lines. All drawings must be made with drafting instruments or by a process which will give them satisfactory reproduction characteristics. Every line and letter must be durable, black, sufficiently dense and dark, uniformly thick and well defined; the weight of all lines and letters must be heavy enough to permit adequate reproduction. This direction applies to all lines however fine, to shading, and to lines representing cut surfaces in sectional views. All lines must be clean, sharp, and solid. Fine or crowded lines should be avoided. Solid black should not be used for sectional or surface shading. Freehand work should be avoided wherever it is possible to do so.

(d) Hatching and shading.

    (1) Hatching should be made by oblique parallel lines spaced sufficiently apart to enable the lines to be distinguished without difficulty.

    (2) Heavy lines on the shade side of objects should preferably be used except where they tend to thicken the work and obscure reference characters. The light should come from the upper left-hand corner at an angle of 45°. Surface delineations should preferably be shown by proper shading, which should be open.

(e) Scale. The scale to which a drawing is made ought to be large enough to show the mechanism without crowding when the drawing is reduced in size to two-thirds in reproduction, and views of portions of the mechanism of a larger scale should be used when necessary to show details clearly; two or more sheets should be used if one does not give sufficient room to accomplish this end, but the number of sheets should not be more than is necessary.

(f) Reference characters. The different views should be consecutively numbered figures. Reference numerals (and letters, but numerals are preferred) must be plain, legible and carefully formed, and not be encircled. They should, if possible, measure at least one-eighth of an inch (3.2 mm.) in height so that they may bear reduction to one twenty-

fourth of an inch (1.1 mm.); and they may be slightly larger when there is sufficient room. They should not be so placed in the close and complex parts of the drawing as to interfere with a thorough comprehension of the same, and therefore should rarely cross or mingle with the lines. When necessarily grouped around a certain part, they should be placed at a little distance, at the closest point where there is available space, and connected by lines with the parts to which they refer. They should not be placed upon hatched or shaded surfaces but when necessary, a blank space may be left in the hatching or shading where the character occurs so that it shall appear perfectly distinct and separate from the work. The same part of an invention appearing in more than one view of the drawing must always be designated by the same character, and the same character must never be used to designate different parts. Reference signs not mentioned in the description shall not appear in the drawing, and vice versa.

(g) *Symbols, legends.* Graphical drawing symbols and other labeled representations may be used for conventional elements when appropriate, subject to approval by the Office. The elements for which such symbols and labeled representation are used must be adequately identified in the specification. While descriptive matter on drawings is not permitted, suitable legends may be used, or may be required in proper cases, as in diagrammatic views and flow sheets or to show materials or where labeled representations are employed to illustrate conventional elements. Arrows may be required, in proper cases, to show direction of movement. The lettering should be as large as, or larger than, the reference characters.

(h) *[Reserved]*

(i) *Views.* The drawing must contain as many figures as may be necessary to show the invention; the figures should be consecutively numbered if possible in order in which they appear. The figures may be plain, elevation, section, or perspective views, and detail views of portions of elements, on a larger scale if necessary, may also be used. Exploded views, with the separated parts of the same figure embraced by a bracket, to show the relationship or order of assembly of various parts are permissible. When necessary, a view of a large machine or device in its entirety, may be broken and extended over several sheets if there is no loss in facility of understanding the view. Where figures on two or more sheets form in effect a single complete figure, the figures on the several sheets should be so arranged that the complete figure can be understood by laying the drawing sheets adjacent to one another. The arrangement should be such that no part of any of the figures appearing on the various sheets are concealed and that the complete figure

143

can be understood even though spaces will occur in the complete figure because of the margins on the drawing sheets. The plane upon which a sectional view is taken should be indicated on the general view by a broken line, the ends of which should be designated by numerals corresponding to the figure number of the sectional view and have arrows applied to indicate the direction is which the view is taken. A moved position may be shown by a broken line superimposed upon a suitable figure if this can be done without crowding, otherwise a separate figure must be used for this purpose. Modified forms of construction can only be shown in separate figures. Views should not be connected by projection lines nor should center lines be used.

(j) *Arrangement of views.* All views on the same sheet should stand in the same direction and, if possible, stand so that they can be read with the sheet held in an upright position. If views longer than the width of the sheet are necessary for the clearest illustration of the invention, the sheet may be turned on its side so that the top of the sheet with the appropriate top margin is on the right-hand side. One figure must not be placed upon another or within the outline of another.

(k) *Figure for Official Gazette.* The drawing should, as far as possible, be so planned that one of the views will be suitable for publication in the Official Gazette as the illustration of the invention.

(l) *Extraneous matter.* Identifying indicia (such as the attorney's docket number, inventor's name, number of sheets, etc.) not to exceed 2¾ inches (7.0 cm.) in width may be placed in a centered location between the side edges within three-fourths inch (19.1 mm.) of the top edge. Authorized security markings may be placed on the drawings provided they are outside the illustrations and are removed when the material is declassified. Other extraneous matter will not be permitted upon the face of a drawing.

(m) *Transmission of drawings.* Drawings transmitted to the Office should be sent flat, protected by a sheet of heavy binder's board, or may be rolled for transmission in a suitable mailing tube; but must never be folded. If received creased or mutilated, new drawings will be required. (See 1.152 for design drawing, 1.165 for plant drawings, and 1.174 for reissue drawings.)

The requirements relating to drawings are strictly enforced, but a drawing not complying with all of the regulations is accepted for purpose of examination, and correction or a new drawing will be required later.

Applicants are advised to employ competent draftsmen to make their drawings.

Models, Exhibits, Specimens

Models are not required in most patent applications since the description of the invention in the specification and the drawings must be sufficiently full and complete and capable of being understood to disclose the invention without the aid of a model. A model will not be admitted unless specifically requested by the examiner.

A working model, or other physical exhibit, may be required by the Office if deemed necessary. This is not done very often. A working model may be requested in the case of applications for patent for alleged perpetual motion devices.

When the invention relates to a composition of matter, the applicant may be required to furnish specimens of the composition, or of its ingredients or intermediates, for inspection or experiment. If the invention is a microbiological invention, a deposit of the micro-organism involved is required.

Filing Fees

Fees are subject to change, so verify each fee before you submit it. Phone the PTO Public Service Center at (703) 557-5168, or write:
Commissioner of Patents and Trademarks
Washington, D.C. 20231

The filing fee of an application, except in design and plant cases, consists of a basic fee and additional fees. The basic fee is $370.00 and entitles applicant to present twenty (20) claims, including not more than three (3) in independent form (see "Specification [Description and Claims"], p. 139). An additional fee of $36.00 is required for each claim in independent form which is in excess of three (3) and an additional fee of $12.00 is required for each claim (whether independent or dependent) which is in excess of a total of twenty (20) claims. If the application contains multiple dependent claims, $120 per application is required.

If the owner of the invention is a small entity, (an independent inventor, a small business, concern or a non-profit organization), the filing fees are reduced by half if the small entity files a verified statement (see form on p. 173). The following formula may be used in the calculation of the filing fee:

Basic Fee $370.00
Additional Fees:
   Total number of claims in excess of 20,
      times $12.00 . . . . ·
   Number of independent claims in excess of 3,
      times $36.00 . . . . ·
   Multiple dependent claim(s) (if applicable), $120.00 . . . . . .
      Total Filing Fee . . . . ·

To avoid errors in the payment of fees it is suggested that a table such as given above be included in the letter of transmittal.

In calculating fees, a claim is in singularly dependent form if it incorporates by reference a single preceding claim which may be an independent or a dependent claim. A multiple dependent claim or any claim depending therefrom shall be considered as separate dependent claims in accordance with the number of claims to which reference is made.

The law also provides for the payment of additional fees on presentation of claims after the application is filed.

When an amendment is filed which presents additional claims over the total number already paid for, or additional independent claims over the number of independent claims already accounted for, it must be accompanied by any additional fees due.

All payment of money required for Patent and Trademark Office fees should be made in United States specie. Treasury notes, national bank notes, post office money orders or postal notes payable to the Commissioner of Patents and Trademarks, or by certified checks. If sent in any other form, the Office may delay or cancel the credit until collection is made. Postage stamps are not acceptable. Money orders and checks must be made payable to the Commissioner of Patents and Trademarks. Remittances from foreign countries must be payable and immediately negotiable in the United States for the full amount of the fee required. Money paid by actual mistake or in excess, such as a payment not required by law, will be refunded, but a mere change of purpose after the payment of money, as when a party desires to withdraw his application for a patent or to withdraw an appeal, will not entitle a party to demand such a return. Amounts of $1.00 or less will not be returned unless specifically demanded, within a reasonable time.

3 PATENT OFFICE PROCEEDINGS

When your application for patent is complete, and all the required parts complying with the rules are received, it is forwarded to the examiner.

EXAMINATION OF APPLICATIONS AND PROCEEDINGS IN THE PATENT AND TRADEMARK OFFICE

The examination of the application consists of a study of the application for compliance with the legal requirements and a search through United States patents, prior foreign patent documents which are available in the Patent and Trademark Office, and available literature, to see if the invention is new. A decision is reached by the examiner in the light of the study and the result of the search.

Office Action

The applicant is notified in writing of the examiner's decision by an "action" which is normally mailed to the attorney or agent. The reasons for any adverse action or any objection or requirement are stated in the action and such information or references are given as may be useful in aiding the applicant to judge the propriety of continuing the prosecution of his application.

If the invention is not considered patentable subject matter, the claims will be rejected. If the examiner finds that the invention is not new, the claims will be rejected, but the claims may also be rejected if they differ somewhat from what is found to be obvious. It is not uncommon for some or all of the claims to be rejected on the first action by the examiner; relatively few applications are allowed as filed.

Applicant's Response

The applicant must request reconsideration in writing, and must distinctly and specifically point out the supposed errors in the examiner's action. The applicant must respond to every ground of objection and rejection in the prior Office action (except that a request may be made that objections or requirements as to form not necessary to further consideration of the claims be held in abeyance until allowable subject matter is indicated), and the applicant's action must appear throughout to be a bona fide attempt to advance the case to final action. The mere allegation that the examiner has erred will not be received as a proper reason for such reconsideration.

In amending an application in response to a rejection, the applicant must clearly point out why he/she thinks the amended claims are patentable in view of the state of the art disclosed by the prior references cited or the objections made. He/she must also show how the amendments avoid such references or objections.

After response by applicant the application will be reconsidered, and the applicant will be notified if claims are rejected, or objections or requirements made, in the same manner as after the first examination. The second Office action usually will be made final.

TIME FOR RESPONSE AND ABANDONMENT

The response of an applicant to an action by the Office must be made within a prescribed time limit. The maximum period for response is set at 6 months by the statute which also provides that the Commissioner may shorten the time for reply to not less than 30 days. The usual period for response to an Office action is 3 months. A shortened time for reply may be extended up to the maximum 6-month period. An extension of time fee is normally required to be paid if the response period is extended. The amount of the fee is dependent upon the length of the extension. If no reply is received within the time period, the application is considered as abandoned and no longer pending. However, if it can be shown that the failure to prosecute was unavoidable or unintentional, the application may be revived by the Commissioner. The revival requires a petition to the Commissioner, and a fee for the petition, which should be filed without delay. The proper response must also accompany the petition if it has not yet been filed.

AMENDMENTS TO APPLICATION

The applicant may amend before or after the first examination and action as specified in the rules, or when and as specifically required by the examiner.

After final rejection or action amendments may be made canceling claims or complying with any requirement of form which has been made but the admission of any such amendment or its refusal, and any proceedings relative thereto, shall not operate to relieve the application from its condition as subject to appeal or to save it from abandonment.

If amendments touching the merits of the application are presented after final rejection, or after appeal has been taken, or when such amendment might not otherwise be proper, they may be admitted upon a showing of good and sufficient reasons why they are necessary and were not earlier presented.

No amendment can be made as a matter of right in appealed cases. After decision on appeal, amendments can only be made as provided in the rules.

The specifications, claims, and drawing must be amended and revised when required, to correct inaccuracies of description and definition of unnecessary words, and to secure correspondence between the claims, the description, and the drawing.

All amendments of the drawings or specifications, and all additions thereto, must conform to at least one of them as it was at the time of the filing of the application. Matter not found in either, involving a departure from or an addition to the original disclosure, cannot be added to the application even though supported by a supplemental oath or declaration, and can be shown or claimed only in a separate application.

The claims may be amended by canceling particular claims, by presenting new claims, or by amending the language of particular claims (such amended claims being in effect new claims). In presenting new or amended claims, the applicant must point out how they avoid any reference or ground of rejection of record which may be pertinent.

Erasures, additions, insertions, or alterations of the papers and records must not be made by the applicant. Amendments are made by filing a paper, directing or requesting that specified changes or additions be made. The exact word or words to be stricken out or inserted in the application must be specified and the precise point indicated where the deletion or insertion is to be made.

Amendments are "entered" by the Office by making the proposed deletions by drawing a line in red ink through the word or words canceled and by making the proposed substitutions or insertions in red ink, small insertions being written in at the designated place and larger insertions being indicated by reference.

No change in the drawing may be made except by permission of the Office. Permissible changes in the construction shown in any drawing may be made only by the bonded draftsmen. A sketch in permanent ink showing proposed changes, to become part of the record, must be filed for approval by the Office before the corrections are made. The paper requesting amendments to the drawing should be separate from other papers.

If the number or nature of the amendments render it difficult to consider the case, or to arrange the papers for printing or copying, the examiner may require the entire specification or claims, or any part thereof, to be rewritten.

The original numbering of the claims must be preserved throughout the prosecution. When claims are canceled, the remaining claims must not be renumbered. When claims are added by amendment or subsitituted for canceled claims, they must be numbered by the applicant consecutively beginning with the number next following the highest numbered claim previously presented. When the application is ready for allowance, the examiner, if necessary, will renumber the claims consecutively in the order in which they appear or in such order as may have been requested by applicant.

FINAL REJECTION

On the second or later consideration, the rejection or other action may be made final. The applicant's response is then limited to appeal in the case of rejection of any claim, and further amendment is restricted. Petition may be taken to the Commissioner in the case of objections or requirements not involved in the rejection of any claim. Response to a final rejection or action must include cancellation of, or appeal from the rejection of, each claim so rejected and, if any claim stands allowed, compliance with any requirement or objection as to form.

In making such final rejection, the examiner repeats or states all grounds of rejection then considered applicable to the claims in the application.

Interviews with examiners may be arranged, but an interview does not remove the necessity for response to Office actions within the required time, and the action of the Office is based solely on the written record.

If two or more inventions are claimed in a single application, and are regarded by the Office to be of such a nature that a single patent may not be issued for both of them, the applicant will be required to limit the application to one of the inventions. The other invention may be made the subject of a separate application which, if filed while the first application is still pending, will be entitled to the benefit of the filing date of the first application. A requirement to restrict the application to one invention may be made before further action by the examiner.

As a result of the examination by the Office, patents are granted in the case of about two out of every three applications for patents which are filed.

APPEAL TO THE BOARD OF PATENT APPEALS AND INTERFERENCES AND TO THE COURTS

If the examiner persists in the rejection of any of the claims in an application, or if the rejection has been made final, the applicant may appeal to the Board of Patent Appeals and Interferences in the Patent and Trademark Office. The Board of Patent Appeals and Interferences consists of the Commissioner of Patents and Trademarks, the Deputy Commissioner, the Assistant Commissioners, and the examiners-in-chief, but normally each appeal is heard by only three members. An appeal fee is required and the applicant must file a brief to support his/her position. An oral hearing will be held if requested upon payment of the specified fee.

As an alternative to appeal, in situations where an applicant desires consideration of different claims or further evidence, a new continuation application is often filed. The new application requires a filing fee and should submit the claims and evidence for which consideration is desired. If it is filed before expiration of the period for appeal and specific reference is made therein to the earlier application, applicant will be entitled to the earlier filing date for subject matter common to both applications.

If the decision of the Board of Patent Appeals and Interferences is still adverse to the applicant, an appeal may be taken to the Court of Appeals for the Federal Circuit or a civil action may be filed against the Commissioner in the United States District Court for the District of Columbia. The Court of Appeals for the Federal Circuit will review the record made in the Office and may affirm or reverse the office's action. In a civil action, the applicant may present testimony in the court, and the court will make a decision.

INTERFERENCES

Occasionally two or more applications are filed by different inventors claiming substantially the same patentable invention. The patent can only be granted to one of them, and a proceeding known as an "interference" is instituted by the Office to determine who is the first inventor and thus entitled to the patent. About 1 percent of the applications filed become involved in an interference proceeding. Interference proceedings may also be instituted between an application and a patent already issued, provided the patent has not been issued for more than one year prior to the filing of the conflicting application, and provided that the conflicting application is not barred from being patentable for some other reason.

Each party to such a proceeding must submit evidence of facts proving when the invention was made. In view of the necessity of proving the various facts and circumstances concerning the making of the invention during an interference, inventors must be able to produce evidence to do this. If no evidence is submitted a party is restricted to the date of filing the application as his earliest date. The priority question is determined by a board of three Examiners-in-Chief on the evidence submitted. From the decision of the Board of Patent Appeals and Interferences, the losing party may appeal to the Court of Appeals for the Federal Circuit or file a civil action against the winning party in the appropriate United States district court.

The terms "conception of the invention" and "reduction to practice" are encountered in connection with priority questions. Conception of the invention *is the formation in the mind of the inventor of a definite idea of the complete and operative invention as it is thereafter to be applied in practice.* Reduction to practice is the actual construction of the invention in physical form; in the case of a machine it includes the actual building of the machine, in the case of an article or composition it includes the actual making of the article or composition, in the case of a process it includes the actual carrying out of the steps of the process; and actual successful operation, demonstration, or testing for the intended use is also usually necessary. The filing of a regular application for patent completely disclosing the invention is treated as equivalent to reduction to practice *and is called a "constructive reduction to practice."* The inventor who proves to be the first to conceive the invention and the first to reduce it to practice, *either actually or constructively,* will be held to be the prior inventor, but more complicated situations cannot be stated this simply.

4 SUCCESSFUL APPLICATIONS

If, on examination of the application, or at a later stage during the reconsideration of the application, the patent application is found to be allowable, a notice of allowance will be sent to the applicant, or to the applicant's attorney or agent, and a fee for issuing the patent is due within three months from the date of the notice.

ISSUE OF PATENT

The issue fee for each original or reissue patent, except in design and plant cases, is $620. The amount of the issue fee is reduced by one-half for small entities. The issue fee is due within three months after a written notice of allowance is mailed to the applicant. If timely payment is not made the application will be regarded as abandoned.

A provision is made in the statute whereby the Commissioner may accept the fee late, on a showing of unavoidable delay. When the issue fee is paid, the patent issues as soon as possible after the date of payment, dependent upon the volume of printing on hand in the Government Printing Office. The patent grant then is delivered or mailed on the day of its grant, or as soon thereafter as possible, to the inventor's attorney or agent if there is one of record, otherwise directly to the inventor. On the date of the grant, the patent file becomes open to the public. Printed copies of the specification and drawing are available on the same date.

In case the publication of an invention by the granting of a patent would be detrimental to the national defense, the patent law gives the Commissioner the power to withhold the grant of the patent and to order the invention kept secret for such period of time as the national interest requires.

CORRECTION OF PATENTS

Once the patent is granted, it is outside the jurisdiction of the Patent and Trademark Office except in a few respects.

The Office may issue without charge a certificate correcting a clerical error it has made in the patent when the printed patent does not correspond to the record in the Office. These are mostly corrections of typographical errors made in printing.

Some minor errors of a typographical nature made by the

applicant may be corrected by a certificate of correction for which a charge is made.

The patentee may disclaim one or more claims of this patent by filing in the Office a disclaimer as provided by the statute.

When the patent is defective in certain respects, the law provides that the patentee may apply for a reissue patent. This is a patent granted to replace the first one and is granted only for the balance of the unexpired term. However, the nature of the changes that can be made by means of the reissue are rather limited; new matter cannot be added.

Any person may file a request for reexamination of a patent, along with the required fee, on the basis of prior art consisting of patents or printed publications. At the conclusion of the reexamination proceedings, a certificate setting forth the results of the reexamination proceeding is issued.

MAINTENANCE FEES

All utility patents which issue from applications filed on and after December 12, 1980 are subject to the payment of maintenance fees which must be paid to maintain the patent in force. These fees are due at 3½, 7½ and 11½ years from the date the patent is granted and can be paid without a surcharge during the "window-period" which is the six-month period preceding each due date, e.g., three years to three years and six months, etc. The maintenance fees are listed on p. 166. The amounts are subject to change every three years and the current fees went into effect April 17, 1989.

Failure to pay the current maintenance fee on time may result in expiration of the patent. A six-month grace period when the maintenance fee may be paid with a surcharge is provided. The grace period is the six-month period immediately following the due date. The Patent and Trademark Office does not mail notices to patent owners that maintenance fees are due. If, however, the maintenance fee is not paid on time, efforts are made to remind the responsible party that the maintenance fee may be paid during the grace period with a surcharge.

Patents relating to some pharmaceutical inventions may be extended by the Commissioner for up to five years to compensate for marketing delays due to Federal premarketing regulatory procedures. Patents relating to all other types of inventions can only be extended by enactment of special Federal legislation.

ASSIGNMENTS AND LICENSES

A patent is personal property and may be sold to others or mortgaged; it may be bequeathed by a will, and it may pass to the heirs of deceased patentee. The patent law provides for the transfer or sale of a patent, or of an application for patent, by an instrument in writing. Such an instrument is referred to as an assignment and may transfer the entire interest in the patent. The assignee, when the patent is assigned to him or her, becomes the owner of the patent and has the same rights that the original patentee had.

The statute also provides for the assignment of a part interest, that is, a half interest, a fourth interest, etc., in a patent. There may also be a grant which conveys the same character of interest as an assignment but only for a particularly specified part of the United States.

A mortgage of patent property passes ownership thereof to the mortgagee or lender until the mortgage has been satisfied and a retransfer from the mortgagee back to the mortgagor, the borrower, is made. A conditional assignment also passes ownership of the patent and is regarded as absolute until canceled by the parties or by the decree of a competent court.

An assignment, grant, or conveyance of any patent or application for patent should be acknowledged before a notary public or officer authorized to administer oaths or perform notarial acts. The certificate of such acknowledgment constitutes prima facie evidence of the execution of the assignment, grant, or conveyance.

Recording of Assignments

The Office records assignments, grants, and similar instruments sent to it for recording, and the recording serves as notice. If an assignment, grant, or conveyance of a patent or an interest in a patent (or an application for patent) is not recorded in the Office within three months from its date, it is void against a subsequent purchaser for a valuable consideration without notice, unless it is recorded prior to the subsequent purchase.

An instrument relating to a patent should identify the patent by number and date (the name of the inventor and title of the invention as stated in the patent should also be given). An instrument relating to an application should identify the application by its serial number and date of filing, and the name of the inventor and title of the invention as stated in the application should also be given. Sometimes an assignment of an application is executed at the same time that the application is prepared and before it has been filed in the Office. Such assignment should adequately identify the application, as by its date of execution and name of the inventor and title of the invention, so that there can be no mistake as to the application intended.

If an application has been assigned and the assignment is recorded, on or before the date the issue fee is paid, the patent will be issued to the assignee as owner. If the assignment is of a part interest only, the patent will be issued to the inventor and assignee as joint owners.

Joint Ownership

Patents may be owned jointly by two or more persons as in the case of a patent granted to joint inventors, or in the case of the assignment of a part interest in a patent. Any joint owner of a patent, no matter how small the part interest, may make, use, and sell the invention for his or her own profit, without regard to the other owner, and may sell the interest or any part of it, or grant licenses to others, without regard to the other joint owner, unless the joint owners have make a contract governing their relation to each other. It is accordingly dangerous to assign a part interest without a definite agreement between the parties as to the extent of their respective rights and their obligations to each other if the above result is to be avoided.

The owner of a patent may grant licenses to others. Since the patentee has the right to exclude others from making, using or selling the invention, no one else may do any of these things without his permission. A license is the permission granted by the patent owner to another to make, use, or sell the invention. No particular form of license is required; a license is a contract and may include whatever provisions the parties agree upon, including the payment of royalties, etc.

The drawing up of a license agreement (as well as assignments) is within the field of an attorney at law, although such attorney should be familiar with patent matters as well. A few States have prescribed certain formalities to be observed in connection with the sale of patent rights.

INFRINGEMENT OF PATENTS

Infringement of a patent consists in the unauthorized making, using, or selling of the patented invention within the territory of the United States, during the term of the patent. If a patent is infringed, the patentee may sue for relief in the appropriate Federal court. The patentee may ask the court for an injunction to prevent the continuation of the infringement and may also ask the court for an award of damages because of the infringement. In such an infringement suit, the defendant may raise the question of the validity of the patent, which is then decided by the court. The defendant may also aver that what is being done does not constitute infringement. Infringement is determined primarily by the language of the claims of the patent and, if what the defendant is making does not fall within the language of any of the claims of the patent, there is no infringement.

Suits for infringement of patents follow the rules of procedure of the Federal courts. From the decision of the district court, there is an appeal to the Court of Appeals for the Federal Circuit. The Supreme Court may thereafter take a case by writ of certiorari. If the United States Government infringes a patent, the patentee has a remedy for damages in the United States Claims Court. The Government may use any patented invention without permission of the patentee, but the patentee is entitled to obtain compensation for the use by or for the Government.

If the patentee notifies anyone that is infringing the patent or threatens suit, the one charged with infringement may start the suit in a Federal court.

The Office has no jurisdiction over questions relating to

infringement of patents. In examining applications for patent, no determination is made as to whether the invention sought to be patented infringes any prior patent. An improvement invention may be patentable, but it might infringe a prior unexpired patent for the invention improved upon, if there is one.

PATENT MARKING AND "PATENT PENDING"

A patentee who makes or sells patented articles, or a person who does so for or under the patentee is required to mark the articles with the word "Patent" and the number of the patent. The penalty for failure to mark is that the patentee may not recover damages from an infringer unless the infringer was duly notified of the infringement and continued to infringe after the notice.

The marking of an article as patented when it is not in fact patented is against the law and subjects the offender to a penalty.

Some persons mark articles sold with the terms "Patent Applied For" or "Patent Pending." These phrases have no legal effect, but only give information that an application for patent has been filed in the Patent and Trademark Office. The protection afforded by a patent does not start until the actual grant of the patent. False use of these phrases or their equivalent is prohibited.

DESIGN PATENTS

The patent laws provide for the granting of design patents to any person who has invented any new, original and ornamental design for an article of manufacture. The design patent protects only the appearance of an article, and not its structure or utilitarian features. The proceedings relating to granting of design patents are the same as those relating to other patents with a few differences.

The filing fee for each design application is $150; the issue fee is $220. A design patent has a term of 14 years, and no fees are necessary to maintain a design patent in force. If on examination it is determined that an applicant is entitled to a design patent under the law, a notice of allowance will be sent to the applicant or applicant's attorney, or agent, calling for the payment of an issue fee. For a qualifying small entity the above fees are reduced by half.

The drawing of the design patent conforms to the same rules as other drawings, but no reference characters are required.

The specification of a design application is short and ordinarily follows a set form. Only one claim is permitted, following a set form.

PLANT PATENTS

The law also provides for the granting of a patent to anyone who has invented or discovered and asexually reproduced any distinct and new variety of plant, including cultivated sports, mutants, hybrids, and newly found seedlings, other than a tuber-propagated plant or a plant found in an uncultivated state.

Asexually propagated plants are those that are reproduced by means other than from seeds, such as by the rooting of cuttings, by layering, budding, grafting, inarching, etc.

With reference to tuber-propagated plants, for which a plant patent cannot be obtained, the term "tuber" is used in its narrow horticultural sense as meaning a short, thickened portion of an underground branch. The only plants covered by the term "tuber-propagated" are the Irish potato and the Jerusalem artichoke.

An application for a plant patent consists of the same parts as other applications.

The application papers and any responsive papers pursuant to the prosecution must be filed in duplicate but only one need be signed (in the case of the application papers the original should be signed); the second copy may be legible copy of the original. The reason for providing an original and duplicate file is that the duplicate file is sent to the Agricultural Research Service, Department of Agriculture for an advisory report on the plant variety.

The specification should include a complete detailed description of the plant and the characteristics thereof that distinguish the same over related known varieties, and its antecedents, expressed in botanical terms in the general form followed in standard botanical text books or publications dealing with the varieties of the kind of plant involved (evergreen tree, dahlia plant, rose plant, apple tree, etc.), rather than a mere broad nonbotanical characterization such as commonly found in nursery or seed catalogs. The specification should also include the origin or parentage of the plant variety sought to be patented and must particularly point out where and in what manner the variety of plant has been asexually reproduced. Where color is a distinctive feature of the plant the color should be positively identified in the specification by reference to a designated color as given by a recognized color dictionary. Where the plant variety originated as a newly found seedling, the specification must fully describe the conditions (cultivation, environment, etc.) under which the seedling was found growing to establish that it was not found in an uncultivated state.

A plant patent is granted on the entire plant. It therefore follows that only one claim is necessary and only one is permitted.

The oath or declaration required of the applicant in addition to the statements required for other applications must include the statement that the applicant has asexually reproduced the new plant variety.

Plant patent drawings are not mechanical drawings and should be artistically and competently executed. The drawing must disclose all the distinctive characteristics of the plant capable of visual representation. When color is a distinguishing characteristic of the new variety, the drawing must be in color. Two duplicate copies of color drawings must be submitted. Color drawings may be made either in permanent water color or oil, or in lieu thereof may be photographs made by color photography or properly colored on sensitized paper. The paper in any case must correspond in size, weight, and quality to the paper required for other drawings. Mounted photographs are acceptable.

Specimens of the plant variety, its flower or fruit, should not be submitted unless specifically called for by the examiner.

The filing fee on each plant application is $250; the issue fee is $310. For a qualifying small entity filing and issue fees are reduced by half.

All inquiries relating to plant patents and pending plant patent applications should be directed to the Patent and Trademark Office and not to the Department of Agriculture.

The Plant Variety Protection Act (Public Law 91–577), approved December 24, 1970, provides for a system of protection for sexually reproduced varieties, for which protection was not previously provided, under the administration of a Plant Variety Protection Office within the Department of Agriculture. Requests for information regarding the protection of sexually reproduced varieties should be addressed to Commissioner, Plant Variety Protection Office, Agricultural Marketing Service, National Agricultural Library Bldg., Room 500, 10301 Baltimore Blvd., Beltsville, MD 20705–2351.

TREATIES AND FOREIGN PATENTS

Since the rights granted by a United States patent extend only throughout the territory of the United States and have no effect in a foreign country, an inventor who wishes patent protection in other countries must apply for a patent in each of the other countries or in regional patent offices. Almost every country has its own patent law, and a person desiring a patent in a particular country must make an application for patent in that country, in accordance with the requirements of that country.

The laws of many countries differ in various respects from the patent law of the United States. In most foreign countries, publication of the invention before the date of the application will bar the right to a patent. In most foreign countries maintenance fees are required. Most foreign countries require that the patented invention must be manufactured in that country after a certain period, usually three years. If there is no manufacture within this period, the patent may be void in some countries, although in most countries the patent may be subject to the grant of compulsory licenses to any person who may apply for a license.

There is a treaty relating to patents which is adhered to by 93 countries, including the United States, and is known as the Paris Convention for the Protection of Industrial Property. It provides that each country guarantees to the citizens of the other countries the same rights in patent and trademark matters that it gives to its own citizens. The treaty also provides for the right of priority in the case of patents, trademarks and industrial designs (design patents). This right means that, on the basis of a regular first application filed in one of the member countries, the applicant may, within a certain period of time, apply for protection in all the other member countries. These later applications will then be regarded as if they had been filed on the same day as the first application. Thus, these later applicants will have priority over applications for the same invention which may have been filed during the said period of time by other persons. Moreover, these later applications, being based on the first application, will not be invalidated by any acts accomplished in the interval, such as, for example, publication or exploitation of the invention, the sale of copies of the design, or use of the trademark. The period of time mentioned above, within which the subsequent applications may be filed in the other countries, is 12 months in the case of applications for patent and six months in the case of industrial designs and trademarks.

Another treaty, known as the Patent Cooperation Treaty, was negotiated at a diplomatic conference in Washington, D.C., in June of 1970. The treaty came into force on January 24, 1978, and is presently adhered to by 39 countries, including the United States. The treaty facilitates the filing of applications for patent on the same invention in member countries by providing, among other things, for centralized filing procedures and a standardized application format.

A number of patent attorneys specialize in obtaining patents in foreign countries. In general, an inventor should be satisfied that he could make some profit from foreign patents or that there is some particular reason for obtaining them, before he attempts to apply for foreign patents.

Under United States law it is necessary, in the case of inventions made in the United States, to obtain a license from the Commissioner of Patents and Trademarks before applying for a patent in a foreign country. Such a license is required if the foreign application is to be filed before an application is filed in the United States or before the expiration of six months from the filing of an application in the United States. The filing of an application for patent constitutes the request for a license and the granting or denial of such request is indicated in the filing receipt mailed to each applicant. After six months from the United States filing, a license is not required unless the invention has been ordered to be kept secret. If the invention has been ordered to be kept secret, the consent to the filing abroad must be obtained from the Commissioner of Patents and Trademarks during the period the order of secrecy is in effect.

FOREIGN APPLICANTS FOR UNITED STATES PATENTS

The patent laws of the United States make no discrimination with respect to the citizenship of the inventor. Any inventor, regardless of his citizenship, may apply for a patent on the same basis as a U.S. citizen. There are, however, a number of particular points of special interest to applicants located in foreign countries.

The application for patent in the United States must be made by the inventor and the inventor must sign the oath or declaration (with certain exceptions), differing from the law in many countries where the signature of the inventor and an oath of inventorship are not necessary. If the inventor is dead, the application may be made by his executor or administrator, or equivalent, and in the case of mental disability it may be made by his legal representative (guardian).

No United States patent can be obtained if the invention was patented abroad before applying in the United States by the inventor or his legal representatives or assigns on an application filed more than 12 months before filing in the United States. Six months are allowed in the case of a design patent.

An application for a patent filed in the United States by any person who has previously regularly filed an application for a patent for the same invention in a foreign country which affords similar privileges to citizens of the United States shall have the same force and effect for the purpose of overcoming intervening acts of others as if filed in the United States on the date on which the application for a patent for the same invention was first filed in such foreign country, provided the application in the United States is filed within 12 months (six months in the case of a design patent) from the earliest date on which any such foreign application was filed. A copy of the foreign application certified by the patent office of the country in which it was filed is required to secure this right of priority.

If any application for patent has been filed in any foreign country by the applicant or by his legal representatives or assigns prior to his application in the United States, the applicant must, in the oath or declaration accompanying the application, state the country in which the earliest such application has been filed, giving the date of filing the application; and all applications filed more than a year before the filing in the United States must also be recited in the oath or declaration.

An oath or declaration must be made with respect to every application. When the applicant is in a foreign country the oath or affirmation may be before any diplomatic or consular officer of the United States, or before any officer having an official seal and authorized to administer oaths in the foreign country, whose authority shall be proved by a certificate of a diplomatic or consular officer of the United States, the oath being attested in all cases by the proper official seal of the officer before whom the oath is made.

When the oath is taken before an officer in the country foreign to the United States, all the application papers (except the drawing) must be attached together and a ribbon passed one or more times through all the sheets of the application, and the ends of the ribbons brought together under the seal before the latter is affixed and impressed, or each sheet must be impressed with the official seal of the officer before whom the oath was taken.

If the application is filed by the legal representative (executive, administrator, etc.) of a deceased inventor, the legal representative must make the oath or declaration.

When a declaration is used, the ribboning procedure is not

necessary, nor is it necessary to appear before an official in connection with the making of a declaration.

A foreign applicant may be represented by any patent attorney or agent who is registered to practice before the United States Patent and Trademark Office.

5 CORRESPONDENCE, FEES, AND FORMS

All business with the Patent and Trademark Office should be transacted by writing to *"COMMISSIONER OF PATENTS AND TRADEMARKS, WASHINGTON, D.C. 20231."* Correspondents should be sure to include their full return addresses, including Zip Codes.

GENERAL INFORMATION

The principal location of the office is Crystal Plaza 3, 2021 Jefferson Davis Highway, Arlington, Virginia 22202. The personal attendance of applicants at the Office is unnecessary.

Applicants and attorneys are required to conduct their business with decorum and courtesy. Papers presented in violation of this requirement will be returned.

Separate letters (but not necessarily in separate envelopes) should be written in relation to each distinct subject of inquiry, such as assignments, payments, orders for printed copies of patents, orders for copies of records, requests for other services, etc. None of these should be included with letters responding to Office actions in applications (see "Applicant's Response," p. 147).

When a letter concerns a patent application, the correspondent should include the serial number, filing date and Group Art Unit number. When a letter concerns a patent, it should include the name of the patentee, the title of the invention, the patent number and the date of issue.

An order for a copy of an assignment must give the book and page or reel and frame of the record, as well as the name of the inventor; otherwise, an additional charge is made for the time consumed in making the search for the assignment.

Printed copies of any patent, identified by its patent number, may be purchased from the Patent and Trademark Office at a cost of $1.50 each, postage free, except plant patents in color, which are $10.00 each.

PATENT FEES

EFFECTIVE APRIL 17, 1989

As this fee list is a summary, and the content of rules may be changing, you should refer to the notice published in the *Federal Register* on February 15, 1989, at 54 FR 6893, and corrections published on February 24, 1989 at FR 8053 and on March 7, 1989 at FR 9431. See also 1100 *Official Gazette* 7.

DESCRIPTION	FEE
Group 1 – Patent Filing Fees	
Basic Filing Fee — Utility	370.00
Independent Claims in Excess of Three	36.00
Claims in Excess of Twenty	12.00
Multiple Dependent Claim	120.00
Surcharge — Late Filing Fee or Oath/Decl.	120.00
Design Filing Fee	150.00
Plant Filing Fee	250.00
Reissue Filing Fee	370.00
Reissue Independent Claims Over Patent	36.00
Reissue Claims in Excess of Twenty & Patent	12.00
Non-English Specification	30.00
Group 2 – Small Entity Patent Filing Fees	
Basic Filing Fee — Utility	185.00
Independent Claims in Excess of Three	18.00
Claims in Excess of Twenty	6.00
Multiple Dependent Claim	60.00
Surcharge — Late Filing Fee or Oath	60.00
Design Filing Fee	75.00
Plant Filing Fee	125.00
Reissue Filing Fee	185.00
Reissue Independent Claims Over Patent	18.00
Reissue Claims in Excess of Twenty & Patent	6.00
Group 3 – Patent Extension Fees	
Extension — One Month	62.00
Extension — Two Months	180.00
Extension — Three Months	430.00
Extension — Four Months	680.00
Group 4 – Small Entity Patent Extension Fees	
Extension — One Month	31.00
Extension — Two Months	90.00
Extension — Three Months	215.00
Extension — Four Months	340.00
Group 5 – Patent Appeals/Interference Fees	
Notice of Appeal	140.00
Filing a Brief	140.00
Request for Oral Hearing	120.00
Group 6 – Small Entity Patent Appeals/Interference Fees	
Notice of Appeal	70.00
Filing a Brief	70.00
Request for Oral Hearing	60.00

DESCRIPTION	FEE

Group 7 – Patent Petition Fees
Petitions to the Commissioner:

–Not All Inventors; Not the Inventor	120.00
–Correction of Inventorship in Appl.	120.00
–Not Provided for Questions	120.00
–Suspend Rules	120.00
–Expedited License	120.00
–Change Scope of License	120.00
–Retroactive License	120.00
–Refusing Maintenance Fee	120.00
–Reinstatement of Expired Patent	120.00
–Interference	120.00
–Reconsider Interference Pet. Decision	120.00
–Late Filing of Interference Settlement	120.00
–Refusal to Publish Sir	120.00
–Access to Assignment Record	120.00
–Access to Application	120.00
–Late Priority Papers	120.00
–Suspend Action	120.00
–Divisional Reissues	120.00
–Access to Interference Agreement	120.00
–Amendment After Issue Fee Paid	120.00
–Withdrawal from Issue	120.00
–Defer Issue	120.00
–Issue to Late Recorded Assignee	120.00
Pet. to Comm. To Make Appl. Special	80.00
Pet. to Comm. — Public Use Proceeding	1,200.00
Pet. — Revive Aband. Appl. —Unavoidable	62.00
Pet. — Revive Aband. Appl. — Unintentional	620.00
Petition — Correction of Inventorship in Patent	120.00

Group 8 – Small Entity Patent Petition Fees

Pet. — Revive Aband. Appl. — Unavoidable	31.00
Pet. — Revive Aband. Appl. — Unintentional	310.00

Group 9 – Patent Issue Fees

Utility Issue Fee	620.00
Design Issue Fee	220.00
Plant Issue Fee	310.00
Statutory Disclaimer	62.00

Group 10 – Small Entity Patent Issue Fees

Utility Issue Fee	310.00
Design Issue Fee	110.00
Plant Issue Fee	155.00
Statutory Disclaimer	31.00

Group 11 – Patent Post-Allowance Fees

SIR — Prior to Examiner's Action	400.00*
SIR — After Examiner's Action	800.00*

*Reduced by Filing Fee

Part III Patents

DESCRIPTION	FEE
Certificate of Correction	60.00
Reexamination	2,000.00
Extension of Term of Patent	600.00

Group 12 – Patent Maintenance Fees – Applications Filed December 12, 1980–August 26, 1982

Due at 3.5 Years	245.00
Due at 7.5 Years	495.00
Due at 11.5 Years	740.00
Surcharge — Late Payment Within Six Mos.	120.00

Group 13 – Patent Maintenance Fees – Applications Filed On Or After August 27, 1982

Due at 3.5 Years	490.00
Due at 7.5 Years	990.00
Due at 11.5 Years	1,480.00
Surcharge — Late Payment Within Six Mos.	120.00
Surcharge After Expiration	550.00

Group 14 – Small Entity Patent Maintenance Fees – Applications Filed On Or After August 27, 1982

Due at 3.5 Years	245.00
Due at 7.5 Years	495.00
Due at 11.5 Years	740.00
Surcharge — Late Payment Within Six Mos.	60.00

Group 15 – Patent Service Fees

Copy of Patent	1.50
Copy of Plant Patent	10.00
Copy of Office Records (each thirty pages)	10.00
Copy of Utility Patent in Color	20.00
Patent Copy — Expedited Service	3.00
Patent Copy Expedited Service Via EOS	25.00
Copy of Application as Filed, Certified	10.00
Copy of File Wrapper, Certified	170.00
Copy of Patent Assignment, Certified	5.00
Cert. Copy of Patent Application Expedited	20.00
Certifying Office Records	3.00
Search of Records	15.00
Patent Depository Library	50.00
List of Patents in Subclass	2.00
Uncertified Statement	5.00
Copy of Non-US Document	10.00
Comparing Copies per Document	10.00
Duplicate or Corrected Filing Receipt	15.00
Filing a Disclosure Document	6.00
Box Rental	50.00
International Type Search Report	30.00
Searching, Inventory Records, Ten Years	10.00
Copishare Card per Page	0.15

DESCRIPTION	FEE
Recording Patent Assignment	8.00
Publication in Official Gazette	20.00
Duplicate User Pass	10.00
Locker Rentals	0.25
Unspecified Other Services	AT COST
Retaining Abandoned Application	120.00
Handling Fee — Omitted Spec./Drawing	15.00
Handling Fee for Withdrawal of SIR	120.00

Group 16 – Patent Enrollment Service Fees

Admission to Examination	270.00
Registration to Practice	90.00
Reinstatement to Practice	10.00
Copy of Certificate of Good Standing	10.00
Certificate of Good Standing — Framing	100.00
Review of Decision of Director, OED	100.00
Regrading of Examination	100.00

Group 17 – Patent PCT Fees – International Stage

Transmittal Fee	170.00
PCT Search Fee — No U.S. Application	550.00
PCT Search — Prior U.S. Application	380.00
Supplemental Search per Additional Invention	150.00
Preliminary Exam. Fee — ISA was U.S.	400.00
Preliminary Exam. Fee — ISA not U.S.	600.00
Additional Invention — ISA was U.S.	130.00
Additional Invention — ISA not U.S.	200.00

Group 18 – Patent PCT Fees – National Stage

IPEA — U.S.	330.00
International Searching Authority — U.S.	370.00
PTO not ISA or IPEA	500.00
Claims Meet Art. 33(1)–(4) — IPEA — U.S.	50.00
Claims — Extra Independent (over three)	36.00
Claims — Extra Total (over twenty)	12.00
Claims — Multiple Dependent	120.00
Surcharge — Late Filing Fee or Oath/Dec.	120.00
English Transl. — After Twenty Months	30.00

Group 19 – Small Entity Patent PCT Fees – National Stage

IPEA — U.S.	165.00
International Searching Authority — U.S.	185.00
PTO not ISA or IPEA	250.00
Claims Meet Art. 33(1)–(4) — IPEA — U.S.	25.00
Claims — Extra Independent (over three)	18.00
Claims — Extra Total (over twenty)	6.00
Claims — Multiple Dependent	60.00
Surcharge — Late Filing Fee or Oath/Dec.	60.00

Group 20 – Patent PCT Fees to WIPO

Basic Fee (first thirty pages)	485.00

DESCRIPTION	FEE
Basic Supplemental Fee (for each page over thirty)	10.00
Handling Fee	150.00
Designation Fee per Country	120.00

Group 21 – Patent PCT Fees to EPO
International Search   1,160.00

GENERAL FEES
Group 29 – Finance Service Fees
Establish Deposit Account   10.00
Service Charge for Below Min. Balance   20.00
Processing Returned Checks   50.00

Group 30 – Computer Service Fees
Computer Records   AT COST

FILING OF CERTAIN PAPERS AND AUTHORIZATIONS TO CHARGE DEPOSIT ACCOUNTS BY FACSIMILE TRANSMISSION

Effective November 1, 1988, certain papers to be filed in national patent applications and reexamination proceedings for consideration by the Office of the Assistant Commissioner for Patents, the Office of the Deputy Assistant Commissioner for Patents, and the Patent Examining Groups (Patent Examining Corps) may be submitted to the Patent and Trademark Office (PTO) by facsimile transmission.

The provision of 37 CFR 1.33(a), requiring signatures on amendments and other papers filed in applications, is hereby waived to the extent that a facsimile signature is acceptable. The paper that is used as the original for the facsimile transmission must have an original signature, and should be retained by applicant or the representative as evidence of the content of the facsimile transmission. No special format, addressing information or written ratification is required for facsimile transmissions. However, the paper size must be 8½" by 14" or smaller to be accepted.

A facsimile center has been established in the Patent Examining Corps to receive and process submissions. The filing date accorded the submission will be the date the complete transmission is received by the PTO facsimile unit unless that date is a Saturday, Sunday or Federal holiday within the District of Columbia, in which case the official date of receipt will be the next business day.

Each transmission session must be limited to papers to be filed in a single national patent application or reexamination proceeding. It is recommended that the Serial Number of the application or Control Number of the reexamination be entered as a part of the sender's identification, if possible. It is also recommended that the sending facsimile machine generate a report confirming transmission for each transmission session. The transmitting activity report should be retained along with the paper used as the original.

The papers, including authorizations to charge deposit accounts, which may be submitted using this procedure, are limited to those which may be filed in national patent applications and reexamination proceedings and which are to be considered by the PTO organizations named above. Examples of such papers are amendments, responses to restriction requirements, requests for reconsideration before the examiner, petitions, terminal disclaimers, powers of attorney, notices of appeal and appeal briefs.

New or continuing patent applications of any type, assignments, issue fee payments, maintenance fee payments, declarations or oaths under 37 CFR 1.63 or 1.67, and formal drawings are excluded, as are all papers relating to international patent applications. Papers to be filed in applications that are subject to a secrecy order under 37 CFR 5.1–5.8, and directly related to the secrecy order content of the application, are also excluded. Informal communications between applicant and the examiner, such as proposed claims for interview purposes, are permissible and are encouraged. Informal communications from applicants will not be made of record in the application or reexamination and must be clearly identified as informal such as by including the word "DRAFT" on each paper. To facilitate informal communications from examiners, applicants are encouraged to supply their facsimile phone numbers on communications to the Office.

The facsimile submissions may include a certificate for each paper stating the date of transmission. A copy of the facsimile submission with a certificate attached thereto will be evidence of transmission of the paper should the original be misplaced. The person signing the certificate should have a reasonable basis to expect that the paper would be facsimile transmitted on the date indicated. An example of a preferred certificate is:

CERTIFICATE OF FACSIMILE TRANSMISSION

I hereby certify that this paper is being facsimile transmitted to the Patent and Trademark Office on the date shown below.

_____

Type or print name of person signing certification

_____   _____
        Signature   **Date**

When possible, the certification should appear on a portion of the paper being transmitted. If the certification is presented on a separate paper, it must identify the application to which it relates, and the type of paper being transmitted; e.g., amendment, notice of appeal, etc.

In the event that the facsimile submission is misplaced or lost in the PTO, the submission will be considered filed as of the date of the transmission, if the party who transmitted the paper:

(1) Informs the PTO of the previous facsimile transmission promptly after becoming aware that the submission has

been misplaced or lost;

(2) Supplies another copy of the previously transmitted submission with the Certification of Transmission; and

(3) Supplies a copy of the sending unit's report confirming transmission of the submission. In the event that a copy of the report is not available, the party who transmitted the paper may file a declaration under 37 CFR 1.68 which attests on a personal knowledge basis or to the satisfaction of the Commissioner to the previous timely transmission.

If all criteria above cannot be met, the PTO will require applicant to submit a verified showing of facts. Such a showing must show to the satisfaction of the Commissioner the date the PTO received the submission.

The facsimile center will have five facsimile units and will be staffed during the business hours of 8:30 A.M. and 5:00 P.M., Monday through Friday, excluding holidays. Although the units may normally be accessed at all times, including non-business hours, there may be times when reception is not possible due to equipment failure or maintenance requirements. Accordingly, applicants are cautioned not to rely on the availability of this service at the end of response periods.

The telephone number for accessing the facsimile machines is (703) 557-9564. In the event that the transmission cannot be accepted at the telephone number above, a backup number has been established at (703) 557-9567. The facsimile center staff can be reached at telephone number (703) 557-4277 during normal business hours.

PATENT APPLICATION TRANSMITTAL LETTER	ATTORNEY'S DOCKET NO.

TO THE COMMISSIONER OF PATENTS AND TRADEMARKS:

Transmitted herewith for filing is the patent application of _____

_____

for _____

_____

Enclosed are:

☐ _____ sheets of drawing.

☐ an assignment of the invention to _____

_____

☐ a certified copy of a _____ application.

☐ associate power of attorney.

☐ verified statement to establish small entity status under 37 CFR 1.9 and 1.27. ——

CLAIMS AS FILED

FOR	NO. FILED	NO. EXTRA	SMALL ENTITY RATE	FEE		OTHER THAN A SMALL ENTITY RATE	FEE
BASIC FEE				$185	OR		$370
TOTAL CLAIMS	—20 -	·	x $ 6=	$	OR	x $ 12=	$
INDEP. CLAIMS	—3 -	·	x $ 18=	$	OR	x $ 36=	$
MULTIPLE DEPENDENT CLAIM PRESENT			+ $120=	$	OR	+ $120=	$
			TOTAL	$	OR	TOTAL	$

* If the difference in col. 1 is less than zero, enter "0" in col. 2

☐ Please charge my Deposit Account No. _____ in the amount of $ _____ .
☐ A duplicate copy of this sheet is enclosed.

☐ A check in the amount of $ _____ to cover the filing fee is enclosed.

☐ The Commissioner is hereby authorized to charge payment of the following fees
associated with this communication or credit any overpayment to Deposit Account
No. _____ . A Duplicate copy of this sheet is enclosed.

    ☐ Any additional filing fees required under 37 CFR 1.16.

    ☐ Any patent application processing fees under 37 CFR 1.17

☐ The Commissioner is hereby authorized to charge payment of the following fees during
the pendency of this application or credit any overpayment to Deposit Account
No. _____ . A duplicate copy of this sheet is enclosed.

    ☐ Any filing fees under 37 CFR 1.16 for presentation of extra claims.

    ☐ Any patent application processing fees under 37 CFR 1.17.

    ☐ The issue fee set in 37 CFR 1.18 at or before mailing of the Notice
of Allowance, pursuant to 37 CFR 1.311(b).

Date _____   Signature _____

OMB No. 0651-0011 (12/31/86)

DECLARATION FOR PATENT APPLICATION

Docket No. _____

As a below named inventor, I hereby declare that:

My residence, post office address and citizenship are as stated below next to my name.

I believe I am the original, first and sole inventor (if only one name is listed below) or an original, first and joint inventor (if plural names are listed below) of the subject matter which is claimed and for which a patent is sought on the invention entitled _____ , the specification of which

(check one) ☐ is attached hereto.
            ☐ was filed on _____ as
            Application Serial No. _____
            and was amended on _____ (if applicable).

I hereby state that I have reviewed and understand the contents of the above identified specification, including the claims, as amended by any amendment referred to above.

I acknowledge the duty to disclose information which is material to the examination of this application in accordance with Title 37, Code of Federal Regulations, §1.56(a).

I hereby claim foreign priority benefits under Title 35, United States Code, §119 of any foreign application(s) for patent or inventor's certificate listed below and have also identified below any foreign application for patent or inventor's certificate having a filing date before that of the application on which priority is claimed:

Prior Foreign Application(s)   Priority Claimed

(Number)	(Country)	(Day/Month/Year Filed)	Yes	No
(Number)	(Country)	(Day/Month/Year Filed)	Yes	No
(Number)	(Country)	(Day/Month/Year Filed)	Yes	No

I hereby claim the benefit under Title 35, United States Code, §120 of any United States application(s) listed below and, insofar as the subject matter of each of the claims of this application is not disclosed in the prior United States application in the manner provided by the first paragraph of Title 35, United States Code, §112, I acknowledge the duty to disclose material information as defined in Title 37, Code of Federal Regulations, §1.56(a) which occurred between the filing date of the prior application and the national or PCT international filing date of this application:

(Application Serial No.)	(Filing Date)	(Status—patented, pending, abandoned)
(Application Serial No.)	(Filing Date)	(Status—patented, pending, abandoned)

I hereby appoint the following attorney(s) and/or agent(s) to prosecute this application and to transact all business in the Patent and Trademark Office connected therewith:

_____ .

Address all telephone calls to _____ at telephone no. _____ .
Address all correspondence to _____
_____
_____
_____ .

I hereby declare that all statements made herein of my own knowledge are true and that all statements made on information and belief are believed to be true; and further that these statements were made with the knowledge that willful false statements and the like so made are punishable by fine or imprisonment, or both, under Section 1001 of Title 18 of the United States Code and that such willful false statements may jeopardize the validity of the application or any patent issued thereon.

Full name of sole or first inventor _____
Inventor's signature _____ Date _____
Residence _____ Citizenship _____
Post Office Address _____
_____

Full name of second joint inventor, if any _____
Second Inventor's signature _____ Date _____
Residence _____ Citizenship _____
Post Office Address _____
_____

(Supply similar information and signature for third and subsequent joint inventors.)

OMB No. 0651-0011 (12/31/86)

Applicant or Patentee: _____ Attorney's
Serial or Patent No.: _____ Docket No.: _____
Filed or Issued: _____
For: _____

VERIFIED STATEMENT (DECLARATION) CLAIMING SMALL ENTITY
STATUS (37 CFR 1.9 (f) and 1.27 (b)) — INDEPENDENT INVENTOR

As a below named inventor, I hereby declare that I qualify as an independent inventor as defined in 37 CFR 1.9 (c) for purposes of paying reduced fees under section 41 (a) and (b) of Title 35, United States Code, to the Patent and Trademark
Office with regard to the invention entitled _____
described in

[　] the specification filed herewith
[　] application serial no. _____ , filed _____ .
[　] patent no. _____ , issued _____ .

I have not assigned, granted, conveyed or licensed and am under no obligation under contract or law to assign, grant, convey
or license, any rights in the invention to any person who could not be classified as an independent inventor under 37 CFR
1.9 (c) if that person had made the invention, or to any concern which would not qualify as a small business concern under
37 CFR 1.9 (d) or a nonprofit organization under 37 CFR 1.9 (e).

Each person, concern or organization to which I have assigned, granted, conveyed, or licensed or am under an obligation
under contract or law to assign, grant, convey, or license any rights in the invention is listed below:

[　] no such person, concern, or organization
[　] persons, concerns or organizations listed below*

　　*NOTE: Separate verified statements are required from each named person, concern or organiza-
　　tion having rights to the invention averring to their status as small entities. (37 CFR 1.27)

FULL NAME _____
ADDRESS _____
　　　　[　] INDIVIDUAL　　　　[　] SMALL BUSINESS CONCERN　　　　[　] NONPROFIT ORGANIZATION

FULL NAME _____
ADDRESS _____
　　　　[　] INDIVIDUAL　　　　[　] SMALL BUSINESS CONCERN　　　　[　] NONPROFIT ORGANIZATION

FULL NAME _____
ADDRESS _____
　　　　[　] INDIVIDUAL　　　　[　] SMALL BUSINESS CONCERN　　　　[　] NONPROFIT ORGANIZATION

I acknowledge the duty to file, in this application or patent, notification of any change in status resulting in loss of entitlement to small entity status prior to paying, or at the time of paying, the earliest of the issue fee or any maintenance fee
due after the date on which status as a small entity is no longer appropriate. (37 CFR 1.28 (b))

I hereby declare that all statements made herein of my own knowledge are true and that all statements made on information
and belief are believed to be true; and further that these statements were made with the knowledge that willful false statements
and the like so made are punishable by fine or imprisonment, or both, under section 1001 of Title 18 of the United States
Code, and that such willful false statements may jeopardize the validity of the application, any patent issuing thereon, or
any patent to which this verified statement is directed.

NAME OF INVENTOR　　　　NAME OF INVENTOR　　　　NAME OF INVENTOR

Signature of Inventor　　　Signature of Inventor　　　Signature of Inventor

Date　　　　　　　　Date　　　　　　　　Date

Form PTO-FB-A410 (8-83)

OMB No. 0651-0011 (12/31/86)

AMENDMENT TRANSMITTAL LETTER

SERIAL NO.	FILING DATE	EXAMINER	ATTORNEY'S DOCKET NO.
			GROUP ART UNIT

INVENTION

TO THE COMMISSIONER OF PATENTS AND TRADEMARKS:

Transmitted herewith is an amendment in the above-identified application.

Small entity status of this application under 37 CFR 1.27 has been established by a verified statement previously submitted.

A verified statement to establish small entity status under 37 CFR 1.9 and 1.27 is enclosed.

No additional fee is required.

The fee has been calculated as shown below:

	(1) CLAIMS REMAINING AFTER AMENDMENT		(2) HIGHEST NO PREVIOUSLY PAID FOR	(3) PRESENT EXTRA	SMALL ENTITY RATE	ADDIT FEE		OTHER THAN A SMALL ENTITY RATE	ADDIT FEE
TOTAL	*	MINUS	**	-	x $ 6 =	$	OR	x $ 12 =	$
INDEP	*	MINUS	***	-	x $ 18 =	$		x $ 36 =	$
FIRST PRESENTATION OF MULTIPLE DEP CLAIM					+ $ 60 =	$		+ $120 =	$
					TOTAL ADDIT. FEE	$	OR	TOTAL	$

* If the entry in Col 1 is less than the entry in Col 2, write "0" in Col 3

** If the "Highest No Previously Paid For" IN THIS SPACE is less than 20, enter "20"

*** If the "Highest No Previously Paid For" IN THIS SPACE is less than 3, enter "3"

The "Highest No Previously Paid For" (Total or Indep) is the highest number found in the appropriate box in Col 1

Please charge my Deposit Account No. _____ in the amount of $ _____ . A duplicate copy of this sheet is enclosed.

A check in the amount of $ _____ to cover the filing fee is enclosed.

The Commissioner is hereby authorized to charge payment of the following fees associated with this communication or credit any overpayment to Deposit Account No. _____ . A Duplicate copy of this sheet is enclosed.

Any additional filing fees required under 37 CFR 1.16.

Any patent application processing fees under 37 CFR 1.17

Date _____

Signature _____

Form PTO-FB-A520 (10-85)
(also form PTO-1083)

Patent and Trademark Office - U.S. DEPARTMENT of COMMERCE

Copyrights Index

Page numbers in boldface indicate reproduction of copyright forms;
page numbers followed by t indicate tables.

Trademarks Index

Page numbers in boldface indicate reproduction of trademark forms.

Patents Index

Page numbers in boldface indicate reproduction of patent forms.